Living Without Regret

Living Without Regret

Human Experience in Light of Tibetan Buddhism

Arnaud Maitland

with Caroline van Tuyll van Serooskerken

Foreword by Tarthang Tulku

 DHARMA PUBLISHING

DHARMA PUBLISHING   www.dharmapublishing.com
35788 Hauser Bridge Rd., Cazadero, CA 95421

Originally published as *Oneindig afscheid;*
ouder worden in het licht van het Tibetaans boeddhisme
© 2004 by Arnaud Maitland and Caroline van Tuyll van Serooskerken
Original publisher: Altamira-Becht, Haarlem, the Netherlands, 2004

Cover and book design and typography: Colin Dorsey
Cover photo: The Main Temple at Odiyan, Ron Spohn

Library of Congress Control Number 2005925228
ISBN 0-89800-367-9
Printed and bound in the United States of America by Dharma Press

9   8   7   6   5   4

To Tarthang Rinpoche,
who showed me the possibility
for human development,
and helped me to hear my calling

What use is the reading of words?
I will read them with my body.
How can a sick person benefit
from reading a book on medicine?
—Shantideva

*Here you will find nothing that has
not been said before
nor do I have any skill in the art of
composition,
Thus I write this not hoping to help
others, but compose it merely to
cultivate my own mind.*

*With these lines,
as I cultivate virtue,
I will increase my own faith.
Should others have similar
inclinations,
when they see these words
they may find them helpful.*
—*Shantideva*

Any errors made in presenting the Tibetan
Buddhist teachings in this book are entirely
the author's doing, for which he takes full
responsibility.

Contents

Foreword

While countless human beings have come into this world,
it is a testament to the remarkable mystery of being that
very few fully understand how we have taken birth, how
we continue to appear, and where exactly we are jour-
neying. For many, the mystery of our entrance into this
world may not even be noticed, and so such questions
may not arise or be regarded as relevant. Like a candle flickering in the wind, each human being uniquely
expresses and participates in infinitely varied ways to
embrace existence. Compounded by nature from diverse
elements, we manifest diverse shapes and forms, and
inevitably and undeniably, a specific character seems to
be expressed through our being. But who we truly are
and how it is that we have appeared still continue to elude
us. At both microscopic and macroscopic levels of either
intellectual or experiential inquiry, we have not yet come
to any genuinely conclusive understanding.

Throughout the course of history, in all the fertile
fields of human knowledge, spanning religion, philosophy,
and modern science, attempts have been made to offer a
coherent answer to the question of our existence, whether
to articulate its ultimate purpose or to probe the causal

nature behind its appearance. While such attempts may offer convincing perspectives, they remain within the province of ordinary conceptual mind: mind attempting to make "sense," a product ultimately destined for consumption by mind itself. How easily we forget that we are the architects of our own designations! Satisfied or even fascinated by our clever answers and elaborations, we cannot see that behind the underlying structure of our thoughts, the essential nature of our being remains a mystery.

How many billions of our ancestors have come before us in the journey taking place on this planet, which the Buddhist tradition calls Jambudvipa? And yet here we are, in the twenty-first century, just beginning to understand the dynamic interplay among the myriad dimensions cohering in a sentient being, that miraculous, invisible coalescence of mind, body and spirit. Modern science, more than ever, is striving to understand the biochemical processes of the body and mind consciousness, and the causal relationship of thought and emotion to body and mind. However, a more subtle, but essential existential awareness is remarkably absent: awareness that the whole of our way of life within the material environment we inhabit is a compounded phenomenal process, itself a product of mind and body and their interactions.

Oblivious to this dialectic, which the Buddhist tradition elucidates as the principle of karma, our inquiry is impervious to genuinely transformative and uplifting knowledge of the meaning of our human being. Our efforts seem condemned to be perpetually conducted and reinforced within the self-structuring corral of thought itself.

The purpose of the vast journey of human being appears all the more impenetrable when we recognize that the mystery of our own fragile individual continuum of being remains hidden despite our sincere efforts to comprehend. Surveying the expanse of our life, from our birth, to living, and dying, we may find ourselves deeply inquisitive about the absoluteness of the beginning of our beginning; we may quite naturally wonder whether there is ever a real and final end to our end. The question of our own genesis invites us into the cosmological perspective that considers the seemingly infinite continuum behind or within the appearance of all the sentient beings who have sojourned in this cosmos. Confounded by the enormity of these macro and micro levels of investigation into the nature of our being, we may retreat into the more comfortable realm of the immediate and the known. Though we may deny the possibility of any theoretical derivation that truly reflects our condition, sooner or later, we cannot avoid the immediately evident, empirical truth: Behind every appearance is a 'from' and a 'to', some kind of parenthood and legacy. Beyond the conditioning of civilization, culture, and personal belief systems, every single life reflects and represents something very precious indeed.

But what is this inexpressibly precious, felt but unseen something that we represent? During our brief embodiment, with this body, mind, and spirit unified in our own unique expression, don't we owe it to ourselves to discover the nature of our being, and still more deeply, the real meaning of the well-being of our being? While certain answers may not come easily, these questions matter a great deal to both our minds and hearts, which in the final analysis, are all that we ever are or have. And so before this life force, these senses, and these elements begin to disintegrate, there can surely be no more valuable inquiry in which we could engage.

With limited time to acquire such knowledge, its necessity seems all the more essential, for there will be even less time to live the gift of our lives in the light of such genuine knowledge. As body, mind, spirit and even knowledge will soon dissolve into fragments destined for unknown configurations and directions, it is difficult to say when we will meet again with such a confluence of good fortune—a human birth where it is possible to awaken a deep wondrous appreciation of being alive that makes that life indeed precious.

While all beings seem to intrinsically yearn for well-being, the preponderance of skepticism today increasingly divorces us from any grounds that affirm and support well-being. With meaning itself attacked on all fronts by new nihilistically-oriented critical approaches to knowledge, our most precious values may even be called into question. The result of this relentless encroachment of meaninglessness is that heart and mind are fragmented and conflicted. As doubt itself becomes increasingly celebrated as the reigning currency of knowledge, we may come to equate our all-encompassing skepticism with intelligence, so that uncertainty itself becomes the ultimate measure and destiny of knowledge. If this trajectory continues unaltered, knowledge could well bankrupt itself, losing the ability, and even legitimacy, to serve the interest of human happiness.

Though over 2,540 years have elapsed since the light of knowledge introduced by the Buddha illumined the hearts and minds of living beings, it continues to prove to be an effective guide in the search for the deepest, most abiding sources of well-being. If we would live as the Buddha invites us all so freely to do, we would take his words to heart. We would be kind, not just to others, but also to ourselves, and lead, not just others, but ourselves as well. Nourished by an intention to kindly lead ourselves toward genuine well-being in order to benefit all beings, step by step we would come closer to realizing the abiding peace of mind that is the deepest wish of every living being. Then with the gift of the Buddha's healing wisdom, we might find our thoughts more friendly and accommodating, so that gradually we could restore trust in our own minds. Once this inner trust is regained, even ordinary thoughts and intentions begin to guide us reliably to the source of an ever-deepening, nonconceptual experience of well-being.

To dismiss this ancient tradition of knowledge and wisdom as anachronistic would only reflect our very limited perspective on the vast span of our human journey. While 2,540 years ago may seem a great distance from our present time and space, relative to the greater narrative of our human journey on Jambudvipa, it was only recently that the Buddha appeared, demonstrating the possibility of enlightenment as the ultimate destiny of every sentient being. To be sure, the present scarcity of enlightened models in our world stimulates our skepticism and makes it all the more tempting to believe that knowledge leading to full awakening is impossible.

Yet, even a brief review of Dharma history reveals scores of great awakaned beings and bodhisatvas who have appeared in our world and will continue to illuminate the long journey into the universal awakening of knowledge. Padmasambhava, for example, the enlightened master who helped establish Buddhism in Tibet in the eighth century is not merely a personality of mythical folklore. Such enlightened masters have demonstrated with their very lives that the karma and emotionality that constrict ordinary experience can be completely transformed into wisdom and compassion.

In the past in Tibet, many ordinary sincere seekers like ourselves, inspired and guided by the lineage of masters such as Padmasambhava, dedicated their lives to the passionate pursuit of enlightenment. When their efforts were consummated by the transformation of body, mind, and spirit dissolving into rainbow bodies of light, everyone could see that the lineage of knowledge was real and effective.

But today in the West, such conviction and confidence are rare. The ordinary mind cannot rationally explain such total transformation, making it difficult to accept the possibility that enlightenment might still occur in the world we inhabit today. So many internal and environmental causes and conditions seem to militate against sustained and effective training of mind. Without the presence of faith, discipline, and merit, the great majestic doors to knowledge remain silently closed. Circumstances for the training of mind may not be available, and even if they are, serious disconnections between the traditional institutions of learning and ordinary lay people, practitioners and non-practitioners, both in the East and West, undermine the framework necessary to support widespread genuine access to the teachings of enlightenment.

In the midst of such impoverished conditions, ordinary mind is lost without any reliable guides to identify and cultivate sources of well-being. Despite our most sincere intentions, mind simply cannot settle itself, and the ensuing malaise, doubt, and anxiety that color untrained consciousness may become so chronic that they seem indelible, natural facets of mind itself. As awareness dims, the memory of awareness or even the longing for it may recede into ever-darker obscurity. Without even knowing what has happened, we may gradually lose our essential human qualities, our inner being hijacked by the forces of confusion and ignorance.

Fortunately, the extremely sensitive nature of mind could also be placed in the service of resurrecting and strengthening awareness. If we learned to settle the mind just a little bit more, we would see increasingly subtle qualities of mind as expressions of its clear and radiant nature. Glimpse by glimpse, this seeing could become clearer, deeper and more sustained, so that our entire being is enriched and transformed with the confidence of knowing our innermost nature. Rather than running round and round in the endless conceptual circles created by our own confusion, like a dog chasing its tail, we could simply stop and see the circle for what it is: a futile attempt to ascribe duality to the brilliant indivisible light of awareness, all encompassing, uncontained by any border, free from any sign. Training our minds in such a gradual way, as countless beings before us have done, we embrace the very faultiness of our fragmented, tormented, and weary hearts as sources of integration into wholesomeness of being.

If knowledge can awaken us to complete freedom of being like this, it is certainly the Right Knowledge taught by the Buddha. Given the momentum of today's knowledge toward the service of utilitarian aims and ever expanding material prosperity, is it possible that such an unrelenting drive could evolve in a new way? If the quest for spiritual prosperity could be affirmed as a measure and purpose of knowledge, spiritual understanding could be shared among all peoples and across all ages, so that knowledge itself becomes a universal symphony celebrating the wonder of being.

It is my belief and my dream that such an evolution of universal consciousness is possible, and so my sincere hope is that works such as this, guided by noble intentions, help readers discover and cultivate the deeply abiding wellness of being that all beings so richly deserve.

Tarthang Tulku
Odiyan Center USA
March 12, 2005

*At the request of Arnaud Maitland and Caroline
van Tuyll, I spent a few hours dictating my thoughts
to Pema Gellek, who wrote up this Foreword, and
Leslie Bradburn, who edited it. I hope this will
encourage readers to consider carefully and seriously
the significance of our human opportunity.*
—*Tarthang Tulku*

Preface

It Is Never Too Late

Living Without Regret was inspired by the story of my mother, who lived most of her life as a happy, healthy woman, but whose last years were spent in a nursing home for dementia patients. This drama, increasingly familiar in recent years, had an impact on the lives of those who were close to her. We were all confronted with situations and emotions for which we had no adequate answers and no effective medicine. Feelings of power-lessness, suppressed guilt and resentment, miscommunication and lack of communication, and above all, gut-wrenching fear made it impossible for us to thoroughly grasp the situation and truly be helpful.

Dementia not only undermines the patient's aware-ness, but also unravels the fabric of the family. While the loved one gradually recedes into shadows, those who stay behind become strangers to themselves, continually say-ing farewell to what is known and familiar. Under such circumstances it seems impossible to find meaning and security anywhere.

Yet, according to Buddhist teachings, there is no need to fear suffering, whether our own or that of others.

The Buddha teaches us to make use of life's opportunities to become more fully human by facing whatever happens without guilt or blame. If those around my mother had been more aware of such other possibilities, the situation might have moved in a different direction.

Living Without Regret deals with impermanence and its accompanying pains, both great and small, and with the related topic of personal responsibility and questions of human possibility and limitation. These topics seem especially timely when an increasingly large segment of society has reached or is approaching old age. Old age and sickness entail a specific form of suffering for which our society does not seem to offer much guidance.

This book may have value for people who work in the field of health care, both professionals and volunteers, as well as people who witness their parents and other family members confronting illness and death. It may be useful as well to those in the prime of life who wish to use the knowledge in this book now, as preparation for their own later years. No matter what our age, we can protect ourselves from fear and confusion, and prepare to approach the final phase of life with wisdom and confidence.

The book may also offer guidance for a wider audience. Reflecting on our relationships with our parents, whether they have passed away or are still living, is healing for anyone, regardless of age. According to Tibetan Buddhist teachings, a healthy relationship with our mothers and fathers sets the tone for a harmonious life.

The portrait painted of my mother in these pages does not do justice to her life. The anecdotes about her at the beginning of each chapter do not fully reflect the situations described. Even the family dynamics that proved to play a major role in events are not discussed at any length. It was not my intention to write a biographical account, or to give an overview of the latest developments relating to Alzheimer's disease. My main purpose is to show the many ways in which Tibetan Buddhist teachings can help us take hold of our lives under all imaginable circumstances, whether happy or desperate, sick or healthy, imprisoned or free, young or old. The possibilities we ignore, the opportunities we pass by, the choices we are afraid to embrace, the missteps we take—these need not be irreversible.

In facing our faults honestly and relinquishing self-pity and shame, we become stronger. With the power of this strength, we can rectify our mistakes. Time never stops giving us new chances. In writing this book, I also hoped to show how we can expand the spiritual dimension of our lives. By accepting the certainty of death, realizing the truth that impermanence is an inextricable characteristic of existence, and daring to live accordingly, we begin to flourish as human beings. Then when we look back on our lives we need have no fear or regrets, for we see a life that has been worth living. It is my hope that this book will inspire readers to find an answer to the question, "How do I really want to live?" And then begin to do it.

I left my country when I was twenty-four. In my fifties, I returned to Holland and began to write, wanting to tell my mother's story in my native tongue, projected against the backdrop of my Tibetan Buddhist training.

Within a year after publication of the book in Dutch, the English edition is being published in the United States, the country where I have lived for more than thirty years. It is under the inspiring tutelage of my Tibetan teacher, Tarthang Tulku, that I have learned what I now know. Because of what he has taught me, I have been able to reflect upon the past, viewing my mother's fate with a new perspective and a deeper understanding of what happened to her and the people who loved her. For it is never too late: We can still heal the past.

Living Without Regret

1

Unending Farewell

The dimly lit temple towers high above us, its silhouette
outlined like a giant candle against gray, red-streaked
clouds. It is the new moon, traditionally a time for prayer
ceremonies for troubled spirits, the sick, and the deceased.
As a participant in tonight's ceremony, I stand waiting at
dusk in front of the bronze entryway on the eastern side
of the massive structure, while incense and conch shells
are being distributed. During the ceremony, we will
blow the conch shells, emitting heart-piercing sounds
like a herd of trumpeting elephants. As the names of the
people to whom these prayers are dedicated are read, I hear
myself adding a name to the list: "Mother."

Tonight it is my turn to ring the bell. In the gathering darkness, I leave the group to walk the hundred paces
from the temple to the bell, a path I have trod many times
before. My heart grows lighter with every step. At the
foot of the bell house, I bend over to pick up pebbles to
use as counters, then turn to climb the small flight of
stairs that leads up to the bell. Above my head, the giant
bronze bell waits, inscribed inside and out with sacred
Tibetan texts. I take hold of the rope and pull on it firmly
to give the clapper speed. Bommmmm. After the sound

reverberates at length, I pull again, and then again, until the bell has sounded twenty-five times. Each new resonance seems to create more space, each tone to travel farther and farther, until the sound ripples outward to the most distant corners of the universe. Borders dissolve; past and present merge into all-encompassing space. The time it takes to complete twenty-five repetitions seems like an eternity.

My mother had died five years before the evening of the ceremony. I am not sure what happens after death, but of one thing I was certain: Nothing is ever truly lost. Her physical body was gone, but everything else remained. Her gestures, the words she had spoken, everything she had done, thought, and dreamt—even her fears in the last years of her life—were all still here, preserved as traces in time. Is it possible to capture this sense in words? The Tibetan language is rich in relevant vocabulary, but in English there are few words; the ones that come closest are *mind*, *soul*, and *spirit*. Regardless of the words, I could still feel my mother's being, in the way a star remains visible even centuries after its death. As the ceremony came to a close, I knew it was time to say goodbye to my life as her son; that phase was now over. For her, the ceremony was a blessing; for me it was the beginning of a farewell.

In the weeks that followed, I revisited my mother's life. There were so many things I remembered about her— things I had been told, things she shared with me—and my feelings of regret could finally be acknowledged.

Her life played itself out before me as though I were watching a film. I saw her as a carefree child, then as a young girl of great promise, and finally as a wife, mother, and full-time volunteer who performed her tasks with cheerfulness and creativity. Her caring and good nature nourished all those who were close to her.

The film of my mother's life did not have a happy ending. At the age of seventy-four, she began to show signs of Alzheimer's disease. As the disease progressed it seemed that she had died long before she actually took her last breath. Gradually she lost control of her body, her speech, and her mind. The ability to express and assert herself as the woman we knew vanished, and the loved ones who gathered around her seemed unable to help. All the time and energy she had invested in making a success of her life and her relationships were of no avail at the end. It seemed that nothing remained of all she had so carefully built; her entire world was obliterated.

For years this vision had plagued me, but after the ceremony, I began to retrace her final years from a new perspective, seeing with the eyes of a practitioner of Tibetan Buddhism. Situations and emotions I had not previously understood began to reveal new depths of meaning.

Looking back on the ten years of her illness gave me insight into how Alzheimer's had affected my mother and her family and friends, and especially me. Years after her death, I was finally able to make peace with some of these events, using the traditional Buddhist methods of observation, inquiry, and the act of increasing awareness. As a result of the insights I gained in the process, her life and death took on a broader meaning, and I was able to let go and begin to say goodbye.

Tibetan Buddhism

All Buddhist traditions tell the life story of Siddhartha Gautama, an Indian prince born more than twenty-five hundred years ago, who set out to find a remedy for human suffering. In his search to make sense of why a human being is born only to die again, the prince left his family and his future kingdom. He studied with the greatest spiritual teachers of his age, but found that they could not give him the answers he sought. After years of meditation, he gained insight into the cause of human suffering and attained enlightenment. From that time on, he was called the Buddha, the Awakened One. For over forty years, he taught his vision, experiences, and insight into the nature of reality to his followers, often giving teachings in response to their questions. Many of these teachings, called *sutras*, are preserved today, and they are the foundation of study in all Buddhist schools.

The teachings of the Buddha describe his path to enlightenment in detail—both the obstacles he overcame and the methods he used to gain complete awareness. Students are encouraged to analyze the inner experience of the Buddha, imitate it, and finally, embody it. Through study, reflection, and practice his followers gain knowledge of both the self and the world, and learn to face reality—the way things really are—without illusions or self-deception.

The great master Padmasambhava, called the second Buddha, brought the teachings of the Buddha from India to Tibet in the eighth century. More than a century earlier, King Srongtsen Gampo of Tibet had prepared the way for the transmission by ordering the creation of a written Tibetan language capable of communicating subtle levels of meaning. Under the direction of Padmasambhava and King Trisong Detsen, the first Tibetan monastery, Samye, was built.

The ordination of the first Tibetan monks and transmission of the inner Tantras marked the beginning of the oldest Tibetan Buddhist lineage, which came to be known as the Nyingmapa, or Ancient Ones. A second infusion of Buddhist teachings reached Tibet in the tenth and eleventh centuries. In the years that followed, the teachings of the Buddha became completely assimilated into every aspect of Tibetan culture.

Until the mid-twentieth century, little was known in the West about Tibetan Buddhism. Only a few teachings by the Buddha and specific Tibetan texts such as the *Tibetan Book of the Dead* had been translated into English, beginning in the late nineteenth century.

This situation changed abruptly in the 1950s with the Chinese occupation of Tibet, when over one hundred thousand Tibetans fled the invader and found refuge in surrounding countries. Many Tibetan lamas—the spiritual leaders and teachers of Tibet—eventually traveled to the West, thus fulfilling an age-old prophecy made by Padmasambhava:

When the iron bird flies
and horses run on wheels,
the Tibetan people will be
scattered like ants
across the face of the world,
and the Dharma will come
to the land of the red-faced man.[1]

HUMAN FLOURISHING

In the Tibetan Buddhist teachings, there is a story that illustrates how the mind tends to mold reality into a familiar size and shape. Once upon a time, there was a frog living in a pond. One day he met a turtle that had come from the ocean. The frog had never been away from home and was curious about the ocean. "What is the ocean like?" he asked. "Does it look like this pond?" "No," said the turtle, "the ocean is much bigger." "Three times as big?" asked the frog with great awe. "No, much, much bigger," replied the turtle. "Ten times as big?" the frog asked with disbelief. Shaking her head, the turtle did her very best to explain the vastness of the ocean, but in the end the frog fainted. The thought of such an immense mass of water was simply too much for him.[2]

On that night of the ceremony, my past and present merged, and my life began to make sense in a new way. My early schooling and study of law in the Netherlands met with the Tibetan Buddhist education I had begun in California. As many young people growing up in the Netherlands after World War II, I had been imbued

8

with the philosophy of Sartre and Camus. But from their writing I drew the sense of a dull and predictable future that fostered melancholy and regret about missed opportunities. In the 1970s, I was exposed to a different worldview when I participated in the human potential movement in California. This experience offered me a glimpse of the possibilities for human growth. It opened a gateway to the Tibetan Buddhist teachings, which would give me the keys for unlocking my own inner resources.

The Tibetan Buddhist teachings brought me into contact with something immeasurable that surpassed everything I had known before. At the age of thirty, the boy who had been floating in a wooden shoe in the canals of Holland had somehow found his way to the ocean. In the very first Buddhist lecture I attended, the main topic was "How can a human being find wholeness again?" It seemed to me that if we could find the answer to this question, we would know the meaning of life. The insights that began to emerge after this initial in quiry were full of knowledge, life, and hope. Studying the Tibetan Buddhist teachings in the Nyingma tradition, which centers on human flourishing, I began to experience a gentle inner revolution.

Intelligence and Energy

From my studies of the Buddhist tradition, I learned that all human potential has two fundamental components: intelligence and energy, or the qualities of knowing and feeling. The study of Buddhism focuses on both of these

9

capacities, developing them by way of both study and practice. Study promotes knowing and practice stimulates feeling. The better we understand the teachings, the deeper our experience becomes. The more fully we experience, the more easily we grasp the teachings.

The written teachings of Buddhism are found in such texts as the *sutras*, which are the spoken words of the Buddha, and the *shastras*, the commentaries written by great Buddhist masters in India and Tibet over the next twenty-five hundred years. Since personal growth requires that we develop the ability to know and feel at the same time, these texts appeal to both our intelligence and energy in order to strengthen both simultaneously. Some of the old texts may seem exacting, but each has immensely practical application. The words and tone are both personal and universal and have survived well over time; some texts over a thousand years old sound as if they could have been written today.

The early teachings encouraged practitioners to leave behind all worldly attachments, including home, family, and society. Retreat from the bustle of daily life still has great value, but we do not need to live as hermits or become monks or nuns in order to benefit from these teachings. The goal is to become familiar with our awareness and at ease with our energy. To do this, we must learn to see that certain forms of attachment are limiting, in particular our attachment to a self-image. Inner detachment paves the way to openness.

Buddhist teachings can be divided into three areas of study. The first area concerns the *individual*. When asked, how one can help others, the Buddha replied, "First learn to take care of yourself." The Buddha encourages us to get to know ourselves, to find out the causes of our suffering, and to follow the path that leads to the cessation of suffering. When we train the body and mind, we come into balance, and we experience the world around us as balanced too.

The second area of study focuses on the nature of *reality*. When we adhere strictly to the laws of logic and common sense, our knowledge and experience are based on assumptions. Thoughts pursued to their logical conclusions either contradict themselves or vanish. Thus we find that everything we have thought, believed, and feared is unfounded, and the nature of reality is revealed to be open.

The third area of study explores the nature of human *being*. In our inner worlds, we can find the source of security we seek. When we unlock the heart of humanness, we understand that the human mind is programmed for perfection. Human beings are by nature good.

Source of Wisdom

"Be a lamp unto yourself," the Buddha said in his last teaching. The questions, "What will become of me? What should I do with my life?" are answered with, "It depends on your own mind." The mind is the source of sadness and pain; our attitude toward life determines our degree of happiness. The obstacles and difficulties we repeatedly encounter and struggle with in our lives do not come from outside us. They originate in our heads and our hearts, and it is there that we must look for solutions. By increasing our awareness, we can gradually transform our negative tendencies and limiting thoughts. We can learn to live heroically, in touch with the vitality that is our birthright; each tear we shed can become a source of renewed courage.

The spiritual path begins as soon as we resolve to make the most of our lives. Accepting our situation and ourselves is the starting point. When the student protests, "How can I do that? It's easier said than done!" the master replies, "Don't be so serious. Relax." Tibetan teachers often tell us to rellax. This does not mean to resign ourselves to our life situation, but to lighten up and allow ourselves to be fully present with whatever we are experiencing. By opening in this way, we naturally relax, and relaxation in turn allows us to embrace whatever is happening more fully. With relaxation everything comes to life.

If we relax and take responsibility for whatever happens, our daily life—what the Buddhist tradition calls *samsara*—with all its joy and sadness, possibilities and limitations, points the way to enlightenment. We find that the answer to every question we ask is already available; we need only ask and observe. Such wisdom belongs to us like wetness to water. When we tap into this inner resource, awareness becomes clear and strong. We realize that the time we are given here on earth as human beings provides us with all the opportunities we need to make the best of our lives.

2

Precious Human Life

Holland was at its most beautiful in early May. Spring displayed her charms everywhere, blanketing our neighborhood with color and perfume. In the garden of our house, the tulip bulbs were nearing their end while the flowering trees and shrubs were reaching their peak. The wild apple tree in the front yard looked just like a calendar picture. Nature was bursting with anticipation at the threshold of summer.

Every year on May 4th my countrymen commemorate the heroes who gave their lives to liberate Holland during World War II. The evening service was the main event, and a solemn mood could be felt throughout the day. Flags hung at half-mast from most houses, people dressed in dark colors, and no one made any unnecessary noise. This day was for remembering the horror of the German invasion and for honoring those who had died during the five war years.

About seven o'clock, as the last rays of the sun slanted through the trees, my mother and I put on our coats and set off for the service. It was the early 1950s and I was eight years old. As we walked through silent streets to the small graveyard on the Schouwweg, about twenty minutes from home, we did not talk much. My mother was always deep in thought during this personal journey into the past.

People streamed to the local war memorial from all sides. Well before eight, we joined the group waiting at the Tomb of the Unknown Soldier. The weather was usually beautiful, but this year a light drizzle covered our somber clothes with pearly drops. At eight o'clock, time stood still. For two minutes, the entire country came to a halt, including buses, trolleys, and the cars on the freeway. Conversations were interrupted; even the radio fell silent. At exactly two minutes past eight, the bells began to peal and everyday life resumed.

On the way home, my mother underwent a transformation. Her gait became springy and graceful and her mood lightened, although she remained thoughtful. She appeared to feel liberated. "This is always such a special moment for me," she said happily, and began to tell stories about how the Allied Forces entered Holland after the winter of hunger in 1944, and how her only brother—a British RAF pilot—had returned from England loaded with delicacies. Hearing her speak about these historic moments sparked my imagination. Would I, like the American and Canadian soldiers, have had the courage to sacrifice my life? If I were living in Canada or the United States, would I, too, have felt the call to leave home and family to fight an enemy in a far-off land?

At that time the memories of those who had lived through World War II were still fresh and we children had heard the stories over and over. It was from a site near

The Hague that the Germans fired their V2s at England. There would be a loud hiss at first, and everyone would start counting seconds. If after twenty seconds there was no explosion, the neighborhood was out of danger, as the bomb was speeding to the other side of the North Sea.

The story I liked best was that of a young German soldier who came up the stairs to the apartment where my parents lived. Dressed in his long, oversized gray coat and seemingly little more than a boy himself, he looked curiously around the room where three children were playing on the floor. My father had quickly hidden in the attic to avoid being caught and deported to Germany, where he would have been put to work in the *Arbeitseinsatz* (labor camps). When the soldier saw the photograph on my mother's desk, he remarked, "Ein netter Mann" (a nice man), then he turned around and went back down the stairs and out into the street.

Like most Dutch people, my mother faithfully repeated this journey through time year after year, remembering the horrors of the occupation and the courage of those who had made the greatest sacrifice. In those few minutes at the Tomb of the Unknown Soldier, she made a focused pilgrimage in her mind, moving straight through destruction and despair to liberation, which she experienced as a kind of purification. By reliving the fear and sorrow of the five years of the German occupation, traumatic emotional knots were undone, so that once again she was able to enjoy life to the fullest. This natural healing process restored her faith that life had meaning in spite of the pain of the human condition.

Remembrance of painful and distressing periods in our lives is a necessary step in a healing process. Human beings learn to cope with sorrow and grief not by suppressing these feelings, but by acknowledging them and working through them. To leave the past behind, we must confront whatever went awry, admitting our own role and accepting our mistakes. This resolve is our freedom.

A day came when my mother could no longer make this essential mental pilgrimage. Her damaged brain refused to obey her command, and her mind lacked the vitality to turn inward. She was incapable of working through her knowledge of human suffering towards the light. Old and decrepit, she herself became a victim, an unknown soldier, lost in the ravages of her illness.

LIVING TRUTHFULLY

Friends, a precious human body,
being a unique occasion and a right juncture,
is very hard to find within the six life-forms.
As delighted as a blind man
who has stumbled on a precious hoard,
use this body for prosperity and bliss.[3]

How can we get the most out of life? For a Tibetan Buddhist, the answer to this question always begins with contemplating our great good fortune in having a human existence. A traditional image says, "It is more likely for a blind sea turtle to stick its head through a yoke tossed into the middle of the ocean, than for us to acquire a human body." Understanding that human life is a rare gift worth appreciating, a traditional Buddhist often begins the day by reciting a text, or even one brief sentence, to invoke appreciation of body, mind, and senses—the means we have to make the most out of life.

There are five truths or Dharma teachings that create a guiding structure for a meaningful life. These truths are always valid, independent of time or space. In their simplicity, anyone can understand them, young or old. These five central truths—appreciation, impermanence, karma, the futility of unnecessary suffering, and freedom—are the heart of daily Buddhist practice.[4]

If we fail to integrate these truths of life with our day-to-day experiences, we feel a vague sense of emptiness. Something indefinable is missing. Our goals remain out of reach; we feel misunderstood. Our frustrations, emotions, tears, internal resistance, and the unfounded hope that someday everything will improve on its own all echo a lack of knowledge.

By embodying these five truths through meditation and practice, we gain the depth we are actually longing for. Our life acquires a spiritual dimension. As they become part of what we think, say, and do, we live more harmoniously with the way things naturally are, free of regret and wasted time. Bearing these truths in mind, we are prepared when death overtakes us. They create a frame of reference in which the mind can unfold towards its intrinsic perfection. In the following pages I present my own reflections on their significance, based on my study and experience over the years as I aimed to comprehend the meaning of these basic but profound teachings.

APPRECIATION

The spiritual path begins when we realize that our lives as well as the lives of all sentient beings have value and deserve respect. Each human being has a body, a mind, and the vital energy to do something useful with them. There are abundant ways to live a happy life and make a positive contribution to the world. Appreciation of these opportunities is the keynote of a meaningful existence.

Our brains and our chemical circuitry thrive on appreciation. Scientific research has shown that just as acquiring a new skill stimulates the production of brain cells, generating feelings of appreciation increases the number of neurons in the brain.[5] Gratitude and appreciation strengthen the immune system and other systems in the body as well. Circulation improves and the eyes become radiant. According to the Buddhist teachings, such liveliness and vitality are our birthright.

Developing appreciation, like any other mindset, is a matter of habit. When we are caught up in negative patterns, it may seem that there is nothing to appreciate; all our energy seems to be focused on problems. Negativity has its own compelling logic. Yet even if we do not feel particularly grateful, we can learn to wake ourselves up to the positive aspects of whatever we are experiencing. Just as we acquired negative patterns by regularly repeating negative thoughts and feelings, we can develop appreciation by cultivating grateful thoughts and feelings. Even the smallest feeling of appreciation stimulates energy and enthusiasm, and this makes it easier to continue. Before long, mind becomes accustomed to the vital energy of positive feelings and thoughts. Soon an inner transformation is set in motion, and our intelligence and energy take on new forms.

We can begin with appreciation for all we have learned and accomplished so far in our lives. Next, we can appreciate the latent possibilities in our present circumstances. How much more wisdom and love can we experience before we die? In times of crisis, appreciation can be a potent medicine. We can ask ourselves, "Despite all my troubles, what good is concealed in this situation and in my life? In the midst of change and uncertainty, what do I know for sure?" Asking these questions generates appreciation.

We look for solutions by asking questions such as, "How can this situation be improved?" and listening for answers. Gratitude for the guidance we receive helps us to understand that no condition is final, no suffering hopeless. Every situation gives us an opportunity to open to greater understanding. As appreciation deepens, love and wisdom are born.

IMPERMANENCE

Understanding impermanence ignites our passion for further exploring our potential. Consider that the average life expectancy of a human being is about four thousand weeks. It is as if we live on borrowed time, tracked by an invisible hourglass that measures out our days by dropping grains of sand. How many days remain? The time left to us is constantly decreasing. We are certain we will die; it is only when and how that is uncertain. We are bound to our breaths. One day, after an unknown number of inhalations, we will exhale for the last time and this life will be over. Every life has a deadline. Every moment—most of all, this moment—counts.

Impermanence may be the main characteristic of human existence. In our daily lives good times and bad times come and go. Children grow up and adults grow old. Life goes on in endless cycles. Everything has a beginning, middle, and end; each beginning contains its end, and in each end, there is the promise of a new beginning. Nothing remains as it is: The present moment does not return. Part of the art of living is to begin each moment well, remain focused, gently let go, and then say good-bye, granting each time its own qualities.

A day that has not been concluded properly will project its unprocessed elements into the next. Perhaps there is something we have ignored or neglected, or a feeling left unfelt—whatever their form, the unresolved elements of the day stay around like unwanted baggage. Today's frustration likely finds its primary cause in the past; if it too remains unquestioned, it becomes another remnant of old experience piled up like trash at the curb.

If we experience the transition from one day to the next with awareness, we can enter the future with a lighter, more open mind. At the end of the day or a phase, we can let everything pass in review: vivid memories, accomplishments, regret and remorse. We accept what has happened and then let it go. In this way, the transition to the next day becomes easier. We no longer carry the burden of strained relationships or painful memories of thoughtless actions. Nothing weighs our conscience down; feelings of self-pity or guilt do not consume us. Even death becomes an occasion for celebration, like a birth—the conclusion of a precious life and the beginning of something new.

Impermanence is not merely a concept, but a lived experience. With practice, our minds and hearts become familiar with impermanence, and we move with change instead of resisting it. One method for establishing a conscious link to the passage of time is to bring awareness to the cycle of breath, focusing on each inhalation and exhalation in a neutral way. As we become attuned to the rhythm of breath, the ever-changing quality of time becomes inseparable from consciousness. Appreciation for time's constant flow becomes a natural part of our daily lives. Intimate with flow, we are at ease with change. Impermanence is no longer an obstacle or a threat, but a gateway to positive change.

Karma

The connection between cause and effect is known in Buddhism as the law of karma. Everything we think, say, and do—or refrain from doing—has consequences. Even the most fleeting thought, the simplest word, the smallest gesture has an effect. Our conduct in the past has led to our present circumstances. Tension in the body expresses the truth of karma, as the body stores the record of our past. If we lack a certain quality in our lives, it is because we have not introduced it previously; without a particular cause, we cannot expect the corresponding result. In the same way, our present actions determine our future happiness. Others cannot fix our lives for us, even if they are willing to try. Grace does not come from outside us, but from within.

Karma can easily be misunderstood as equivalent to fate. "Oh, that's my karma," we may say, sighing in resignation. This response tends to excuse us from responsibility, as if we were actually saying, "It's not really my fault." The root of the word karma is "kr," meaning to make, do, or accomplish. Karma refers to action, or motivation, as well as result. If the motivation for thoughts or actions is impure, it is impossible to achieve a wholly positive result. A negative intention undermines the value of human being and causes unnecessary suffering for both ourselves and others; it cannot produce a constructive outcome. Only a positive attitude eventually bears fruit in a positive result.

Since our behavior tends to be a mixture of positive and negative intentions, the effects of our actions may be difficult to sort out. Yet by training ourselves to notice how our motivations wander, and repeatedly straightening them out, in time we will achieve the desired results. Actions will mature in the same way they are performed.

The results of actions display our intent. If the qualities of caring and focused attention are part of a project, these qualities are bound to manifest in the results. Raising a family in harmony, creating a work of art for others to enjoy, working for a good cause—these actions generate positive karma. Our good karma will multiply exponentially to the degree in which other people benefit from our work and its results endure. Positive karma is wisdom in action.

Unnecessary Suffering

In one sense, the mind is neutral, equally capable of producing happiness or pain. It holds no preference for a cheerful expression over an angry one or vice versa. It is true, however, that the way the mind functions—on either a limited or larger scale—determines the way we live. If the mind produces happiness, our experience will be positive; if the mind functions so as to produce suffering, our experience will be negative. Since mind's nature is neutral, it is possible to diminish the causes of suffering and strengthen the causes of happiness.

A piece of cloth dipped in oil will reek of oil; similarly, human beings take on the characteristics of the environment. Some people learn as children to distrust their own feelings and thoughts, resulting in alienation from both themselves and others. Once such a pattern of self-distrust is established, it tends to shape all subsequent experiences. At any age, we may seek validation by adhering to other people's norms and values, taking the expectations of the world around us as the standard by which we measure ourselves. Not recognizing our own

23

value, we are unable to acknowledge and appreciate the special qualities of others.

Athletes strive to overcome personal patterns that undermine their performance, setting their intention to learn from obstacles and make the best use of their talents. Similarly, we can set our intention to approach the obstacles in our paths as teachers, opportunities to strengthen our resources of mind and energy. We can grow wiser by acknowledging mistakes and learning from them. Our frustrations, helplessness, and resistance to life can become important sources of knowledge. Looking beneath the surface of these experiences, we can learn to decipher their hidden messages. Then setbacks no longer throw us off course, because we know they offer invaluable self-understanding.

Suffering takes place in body and mind, so it is in body and mind that we must search for solutions. Through sorrow and pain, life feeds back to us aspects of our being that remain poorly developed. Even if we cannot always decipher the message or are oblivious to most of the knowledge buried within us, we can still gather enough confidence to go deeper, reminding ourselves that we are responsible for our own disappointments. Instead of allowing ourselves to look for a culprit elsewhere, we can choose the wiser path, examining the cause of our hardship and the dynamic that sustains it. A firm foundation of self-knowledge can gradually replace the unstable ground of the self that suffers without knowing why. Because it helps us to discover the conditions that lead to happiness, suffering shows the way to freedom.

FREEDOM

Tibetan Buddhist teachings suggest that there are four gates to freedom. The first gate has a sign saying "Forget the past." Do not cling to what happened to you earlier in life, or you may miss whatever life has to offer. View the past as a city you have left behind and walk through the first gate, without regret. The sign on the second gate reads, "Participate in what is happening now; do not hold back." The key that fits the lock to this gate is total participation. Whenever you give yourself with heart and soul, the second gate will open. When you are not obsessed by the past and are totally immersed in the present—in your work and in your love of life and other beings—you naturally find yourself at the third gate, where the sign says: "Drop any sense of *I*." Instead of egocentric concerns, centering around what good your actions will do for you—such as bringing fortune and fame—you focus on being and doing with passion: on experience and life without *I*. Now you unexpectedly find yourself in front of the fourth and last gate: "Let go of all notion of the future." When your mind ceases to wander into the future, to what you will do or be later on, you stay with "now," and the last gate swings open. Without past, totally involved, liberated from *I* and without expectations, you are free.

We have been conditioned to believe that human beings cannot essentially change, that "this is how I am." While we sometimes feel cheerful, free, and self-assured, we are not in charge of these moods and cannot sustain them. Eventually we grow frustrated with this powerlessness, with our inability to direct our lives. If we fail to work with this frustration, we may end up with no real way out, expressing our hunger for inner freedom to a secret diary or locking it away in a private corner of our minds.

There is another way. When we succeed in paying attention to negative emotions without being compelled to act them out, our awareness increases, and we discover that we have the freedom to choose the quality of our attitudes and responses. Compulsive behavior releases its grip, while constructive thoughts and positive actions become easier, even natural. We stop chasing after what makes us happy or avoiding what offends us. We make our home within the space and power of the open mind, rather than within the confines of the self. Life is what we make of it, and time gives us opportunities to change and grow.

Reflecting on these five truths—appreciation, impermanence, karma, unnecessary suffering, and freedom—can spark an inner transformation that puts an end to the sting of powerlessness. We realize that not knowing how to give our emotions a positive turn is knowledge too. We know that we do not know—we do not yet have the knowledge we need. But the answers are not produced through the intellect. Buddhist teachings offer insight and a path of action to strengthen our ability to know. It is up to us to choose it. This freedom of choice is the freedom of being.

In Buddhism, all of us are students for life. The process of becoming aware is similar to cutting a diamond; patience and expertise bring out the stone's finest qualities. The process of awakening awareness has multiple facets that gain meaning and beauty with work and time. As we begin to understand and embody the five truths, hope and fear turn into certainty and confidence. Classical Buddhist texts refer to this journey as the Path of Heroes. Overcoming personal and cultural patterns requires heroic courage and resolve. According to an old Tibetan saying, we must grow a bone in our hearts.

3

Mind Is Captain of the Ship

On her birthday my mother always had a cold; she called it being "stuffy." Otherwise she was never ill, but on that day she sniffled all day long. Actually, everything was upside down that day; instead of being able to enjoy some time off, she bustled about from morning until night. Her birthday was one of the busiest days of the year for her.

The day would start out with presents in bed, an exciting moment for us children. How would she react to our gifts? My father and I always bought my present in the same store. One year, it was a bottle of Chanel No. 5, the next year a silken corsage that she would wear on a dark evening dress, and a pair of dainty, too-narrow shoes. With the money I had earned from mowing the lawn and washing the car, I was able to put in ten guilders, which my father always supplemented so we had enough. Driving home, I would hold the present in my lap with both hands. The next morning, my mother would react with delighted surprise, "How did you know?"

After breakfast, when we had left for school, she would begin to hurry about, with barely a moment to spare. In the morning, she received the women from the Kaleidoscope Club, at afternoon tea all her women friends from the neighborhood, and after dinner the couples and relatives. She ran back and forth, to and fro, with coffee, cake, sherry, tea, cookies, more cake, drinks, and finally dinner. On our own birthdays, my father, my brothers, and I could choose our favorite dishes for dinner, but this was not true for mother, as none of us would eat the kidneys with Brussels sprouts that she loved.

In my first years of high school I enjoyed helping her with the birthday guests; in the kitchen we would laugh and talk incessantly. Once I told her a joke: "What's green and has white stripes?" Of course she had no idea. "A pickle with suspenders!" We both burst out laughing. "Really?" she said. "I'll have to remember that one." Then the doorbell rang, and new guests made their way inside. When they had all found a place to sit she took their orders for coffee or tea, while passing around cookies and chocolate candies. Then she hurried back to the kitchen.

A few minutes later, I found her leaning on the kitchen counter. Her face looked ashen, and the empty pan she always used to warm the milk hung loosely from her hand. I had never seen her look so pale and defeated. "Who wanted what?" she whispered. For a moment we seemed like two actors who had forgotten their lines, until she began laughing and mumbled, "Who knows?" That sounded like my mother again. Together we prepared a large tray with tea and coffee and a lot of cups and saucers. She walked ahead of me, relieved and triumphant. It took a little while before everybody had found a seat and was served. There was a moment of silence after mother took a seat, and in order to break it she said, chuckling, "Arnaud, why don't you tell that funny joke about the pickle with suspenders?"

Maybe that was the day I first saw signs of the illness that was already working on her and would manifest itself many years later. Then again, forgetfulness does not necessarily indicate the onset of dementia. Most people are familiar with the experience of losing something they had in their hands only a moment ago or forgetting a word that was just on the tip of their tongue. This is not likely to destroy their self-confidence or their faith in themselves, as they feel they can still trust their mental capacities. Only when the same questions and stories are repeated over and over again—when the connection with time is lost and spatial orientation is gone— are we clearly witnessing the signs of dementia. Then the patient will start to lose ground, setting the stage for confusion and fear.

My godfather and uncle, mother's only brother and an Alzheimer's patient just like her, had to repeat the same question, "Nice weather, isn't it?" over and over. He craved human contact but had lost the capacity to sustain normal conversation. His wife helped him by referring to a major period in his life, the years of World War II. My uncle had always refused to discuss his war memories; as a young man he had joined the British RAF at the age of twenty-three, and as a bomber pilot during the war he made hundreds of flights over Germany. After developing Alzheimer's, the images no longer tortured him, although the facts, names, and numbers of that time still remained crystal clear in his mind. Instead, it was the present that eluded him. In his final hours, his wife soothed him with the words, "You go take your last flight."

Clear Mind, Impure Mind

"All things have the nature of mind" are the opening words of the *Dhammapada*, an eloquent collection of teachings given by the Buddha. "Mind is the chief and takes the lead. If the mind is clear, whatever you do or say will bring happiness that will follow you like your shadow. If the mind is polluted, whatever you do or say leads to suffering, which will follow you, as a cart trails a horse."[6]

Sometimes it may seem that there is someone in our heads who controls everything, an independent authority we call *I* who is responsible for our actions. We tend to equate this *I* with our minds. The Buddha teaches, however, that the belief in *I* reveals a lack of insight into the nature of mind. In Tibetan philosophical language—which was developed to translate Buddhist texts from Sanskrit—there are many words for mind, depending upon the activity being performed. All Buddhists realize that mind has a great variety of functions. In the broadest sense, we might say mind means something like our total response to being alive.

All of our responses to the world around us are produced in the mind. Whether we are confident or insecure, trusting or suspicious depends on how our minds have been trained. The way we live, the actions we perform, and the words we speak all reveal the quality of mind.

If we sprawl in a chair, for example, the mind cannot be alert or open. Sitting on the edge of our chairs, wholeheartedly participating without holding back, we radiate energy and warmth.

Mind is the captain of the ship: setting the tone, determining the cargo, and plotting the course. The captain sets priorities and decides what to record in the logbook—what is worth remembering and what should be ignored. Where we are today is a result of our choices in the past, and the future depends on what is happening in our minds right now. Our state of mind determines our lives.

The mind is infinitely complex, possessing a potential we may not be able to imagine even in our wildest dreams. Still, the way it tends to function is rather limited: The engines of our ships run at half power. Despite the vast options that mind has to offer, we typically draw from the same narrow repertoire of four or five possibilities. We are primarily motivated by hope, fear, and responses made familiar by habit. What appeals to us, what is dear to us, what we ignore, what we would rather push away, and what we do only out of pure necessity—this is the scope that tends to dictate the field within which the mind operates.

Refining our Resources

The two main inner resources of human being are mind and body, or intelligence and feeling. Human development entails the refinement of these two resources.

Intelligence and feeling are always active simultaneously. Each experience consists of an intelligently directed
activity and a feeling tone. Ideally both are fully realized, balanced and integrated, creating inner harmony.
In practice, however, intelligence and feeling generally
do not relate well to one another, causing imbalance.

Reintegrating thinking and feeling is not easy. The
gap between our thinking and feeling often makes us
express the complete opposite of what we feel. We may
use our intellect as a compass while suppressing our
feelings, or conversely, emphasize our emotions at the
expense of our intellect. Eventually, we may become so
accustomed to the resulting confusion and conflict that
we no longer recognize our true feelings.

Thoughts move very quickly, pushing and shov-
ing and demanding our attention. The thought process takes place faster than our eyes can blink. At times
thoughts jump all over the place, like monkeys. At other
times, they seem to be carved out of stone, or surrounded
by a dense, impenetrable fog. Whatever their character,
thoughts pop up relentlessly.

Far below the carnival of the thought-world lies the
subtle landscape of feeling, hidden within the body.
Feelings are inseparable from physical sensations, which
have a feeling tone that may be described as pleasant,
painful, or neutral. Whatever their tone, feelings are
shy and tend to linger in the background. In this they
are unlike emotions, which can be thought of as judgments about feelings and are therefore in large part the
product of thought.

It takes time and awareness for feelings to become apparent, and thus they are often overlooked. While thoughts trip over one another, urging us to act, feelings move at a slower pace. Well before feelings can transmit a faltering message, thoughts may have already moved on. Often our thoughts evaluate a situation and prompt action before our feelings have had time to surface. At the end of the day, or perhaps in the quiet of the night, when the time to relax and listen to our feelings has finally come, it may be too late. The letter has been mailed, the words have been spoken, the contract has been signed. Our feelings have lost the opportunity to join with intelligence in making a contribution.

Feelings, through their connection with the body, supply our energy. If feelings are not allowed to integrate with thoughts and actions, the messages they contain are lost. Without the feeling-energy that could have empowered us, tension arises. Suppressed feelings will fester in the body, feeding a deep sense of frustration, which may "suddenly" erupt in physical symptoms or in an outburst of spiteful words that we later regret. Such occurrences are a signal that the thinking mind with its attendant emotionality has too much control. We are out of balance. To restore harmony we need to relax and take time to connect to feelings.

Exercise: Consciousness of breath forms a bridge between thinking and feeling, as the breath connects the head with the body. Concentrating on the breath for even five minutes, three or four times a day, restores equilibrium to thinking and feeling. Begin by focusing on the in-breath, without trying to manipulate the breath in any way. If you forget to focus on the breath, simply begin again. The constancy and rhythm of the breath activate a process of integration. You arrive in the moment; you are present in your body. Intelligence and feeling are merging.

Mental Fabrications

Thoughts monopolize our attention. At night, we fall asleep as soon as the last unfinished thought disappears into nothingness. When we wake up in the morning, the first thought is already waiting. Thoughts rule our days like a master commanding a slave. It seems as if we have no say about what goes on in the mind: We are compelled to think our thoughts.

If we studied our internal world as seriously as we study the external world, the mind would reveal to us a wealth of possibilities. We need not start from scratch, however, in studying the mind, for we have available today the support of the Buddhist tradition. Countless Buddhist texts are concerned with the mind. The texts of the Abhidharma contain the psychological teachings of the Buddha, an in-depth study of the human mind. The inner activities of mind are catalogued with meticulous detail and provided with commentary.[7]

Human experience is sparked by events that the mind considers important. For instance, the senses are attracted to an object like iron to a magnet. Contact between one of the senses and its object ignites a sensation, and we see, hear, feel, taste, or smell something. The sensation leads to an interpretation; the experience is labeled, and a thought is born. A thought is thus the last link in a complex inner process, a mental chain reaction.

Once the thought is in place, the direct experience disappears. We may believe the thought reflects reality, but it is really nothing more than a poor surrogate for the lost experience. If we start giving an extensive commentary on the food we are eating, do we still enjoy the flavors of the meal? If we classify the plants while walking through a luxurious garden, do we perceive its beauty? Interpretations of experience take us out of the present; the moment passes without notice. When we think about an experience, it is already past, already "dead."

In the process of beginning to control the mind, the first step is identifying the precise moment when a thought appears on stage. By remaining still and turning inward, we can observe the initiation of a single thought. We can also witness the stream of thoughts. Paying close attention to the subsequent interior events prevents us from becoming lost in mental fabrications.

Knowledge of Awareness

One function of mind is to evaluate and select what is advantageous for us and what is not. This discriminating capacity is indispensable for making practical decisions and choices, like filling out a form, crossing a road, or paying a bill. But this critical consciousness tends to stifle other forms of mental activity. As we exercise it more and more, the rational aspect of mind cannot help but form opinions and judgments about everything it observes. Unless we consciously develop awareness of mind's activity, all experience is filtered through the intellect, leaving feeling aside. The mind becomes obsessed with pulling or pushing; critical judgment overrides open awareness and the wholeness of experience is shattered.

Intelligence includes other sources of knowledge besides thought and intellect. Attention, mindfulness, interest, focus, concentration, introspection, fantasy, creative imagination, and presence of mind can all contribute to knowing. The quality of our wisdom depends on the extent to which these various aspects of intelligence cooperate with the world of feeling to create balance.

Spiritual awakening is a process of becoming aware, and awareness is linked to realizing fully all intelligent capacities, including thinking. Interest is the engine that drives this process. Being interested is not just being curious, however; interest maintains involvement and persists—this is how human beings learn. Paying attention fosters interest. Interest can gradually grow into concentration; concentration in turn produces knowledge and finally, wisdom. When we have genuine interest and are able to sustain it, our intelligence leads us to wisdom.

The teachings of the Buddha aim to restore wholeness to the shattered experience. There are numerous methods for returning to direct experience and reestablishing integrity; traditional texts speak of eighty-four thousand methods. Mindfulness is pivotal, and in many Buddhist traditions, mindfulness begins with awareness of the breath. By practicing mindfulness in the midst of the countless confusing experiences we move through each day, we arrive at the wholeness of the present moment. Here there is no fragmentation.

Trusting Is Believing

For constructive mental activity to occur, we need to apply our intelligence. Maintaining a calm and balanced state of mind means neither giving in to destructive emotions, nor forcefully suppressing them. Instead, the way through is to consciously cultivate positive mental events. When positive, constructive qualities are at work, there is no room for destructiveness. By consciously cultivating positivity, we thwart negativity.[8] A negative mind-set contracts consciousness, whereas a positive outlook opens up the mind. Confidence, appreciation, gratefulness, cheerfulness, contentment, satisfaction, and willingness are positive mental states that strengthen awareness and provide energy and stability. By cultivating positive mental events we can gain control of the directionality of mind.

In the Abhidharma, confidence or faith is the first of the positive mental events, the indispensable basis for training the mind. Without confidence, we are bound to end up in fear. Buddhist faith is traditionally described in terms of three kinds of confidence, based on admiration, longing, and conviction. But one could also put it this way: First, one has faith in the ability to tame and awaken the mind: not blind faith or senseless hope, but rather the certainty that we can wake up by putting our trust in what is valuable. Second, there is confidence that our actions have results; we put our trust in what is real. Third, one realizes that most suffering is needless; we put our trust in what is possible.[9]

The first kind of confidence is the certainty that human beings have the potential to become fully aware. The lesson implicit in the life of the historical Buddha is that human beings have the capacity to attain full realization. Just as water can be purified, the mind can be cleansed. This happens on the path of enlightenment.

In daily life the simple recognition that every experience has a positive aspect we can nurture may be considered a milestone. Trusting in this, we come to trust the dynamic inherent in solving problems: Each time we solve a small problem, a positive change ensues. This positive energy gains momentum with each challenge, until we come to enjoy handling more difficult situations. In time, even serious predicaments no longer weigh us down, for we do not feel victimized by them; we know the knowledge we need to respond to them is available to us. With expanding insight comes unshakable faith in the strength and power of awareness.

The second kind of confidence is faith in the law of karma. We cannot expect to achieve a result if we do not first create the cause. This insight provides security for our personal development. If we place a tulip bulb in the earth and give it water and proper nutrients, then a tulip will emerge—not a pine tree. If we do not plant anything, whether accidentally or on purpose, nothing will grow. Our actions make a difference. To every result there has been a cause.

The third kind of confidence is certainty that many of our disappointments and frustrations could have been prevented, that much suffering is senseless and unnecessary. Senseless suffering decreases as soon as we understand the patterns that perpetuate problems. At the very least, a constructive mental attitude prevents problems from intensifying. With sufficient interest, faith, and persistence, we can abolish suffering entirely.

THE ELEVEN POSITIVE MENTAL ACTIVITIES

In the Buddhist Abidharma teachings, confidence or faith is the first of eleven positive mental events. By developing these eleven attitudes, we begin to control our inner lives, and thus our possibilities. In the beginning, it may seem forced or insincere to work deliberately on developing positive mental structures. But before long positivity acquires momentum and fosters tangible results--it works Confidence is followed by self-respect, decorum, non-attachment, non-aversion, non-deludedness, effort, alertness, caring, equanimity and finally, non-violence.[10] The first ten of these positive mental activities provide a path of personal growth that ultimately results in the positive factor of non-violence. Such non-violence is both physical and mental, and is manifested toward ourselves as well as others. This non-violence has been described as the culmination of a fully actualized mind, which bears no harm toward anyone.

In traveling the path of personal growth, we may meet with a variety of obstacles. The greatest impediments are within us. There is a long list of possible obstacles, depending on personal habit. In addition to insecurity and laziness, we may suffer from arrogance, disinterest, distraction, stress, dullness, and the wish that the path were different.[11] Such internal attitudes are described in the Abhidharma as "mind ailments," meaning that they can be cured.

By becoming acquainted with the mind, we understand who we are and what we can make of our lives. Once we have this knowledge, our inner compass can no longer be ignored. With mind as captain of the ship, we know the course that we must take.

And yet—what if the ship is rudderless? What can we do then?

4

We Are Who We Think We Are

My mother had a personal philosophy about love. When I was about twelve years old, she revealed it to me: Somewhere on the face of this earth, there is somebody who belongs with you. No matter how different the two of you are, there is no doubt but that you belong together. Think of an apple that you cut in half. Only these two halves fit together to make the apple whole. "How do the two halves find each other?" I wanted to know. "If you really believe in it, you will find your other half sooner or later."

To my ears this made perfect sense. When I was very small I had once asked her, "If you had to choose between Daddy and us, who would it be?" She protested, "What an impossible question!" But I persisted and finally she gave in. "Daddy." The disappointment had been bitter, but years later I understood. I was simply a piece of her half of the apple.

Actually, I knew little about the relationship between my parents; their marriage was strictly private territory. At night, their bedroom door was locked. Only during heavy thunderstorms, or when one of the children had a nightmare, would my mother leave their bedroom and sometimes take us back into their big bed. My father usually continued sleeping, but she would wait to fall asleep until she heard us breathing evenly.

Together my parents formed an imposing bastion. If you asked either of them a question, he or she first wanted to know if the other had already given an opinion; if so, there was no further discussion. The outside world never heard a cross word spoken between them, and even we saw only rarely a gesture of impatience. Nor were there open displays of love. In the morning, when my father left for the office, my mother gave him a kiss; it never seemed to bother her that he received her show of affection passively.

My parent's unity was indisputable, and nothing could come between them. But what were their higher values and aspirations? Was there a guiding principle in their lives that they held high and cherished? As children we never received rules of behavior or a clear code of conduct, except that we should not throw away food or waste money. My parents had strong feelings about treating their four sons equally, not favoring one over another. And there was no question but that they expected each one to succeed in a career, preferably business.

One evening in January 1964, we observed an intimacy between my mother and father that we had not witnessed before. The day of their silver wedding anniversary was celebrated with a festive family dinner. Silver candelabras decorated the table, which was set with the fine china and had an exquisite flower arrangement as the centerpiece. Rows of tea lights burned in the windows.

As usual, my father sat at the head of the table and my mother at the foot, with two sons on each side. All of us were formally dressed: my mother in an evening dress with corsage and jewelry, my father and the four sons in dark suits. My father was the first to speak and he rose, addressing each of us individually. Finally, he turned to his wife. Tears rolled down his cheeks as he said, "You are the light in my eyes." I had never seen him cry before.

As he kept talking, details about his cheerless youth were revealed to us. As the eldest son, it had fallen to him to bridge the gap between his parents. His father, a silent, commanding man with a moustache, seldom talked to him; his mother also spoke sparingly. Later, during his years at the University of Amsterdam, my father, despite his gruff shyness, became president of a student organization. The time came for the club's anniversary celebration. He did not have a date, but somebody on the organizing committee had a cousin in Paris—why not ask her? After a few months my parents became engaged. They married six years later, just before World War II began.

"When you entered my parents' home, it was like the lights came on," my father said to my mother. The silence at the table was palpable. He muttered, "That's all I have to say." and sat down abruptly. Chairs were moved and the clinking of silverware resumed.

Suddenly my mother rose. "I want to say something, too." I beamed with pride. All eyes were on her. Usually, one of my brothers would make a silly joke when she attracted attention, but not this time. There was an expectant silence. Mother was not shy about expressing herself to others, but it was unusual for her to step into the limelight this way.

As she spoke, she was like a captain standing on the bridge of her ship, eyes focused on the horizon. She talked of starting a new phase in her life, now that the children had left home. It was clear that she did her best to envision the future positively. Instead of dwelling on the past she had left behind and the melancholy of an empty nest, she was determined to give her life new meaning.

We all remained silent for quite some time, impressed by her sense of leadership and the way she took charge of her destiny. She appeared to know her own mind. It did not occur to us to ask questions about what guided her vision of the future.

Looking back on that night, I still cannot tell what she believed in then. Were the old ideas of motherhood and two halves of an apple still her main reference points? Or were her thoughts changing with her, as she grew older? She was only fifty-one years old, and she held her future in her hands.

Circle of Thoughts

"We are who we think we are," said the Buddha, "having become who we thought we were." Thoughts create our reality. Viewing ourselves and the world around us, we draw conclusions based on our thoughts and observations. We are constantly seeking confirmation of our views, finding security there. With the years, *what* we think and *how* we think become the standard for our reality. We begin to consider our thoughts and. impressions as representations of absolute truth.

To the one who thinks, thoughts may seem fresh, but actually thoughts spin endless variations on a few themes, supported by recurring patterns of opinions and inter-pretations. Believing that our assumptions are based on objective truth, we are attached to our way of thinking. And should we suspect that our thoughts and perceptions are channeled into old grooves, it still seems impossible to change our perception. We always encounter the same problems, provoke the familiar responses, and react in the only ways we know—a *perpetuum mobile*. Ultimately everything remains the same. Life becomes a repetitive cycle that holds us captive. This repetitive cycle is char-acterized by an underlying restlessness and confusion. In Buddhist teachings this cycle, and the ultimate aimless-ness of the wanderings within it, is called *samsara*.

The mind constantly produces thoughts. As we grow older, we become more attached to the content of our thoughts and less receptive to unfamiliar positions. Having experienced most things more than a few times, we grow accustomed to our opinions and consider our-selves expert in certain fields. It is not simple to "change" our minds, nor does it seem wise to do so. What would happen if our minds changed? Who would we be? What would others think of us?

Still, if we want to grow as a person, we must make a conscious effort to alter our thoughts, challenging our-selves by asking such questions as, "What thoughts would I like to carry through the day?" "What is important in this thought?" "Have I had this thought before?" "Can I think a thought I have never had?" We can experiment with changing our minds by trying on another person's perspective, or perhaps by refusing to elaborate on an entrenched theme. The best remedy for repetitive thought patterns might be simply to forget them.

Whatever approach we choose, in order to change our minds we must learn to refrain from following our automatic tendencies. Ingrained thoughts weigh us down, whereas the slightest change in a habitual pattern lightens everything. With each conscious change in the way we apply our minds, a burden is lifted off our shoulders.

Tyranny of *I*

Our thought-world is similar to a movie theater that runs continuous films, all featuring *I* as the main character. All supporting roles serve *I*, and the world depicted in the story line is merely a backdrop for *I*'s life. *I*'s obsessive nature demands constant attention. Scenes follow one another haphazardly, according to how *I* sets the stage. All other characters in the story are seen through *I*'s eyes, and in a real sense are figments of *I*'s imagination. Characters act out their roles as if in a soap opera, the story line of each new episode shared with *I*.

The more the mind identifies with the self, the more confined our world becomes. Separated from the whole, we attempt to ease the sense of isolation with emotional dramas. While these dramas provide a semblance of contact, our self-absorption makes a positive connection

47

with others impossible. At times, the self-image may appear to be asleep, as when we are engrossed in work or a game, or faced with an emergency that makes us act spontaneously. Yet invariably the self reappears from the wings, anxious to be right and to draw attention to itself. "Did *I* perform well? Did they see that *I* saved the situation?" Spontaneity and authenticity are replaced by petty concerns about ego.

We are inclined to surround ourselves with individuals like ourselves, people with similar experiences who share our opinions and emotions, who accept us and want us to stay the way we are. Each of us participates in a conspiracy to prevent anyone and anything from changing. In this way, our beliefs are repeatedly confirmed and reinforced. Any change provokes feelings of insecurity and fear, as if the ground were shifting under our feet.

How can we dispel the power of *I*? Simply witnessing the fabrications of *I* without manipulating them can create the beginning of a new stability. Whenever a persistent thought reflects an assertion, the witness can ask, "Says who?" For each answer that emerges, the witness again inquires, "Says who?" By asking this simple, neutral question over and over, we become more genuine, rediscovering our authenticity. In this way we lay the groundwork for the self to be gradually dismantled.

String of Thoughts

Rarely is a thought finished before the next one takes its place. An inner restlessness forces us to produce more and more thoughts; they billow out like the cloudy breath of a fire-breathing dragon. If we can stay with one thought, not grasping it but thinking it through until there is nothing left to think, an insight will follow. For example, we may find that there was an unjustified assumption at its origin and we were off the mark from the start. Or the end of the thought may reveal an answer we were searching for, knowledge we did not realize was available or had ignored because it was uncomfortable, or perhaps entailed frightening conclusions. For example, we may think, "I will have to make a change in my responsibilities at work." If we were to think the thought through, we might decide to make the change right now, instead of waiting for the inevitable to happen later, when the situation might have spun out of control. Thinking thoughts through, and questioning relentlessly our responses ("But I don't know how," "I am doing my best," "I am only human") enables us to change.

Exercise: To explore the possibilities of thought we must learn to look inward until we can glimpse the thought world.

1. Sitting still in meditation, you can discern the stream of thoughts. You may at first be taken aback by the chaotic activity that takes place in the mind—a great tumbling parade of mental events: perceptions, emotions, images, memories, and associations, all of them impulses resulting from sensory stimuli, ending up in thoughts. Let yourself relax and take an inventory

of your thoughts, without judgment or manipulation. "Oh, this is distrust; here is greed; this is about wanting my father's recognition; this is about pride; now jealousy is talking; here is the need to be the ringleader again." By simply observing, recognizing, and allowing thoughts to pass, awareness shines light upon itself.

2. You can also observe your thoughts while you are at work. Keep a sheet of paper near your workspace. For a short period, maybe no more than ten minutes, tally the thoughts that arise in the mind. Keep a separate tally of each distracting thought that is unrelated to the work at hand. This exercise makes the mind clearer and more alert, and improves concentration.

3. You can also categorize thoughts according to their quality: positive, negative, or neutral. In a split second you must decide to which category a thought belongs, but upon closer scrutiny, every thought, regardless of its content, has a positive, negative, and neutral aspect. Eventually, awareness of this threefold aspect of thoughts can strengthen your ability to cultivate positive attitudes in your daily life. Knowing you have a choice, you begin to look for the positive quality in everything and build upon it.

Once you become aware of a thought as it enters the mind, you have reached a milestone in meditation on thoughts. At this point, awareness is no longer wedded only to the content of thought. Two mental activities manifest simultaneously: the thought, i.e., "Is it already that late?" and awareness of the thought, separate from its content. With this expansion of awareness, you find freedom from the flotsam and jetsam of the mind. Released from bondage to whatever thoughts happen to arise, awareness begins to exercise its potential to determine the content of thought.

Once awareness manifests this potential, you begin to understand how the mind operates and are able to leave thoughts alone. The less you identify with what you think—with whatever comes to mind—the less fixed your patterns become. You no longer take your moods and prejudices so seriously; they are just passing through, like temporary guests who come and go in the uninhabited house of the mind. If you do not pay them much attention, they leave as quickly as they arrived. This is the fruit of meditation.

Our thoughts may appear to be securely linked, like the pearls on a necklace. But when mind is quiet, we see that there is no connecting thread—only a handful of pearls. In fact, thoughts generally arrive in disorganized groups. If we observe streams of thoughts closely, we see that the mind can appear clear and quiet in one moment, and then, without warning, be overflowing with mental activity in the next. Close scrutiny may reveal that one thought contains a host of others, although we tend to select out the one that is most familiar. Upon further investigation we may find that one single thought contains all thoughts, in the sense that at the heart of every thought is space active with an agitated quality of energy.

If we try to trace either the origin or destination of thoughts, we come up empty-handed. Where do thoughts come from and where do they go? They appear suddenly and then simply disappear, we know not where, leaving behind in our bodies and our energy a trace that instantly tends to establish a pattern.

As we learn to relax the mind and let thoughts come and go without clinging to them, a tiny gap between thoughts is revealed. In the space before the next thought arrives, there is emptiness, stillness. For a moment even *I* is absent; without thought, there is no *I*. In meditation, it is possible to discern and enter these still spaces in the string of thoughts. As if beneath, behind, below, or inside this dense emptiness, we find the true nature of mind—open, spacious, and free.

Where Is *I*?

Senses, feelings, and thoughts collaborate to produce the *I* that causes so much unrest. But where is *I* located? If we look for *I* in the body, we will not find it there. If we look in the mind for a distinct and autonomous *I*, we come up empty-handed as well. The thoughts, feelings, projections, and memories that are acted out in the mind are constantly changing. We have no idea what our next thought will be. Thoughts come and go uncontrollably, and the self that supplies the content for so many thoughts is as elusive as thought itself. One moment we feel deeply satisfied, the next moment bitterly disappointed. If *I* were a constant factor in the mind, would not our experience remain constant too?

But the mind has no constants. It is formless, colorless, odorless, and tasteless. Regardless of the limitations and boundaries we impose upon it, mind remains immeasurable, its power inconceivable. A nineteenth-century Tibetan lama, Lama Mipham, was once asked, "What knowledge do we need to become wise human beings?" He answered, "The knowledge that penetrates the despotism and illusion of *I*."[12] In ten different ways Lama Mipham demonstrated that it is not *I* that suffers and becomes free—it is mind that suffers and is liberated from the tyranny of *I*.

Through deeper knowledge of *I*, we learn to appreciate the true nature of the mind and its potential for our lives. When the sword of self-knowledge cuts through belief in a permanent, substantial *I*, unnecessary suffering comes to an end. The mind begins to awaken. The more translucent *I* becomes, the less likely we are to fall victim to its whims. When *I* no longer dominates and the open mind can play freely, our full being emerges and blossoms.

Still, it makes sense to say that there is a life phase in which *I* has a constructive role to play. When we are young, it is important to develop a balanced *I*. A healthy self-image nurtures the confidence vital to shaping young life. A strong dose of self-esteem awakens a sense of personal responsibility; a pinch of pride is like the salt that draws out the taste of a dish. With a balanced *I*, ego, or self-image, young people can blaze their own trails instead of merely following well-worn paths. Scientific research suggests that the part of the brain that creates order and takes care of long-term planning, the CEO of the brain, is developed in one's late twenties. Until that time, we are "future-blind."[13] Perhaps this is one reason why Siddhartha Gautama, who was to become the Buddha, began his journey to enlightenment at the age of twenty-nine.

Early in life, *I* helps us find our way. However, as we get older we begin to see that self-absorption constricts our nature. *I*'s limited repertoire is only capable of creating duality: self and world, like and dislike, we and they. It repeatedly isolates and separates us. Within such duality, living and working together in harmony is impossible. Only an open, undivided consciousness can perceive a larger picture and the contributions each of us can make within it.

Exercise: Sitting quietly, let the following question resonate: "Who am I?" Listen briefly for the reactions that arise and after a while ask again, "Who am I?" Try answering: "I am not my body. I am not my feelings. I am not my thoughts." By repeating both question and answers, mind becomes aware of itself. Consciousness becomes a neutral witness of the inner processes. When silence descends, ask once more, "Who am I?" Question each reaction, "But who am I?" Now and then, quietly call your own name and ask again, "Who am I?"

Just before attaining enlightenment, Prince Siddhartha Gautama was threatened by demons—illusions of *I*—that attacked him with all the weapons at their disposal. The demons can be understood as signs that the subconscious is breaking through. All that lies hidden emerges: primeval terrors from the distant past, fears carried from bardo to bardo, repressed memories from childhood, or emotional devastations from this present life.

Understanding that neither the demons nor their weapons in themselves had the power to harm him, Prince Siddhartha transformed all the weapons into flowers. We, too, can understand and transform the destructive machinations of *I*. Supported by knowledge, awareness has the power to defeat *I* and emerge victorious. The process begins when we have faith in this possibility.

In some Buddhist traditions, the defeat of *I* is called *small nirvana*. Release from the shackles of ego ends unnecessary suffering. A person who reaches this level of awakening is called an *Arhat*: one who has overcome the enemy. In Buddhist art, this stage is often illustrated by miniscule human figures trampled underfoot, or by a headdress made of human skulls. These symbols signify the defeat of *I*'s tyranny.

Some people experience great bliss just before the moment of dying. *I*'s role is over; redemption and liberation are near. The mind separates from the body, while *I* and its emotional patterns vanish. The light of awareness that has made it possible to see thoughts and images throughout life finally shines unfiltered, clear and soft. For the moment, we are free.

5

Beginningless Continuity

In the fifties, my mother founded a women's group called
The Kaleidoscope. She selected eight women of diverse
backgrounds who would have much to discuss. They met
on the first Friday of each month. Several members had
to come from far away, but by nine-thirty in the morning
everyone was settled in. They began by catching up with
each other's lives, a cup of coffee in hand. The prelim-
inary chats were often personal, and it was understood
that everything would be kept private. When everyone
was up-to-date, one of the members would give an informal lecture for about an hour, followed by a lively discussion in which everyone took part.

When it was my mother's turn to give the lecture, she
would study her subject for months. One of her first topics was the psychology of color. My mother believed that
each human being is characterized by a specific color. At
the birth of each of her four sons, she bought an album
in which she collected anecdotes, photos, and clippings
illustrating the highlights of the child's life. The color of
the album cover was an important choice—green for the
oldest one, then blue, yellow, and red for the youngest. In
spite of her interest in colors, I never found out what her

favorite color was. My father was the one who picked out the curtains, the couch upholstery, and sometimes even my mother's clothes.

Another interest my mother brought to the club was handwriting analysis, a subject she studied at the University of Leiden. The Kaleidoscope offered her an opportunity to share her knowledge, for otherwise her expertise in this field was seldom enlisted, except by my father, who occasionally employed her skill to help evaluate job application letters. His main concern was detecting a talented manager through handwriting analysis. We children also benefited from her knowledge; once we learned which characteristics indicated a bold and energetic personality, we adjusted our handwriting accordingly. For instance, she taught us that underlining or placing a period behind one's signature, or crossing two t's with a single bold stroke, showed character.

On another occasion my mother's lecture for The Kaleidoscope was about the fourteenth Dalai Lama, the spiritual leader of the Tibetan people who, together with thousands of other Tibetan refugees, had fled his home country in 1959. In the sixties relatively little was known about the tragic events taking place in that remote part of the world. Only in 1989, when the Dalai Lama won the Nobel Peace Prize and became world-renowned, did the West become intrigued by Tibet.

For twenty years The Kaleidoscope blossomed, with my mother as instigator and guiding force. When finally Alzheimer's disease had frayed her mind so that she lacked the necessary resourcefulness, the club abruptly disbanded.

Without any closure, not even a formal farewell, the circle of friends fell apart. Whenever I encountered one of the members later, usually at funerals, she would express a fond wish to revive the club. Raked embers would flare briefly, wistfully. "It was really becoming too much for your mother," each would conclude ruefully.

Why were these eight women unprepared to step in as my mother's health faded? For years they had witnessed my mother's gradual decline, and yet the end came as a surprise. When she was no longer capable of organizing the meetings, no one else took the initiative. Allaying their concerns, they hoped all would work out. In brushing aside worry they also discarded valuable insight, precluding any constructive action on their part. The promptings of intuition were missed or ignored, and the opportunity to act in a timely manner passed by, unheeded. Thus knowledge vanished, and regret was born.

Securing Closure

Everything has a beginning, a middle, and an ending. Beginnings require energy and creativity; in the middle one needs to persist and follow through. Endings demand the courage to consciously bring matters to a close, enjoy what has been accomplished, and then let go.

People who are full of energy and ideas tend to launch new plans with zest and enthusiasm, eager to take on the challenge of another adventure. At the beginning all goes well, but after the development stage, when routine sets in and there is a need for perseverance, the sense of fun and excitement soon vanishes. Remaining motivated is difficult.

Others may not want to take responsibility for beginning a new venture on their own, but will readily support someone else's plan. They are the doers who are able to remain motivated, to persevere, follow up, and keep things going. They handle all kinds of difficulties, have steady energy, and are able to exercise creativity within the given structure.

Once the development stage of the project or venture has run its course, the project heads into the home stretch, which most people find the most challenging of the three stages. Proper closure requires time, energy, endurance and most of all, caring. When the finish draws near, we are confronted with the truth of impermanence. Whatever the situation—the end of a club, a job or a business, a relationship, or an era—the knowledge that everything comes to an end, ourselves included, urges itself upon us, although we may avoid acknowledging this message.

Even though we have already witnessed this truth in countless different ways, we continue to resist knowledge of transience. If something new lies on the horizon, it is tempting to skip closure and rush off to the next challenge. Conversely, without new challenges ahead we may persist with old routines out of fear, even if they have outlived their usefulness. Either way there is a lack of closure, and regret will be the result.

The beginning and middle of The Kaleidoscope were successful, but at the end it fizzled out. Could it have turned out differently? Perhaps the talks could have been gathered together into a memorial volume. Or the women could have come together one last time, allowing each member to express what the group had meant to her. The truth of impermanence could have penetrated the consciousness of the group: The Kaleidoscope had a beginning; therefore it must have an end. Perhaps a new club could have been formed, to support those in need of warmth and friendship in their old age. Instead, a part of the women's lives abruptly ended. The loss of the club may not have weighed heavily on them, but a nagging regret meant that they could not let go of it. Some part of them was bound up in the past.

A happy conclusion is not always feasible, and there is no such thing as ideal closure. When a period of our lives is over, however, there is considerable value in taking the time to reflect on what has happened, if possible with the other people involved. It may be tempting to ignore the end, but by doing this, we miss the opportunity to bring what was valuable in this phase into the next. Without closure, we risk losing a part of our memory.

Impermanence is a fact of life, simultaneously one of the most painful and most beautiful. In its beauty, imper-manence allows us to move on and still retain what we have held dear. A time that has been brought to an appro-priate close can be remembered in its fullness, without anxiety or regret. Such memories, knowledge, and feel-ings fuel and nourish our lives; they become part of us.

Nothing Lasts Forever

Change is inherent in the fabric of the cosmos. Our universe, one of many, according to Buddhist teachings, is constantly changing. Creation and decline follow one another ceaselessly; in the rhythms of time, beginning and ending, birth and death are inextricably linked. Nothing that seems natural and even indispensable now will remain with us until the end. The towns where we live may seem to be fixed realities, but those who live in areas where earthquakes or other natural disasters occur know better. If in twenty-five years we return to our present location, much of it will have disappeared or changed beyond recognition. The ground on which an old building now rests was once a swamp or a forest, and before that, many millennia ago, perhaps a sea or an ocean. The families in which we grow up or that we start, the organizations for which we work, the society to which we contribute, the culture that has shaped us—everything that exists due to causes and conditions will change and ultimately, disappear.

Nothing lasts or stays the same; everything is in motion. A butterfly may last for a week, redwood trees for thousands of years, and stars for billions of years, but each has its appointed time, and within that time, keeps changing. Likewise, the human body undergoes constant transformation within its appointed span of time, no matter how we try to deny or prevent it. At middle age, not one cell in the human body (except for brain cells)[14] is the same as it was at birth. Not even our planet or the sun will last forever. Even the universe—vast space within which the life of a human being appears like the volume of a single breath of air—is constantly undergoing transformation. Change is the dominant flavor of reality.

What if we could taste change as if it were a delicacy? No longer would we have to cling to the illusion that ignoring time lets us hold it at bay. We could let go of the need for control, knowing that it serves only to mask fear of the uncertainty inherent in change. Instead, rejoicing in the fact that nothing is fixed, we could allow ourselves to yield to transformation. Change offers wonderment and vitality. Since everything is open, things can always improve; we can take refuge in that knowledge. Time is our partner and our teacher.

CODEPENDENT ORIGINATION

The forces of the universe have their own momentum. Following the law of karma, all things arise from what has come before. All appearances are the result of a complex array of causes and conditions, which together produce a particular outcome.[15] When a business receives an order for merchandise, successive steps are set in motion that result in delivery of the finished goods. The same sort of chain reaction occurs in nature. A seed sprouts, leaves form; a plant takes shape and grows. A bud appears that, if all goes well, turns into a flower and in time into a seed-bearing fruit. Change is a spiral of never-ending recycling processes.

The transformation from seed to fruit to seed, from beginning to end to new beginning, always takes place in time. Every phase is preceded by something else: *Ex nihilo nihil fit*—no thing can ever emerge from nothing. There is always a chain reaction. This is true of mental processes, of the world around us, and of events on a collective and universal level. The present is the product of the past; what we think, say, and do now provides seeds for the future. When we are aware of the seeds we are sowing, we have more control over our crops.

According to Buddhist teachings, there is no higher authority that rules and directs this ever-unfolding process. Appearances operate according to a self-organizing principle, establishing order out of chaos, both at microscopic and macroscopic levels. "This is a consequence of that, and that in turn is the basis for what follows," as the Buddha taught in the *Pratityasamutpada Sutta*. The law of karma is in charge.

One thing is certain: Neither the cause nor the result is permanent. A sprouting seed disappears once a plant takes its place. Water in the kettle boils and takes the form of vapor. These processes have no "doer," but are part of a continuous flow of transformation. The only constant is that everything changes. Therein lies our hope.

It is not *I* that plays a decisive role in this process. The self is not an independent entity that enjoys, initiates, or suffers. Consequences result from a many seeds that have borne fruit. Happiness, suffering, and success are neither predetermined nor coincidental. They are the result of causes and conditions.

Awareness of the interplay of causes and conditions can become a guiding principle in our lives. Usually, we tend to look for "the" cause of what befalls us. But if we focus on trying to find a single cause, we could spend an entire lifetime searching unsuccessfully. Put differently, the only single cause may be our ignorance concerning karma, the web of causes and conditions. We do not realize that all composite things, such as human life, natural phenomena, states of mind, even the ebbing and flowing universe, are transitory and unable to exist independently. Interwoven causes and conditions—in Buddhist terminology, "codependent origination"—create a tapestry of both good and ill.

In a moment of distraction, I let the milk boil over. The whole house smells sour, so I open the windows wide. Not noticing the draft, I catch a cold. Feeling unwell, I stay at home and miss a meeting that could have changed my life. Such a seemingly random sequence of events actually fits together like the pieces of a puzzle. For answers to the questions, "Why is my life this way? Why is this happening to me?" we must look not only to the present. Present circumstances reveal what has become of seeds that have previously been sown. Exploring the foundation of karma lies at the heart of the Buddhist path.

CERTAINTY IN UNCERTAINTY

When Siddhartha Gautama, who became the Buddha, sat under the Bodhi tree in Bodh Gaya, India, he resolved not to arise until he completely understood the nature of human existence. In order to penetrate to the heart of things, his mind had to be calm and clear. He focused on the rhythm of the breath. In the *Sattipathana Sutta*, the Buddha describes how he witnessed this process: "The breath comes in, and the breath goes out. The breath is large, the breath is small. The stomach expands, the stomach pulls in. The breath comes in, the breath goes out again."

When we follow the Buddha's example and focus on the breath instead of on thoughts, the mind grows quiet. The energies of body and mind, of feeling and intelligence, harmonize with the rhythm of breath and with one another. Agitation subsides, consciousness relaxes, and the mind becomes clear. With the coming and going of the breath, the unfolding experience of impermanence, which the breath exemplifies, permeates awareness. As knowledge of impermanence merges with awareness and becomes an inseparable part of it, the nature of life becomes clear: Everything that is born will die; nothing remains untouched by impermanence. We need not cling to the status quo nor deny that change is imminent. Change need no longer cause us to panic. We find our ground when we feel certainty in uncertainty.

How We Breathe Is How We Become

The way we breathe determines our physical, mental, emotional, and spiritual well-being. When the flow of breath is uneven, its energy does not nourish certain areas of the body. These parts eventually become numb, while other areas where breath is concentrated tend to become overactive. When our breathing is gentle and even, however, our senses are refreshed and our heart relaxes. As we refine our breathing, awareness can contact a subtle inner energy of the breath that provides both mind and body with vitality. In classical Greek, this inner breath is expressed in the word *psyche*, which refers to both breath and soul, inseparable in their unity.

Our state of mind determines the way we breathe, and vice versa: The way we breathe is the way we become. When we are nervous, for example, we emphasize the inhalation, gulping anxiously. We stumble over our words and fail to communicate adequately, because we cannot slow down enough to allow breath and speech to join together. When we feel lazy and negative, on the other hand, we emphasize the exhalation, puffing out expressively. Heaving deep sighs, we find it impossible to muster any enthusiasm, and feel tired and apathetic, indifferent to time passing us by. Feelings of depression are accompanied by shallow breathing; we feel empty and drained, lifeless. Everything seems to require an inordinate amount of effort. Overcome by emotion, we can hardly breathe at all. Cut off from breath, we feel paralyzed and fail to see any alternatives.

When we breathe as we normally do, without much awareness, the breath fills only the upper region of the lungs, and the vitality of breath is directed primarily toward the head. Our thoughts receive too much fuel, while our bodies do not receive enough. We drift off into a world of thoughts and lose touch with our deeper feelings. Generating more ideas than we can handle, we easily become emotional, and tend to succumb to impatience, despair, or panic. It is difficult to act or to persist in a course of action.

We can break this vicious cycle by becoming more aware of our breathing. Awareness of breath creates space in our minds and expands our sense of time. It becomes easier to pause and take a deep breath. Even one deep breath in the middle of a tense situation can provide enough space and time for us to ask, "How do I want to react?" Taking several deep breaths may prevent impulsive action. Walking around the block or taking a bike ride literally offers a breath of fresh air, clearing the brain and supporting the functioning of the body as a whole.

With practice, the breath can become our refuge. When we practice awareness of breath in calm situations as well as emergencies, we build up a reliable dynamic. As awareness merges with the rhythm of breath, whatever is overactive in the body or mind quiets down, while whatever is dull and sluggish becomes more alive. Thinking and feeling integrate, and our lives grow healthy and harmonious.

Mindfulness of breath as it comes and goes gradually brings the breath to an even level. As the breath slows down and grows gentle and steady, the subtle breath awakens and begins to nourish head and heart, intelligence and feeling. The senses relax and open; colors become brighter and tastes richer. We discern the hidden meanings behind words. A balance emerges

67

between inner and outer: Our internal experience becomes open, and we are attuned to the energies of the external world.

When preparing a recipe from a cookbook, we invite the chef who created it into our kitchen for inspiration. When we play a sonata for violin, we invite the composer or the performer into our living room, to find the right tone and maintain the rhythm. In drawing on the talents of the masters, we access greater knowledge than if we relied solely upon our own beginner's mind-set. Similarly, when we practice the "mindfulness of breath" method taught by the Buddha, we summon the Buddha-nature in us to come forward. This is a major benefit of this meditation: Tapping into the mind and energy of the Buddha within, we plant the seed of awakening.

> *Exercise*: To become mindful of your breath, sit quietly, initially with eyes closed, and turn your attention inward. Let your body become relaxed and still. Stillness refreshes the body, especially the senses, which can become so overstimulated by impressions during the day that it is difficult to find relaxation, even while sleeping.
>
> As you sit in silence, imagine that the pores of your skin absorb the silence. Allow the silence to penetrate deeply into your body, saturating the muscles and sinews, and even the organs. Open your mouth slightly, and breathe through both nose and mouth; let the tip of the tongue touch the upper palate, just behind the upper front teeth. This kind of

breathing may be uncomfortable at first, but with practice, you will find that it helps to balance the flow of the breath to both head and heart. You become more relaxed and alert, and able to sustain your efforts for a longer period of time.

As you breathe, simply observe the breath, without judging or trying to change it. Simply notice: "The in-breath is short," or "the in-breath is long." When thoughts distract you, inhale more deeply and exhale slowly. Once the pull of thoughts subsides, return to observing the breath without manipulating it. In the beginning, it is advisable to practice this meditation briefly five or six times a day; several short sessions are often more fruitful than a single long one.

THE SUBTLE BREATH

Stillness linked with mindfulness of breath brings many benefits. With growing awareness of body and breath, presence of mind increases. Thoughts and interruptions still occur, but no longer distract us. Awareness settles within itself. Breathing patterns change; the breath goes deeper and becomes softer, gentler, until it is barely noticeable. When the body is still and the mind is calm, the subtle internal breath reveals itself. Sometimes we hardly seem to be breathing at all, yet we experience a delicate flow that permeates the entire body and mind. Integration of the energies of body and mind has begun.

It is easy to lose track of the subtle energy when we go off into thoughts or waste the breath on meaningless chatter. Silent awareness of the breath allows the energy of the subtle breath to accumulate in the body and increase in power, like water building up behind a dam. This accumulation is healing, a natural antidote to stress and tension.

When the subtle breath circulates throughout the body, meditation opens up to a deeper level of integration.[16] Body and mind, inner and outer become united. Boundaries dissolve and time expands, until a single moment becomes an eternity in which everything seems to be knowable.

THE GROUND OF COMPASSION

The Buddha said that an atom contains many universes and that a single hair on our heads encompasses innumerable worlds. Everything is connected, and all is constantly in a process of change. Long before the earth came into being, the oxygen atoms now in our lungs, the carbon in our cells, the calcium in our bones, and the iron in our blood were part of a distant star.[17] Long after we are gone, the elements and minerals of our bodies will continue to contribute to many different forms of life. The handful of raw materials that make up our bodies and minds constantly manifest in new shapes and events. Like a kaleidoscope that with each turn displays new manifestations, time continuously transforms the same elements, while space is infinitely pliable, accommodating all appearances.

This recycling process continues forever; according to the Buddhist teachings, there was no beginning and there will be no end. When the earth and our universe cease to exist, there will still be space, full of activity, eternally pregnant with the vitality that manifests as breath in sentient beings. Enlivened by the energy of the universe with each breath, we are children of space and tap one source ". . . all of them from one breath."[18] Awareness of our interconnectedness is the ground for compassion: one in all and all in one.

6

Loss of Memory

As an eighteen-year-old, what did my mother dream of? As a young woman, what did she long for? When the youngest son left home she was in her early fifties—what would she do with the rest of her life? Women of her generation were generally not encouraged to have aspirations other than giving emotional support to their husbands, educating their children, and keeping an impeccable household. Half her life had been devoted to the care of her family and that task was almost completed. With her many talents and capabilities she was still young enough for new challenges. My mother might never have this unique opportunity again. Did she hear a small voice expressing a longing that had not yet been fulfilled? For the first time in her life the future was open and time presented her with a clean slate.

I never knew what her inner voice said, and no one in our family seems to remember exactly how she started on her new career. Did someone recommend it to her? Did she read about it in the local newspaper, *De Haagsche Courant*? She never kept a diary and in none of her letters is it mentioned. But maybe her actions spoke clearly enough. She joined the executive board of a national care organization, *Pro Senectute,* meaning For the Aged. As a full-time volunteer she managed a home for the elderly called Salomonson, in The Hague. Soon after she began, the house had to close down. The board decided to build a new dwelling for the thirty inhabitants. In a nearby rural area my mother located a suitable plot of land for construction. The site was near a school, so the inhabitants would benefit from youthful energy. In the local archives she unearthed the historical name of this small town, "Foreschate," which became the name of the home.

Under her direction, Foreschate was split into small apartments, each with a kitchenette, combined living room and bedroom, and bathroom with shower. This was a novel concept at the time, and my mother had to convince the mayor to support the revolutionary plan. As a member of the building commission, she made many choices and decisions, all of which were guided by a single criterion: the best interests of the elderly people who would have to live with them. She felt that they had already given up much of their lives in order to move to Foreschate, and she wanted to ensure that their autumnal years were as comfortable as possible.

An annual report of Pro Senectute describes how in February 1971, my mother drove the first stake into the ground; on May 11, 1973, Foreschate officially opened. The opening ceremony was well attended, not just by the board of directors and friends of the organization, but also by the mayor and all the students from the neighboring school. One of the guests was so taken with the new home that he immediately committed a million guilders to build another Pro Senectute House. The chair of the board called my mother the godmother of Foreschate. Three years later, in 1976, when my parents retired to their home on the Italian island of Elba, the annual report mentioned her departure in these words: "At this time, we realize how much work she has accomplished. In her farewell speech, Mrs. Maitland expressed gratitude for the opportunities she was given by Pro Senectute. But surely, the appreciation and gratitude of all the residents and staff of Foreschate are much more in order."

Memory Is Outdated

My teacher Tarthang Tulku once said that memory loss should be considered one of today's most serious illnesses. He was not referring to Alzheimer's disease, but to our limited capacity to remember, or rather, our limited use of this capacity. The human brain is like a well-stocked toolbox, useful in almost any situation, but subject to rust if neglected. "Use it or lose it," as the saying goes. Inactive brain cells receive the message that they are no longer needed. As cells begin to atrophy and synapses (contact points between the cells) wither, the connections between parts of the brain that exchange vital information grow weak. Memories, names, and facts increasingly elude us and can no longer be brought to mind. The power of the mind deteriorates.

It is so easy to forget; most of our experiences disappear out of our mind right away. We hardly remember the emotions we felt last week or even yesterday. We are probably not aware of much of what we thought and said even five minutes ago. Things that kept us awake at night six months ago have fallen into oblivion. Our own birth, our dramatic entrance into this world, is completely beyond the scope of our memory.

Yet memory is the foundation of our worldly wisdom. Where we come from and what we have done in the past dictate who we are and what we do today. Likewise, what we think and say today determines what we will be capable of tomorrow. If we want to fully mobilize our mental capacities, we need to use our memory.

Memory has been indispensable for the development of human civilization. Knowledge required for survival has always been transmitted from parent to child through example and the spoken word. In ancient traditions, some of which survive today, history and culture were kept alive through oral accounts passed on from generation to generation. The use of mnemonic devices to support prodigious feats of memory was a sophisticated art. Various techniques, such as story, rhyme and song, or so-called memory palaces—imaginary edifices for storing information—strengthened memory and made it reliable. A good memory was the first requirement for success. Poets recited entire bodies of work, musicians played concerts by heart, and public speakers memorized speeches word for word. Communal wisdom was a collective inheritance, a shared memory that resided within individual awareness.

Today, much spiritual and practical wisdom has been lost. Too often the wisdom and insight of ancient peoples live only on paper. Human beings are forced to continuously rediscover perennial truths that were once common knowledge. In modern societies, where computer technology allows information to be externally located with exceptional speed and accuracy, reliance on human memory seems outdated, redundant, and pointless. Even if we endeavor to improve our memory, we may believe we have little real use for it. Doing arithmetic by heart, reciting poems, or telling long and complex stories are no longer considered vital or respected skills. We may occasionally hear of a young genius who performs astounding feats of memory, but most young people do not expect to develop a strong memory, and do not consider the lack of it a loss. Reference materials abound, and memorization seems tedious and unnecessary. Why make something difficult, when it can be so easy? Perhaps we do not realize that as memory declines so do the concentration, discipline, and patience necessary to build a powerful mind. This realization may come belatedly, when even the limited memory we have now can no longer be relied upon.

A HEALTHY BRAIN

Scientific research has shown that simple mind training shapes the brain, and influences the quality of life positively. Given a stimulating environment and an active existence, the brain builds new cells and synapses, even late in life. When cognitive abilities are challenged, the synapses, contact points, multiply accordingly. The greater the number of contact points, the better the

communication amongst the cells, and all brain functions, including memory, benefit. As we grow older, synapses function like money in the bank: The more we save,
the more we can spend, and the longer it will take before
our wealth is exhausted. Healthy synapses are a "brain-
reserve," a buffer we can draw on during times of adversity, such as illness and debilitation. By stimulating the
brain to grow, we protect ourselves against the future
when, due to a variety of circumstances, the health of the
brain declines. Those who continue to learn new skills,
explore new ideas, and show interest in the outside world
keep the brain active and run less risk of memory loss,
and (so it seems) of developing Alzheimer's disease.[19]

Meditation is one form of mind training that has
proven to have positive effects on the brain and the nervous system. Since the 1970s scientists have investigated
the effects of meditation on stress. A meditative state of
mind slows down the heart rate, strengthens the immune
system, and alleviates pain, including pain caused by
cancer and heart disease. Researchers also discovered
early on that meditation improves concentration. While
they started with the assumption that concentration was
tiring, they found to their surprise that meditators experienced concentration as a pleasant and effortless activity that increased energy rather than depleting it. Overall,
scientific research suggests that the long-term effects of
meditation are entirely positive.

In the 1990s the development of brain-scan technology began to accelerate scientific research on brain functions, revealing the impact of meditation on the brain.

Until recently, scientists believed that the number of human brain neurons remained stable after birth. Yet, new research shows that the adult brain is constantly producing new neurons. Recent scanning technology reveals that meditation stimulates the building of new brain tissue and circuitry that effectively reconfigures the brain. Meditation relaxes the "fight or flight" response and its accompanying negative emotions, such as fear, anxiety, and depression. Activity shifts to the parts of the brain where positive emotions like appreciation, enthusiasm, and interest predominate. Biological changes in the brain cause a positive ripple effect throughout the body, benefiting overall well-being, increasing intelligence, and fostering happiness. This development counters the decline of the brain, stimulating a vivid, creative memory, with appreciation for everything it comprehends.

Transmission of Knowledge

In Tibet, children traditionally grew up learning certain truths: A human life is a rare gift; our time on earth is brief; it is possible to master the mind and understand the law of karma. Knowledge of the Dharma was imparted at a very young age and reflected everywhere in the environment—the countryside, cities, houses, and monasteries. Dharma symbols, including stupas, prayer flags, and mantras carved on stones, as well as sculptures and paintings were everywhere, creating a pervasive atmosphere of spiritual values that constantly worked to refine consciousness. The flavor of enlightenment was carried on the air and united with the breath.

Memorizing used to be a fundamental part of Tibetan education, and is still practiced today in the remaining monasteries in Tibet and in the Tibetan refugee communities in Nepal, India, and other countries. As children, young monks and nuns learn by heart the names of the Enlightened Ones, as well as entire classical texts. Even if they are too young to understand the meanings of the texts, chanting the words of wisdom provides a wholesome framework for the unfolding of their potential. At a subtle level, the meanings of the texts are imprinted upon their consciousness. As their understanding matures, these meanings can be brought more fully into awareness. Thus memorizing stimulates the active capacity for knowing and encourages young people to appreciate the value of developing the mind.

Once knowledge has been imprinted through memorization, and awakened, developed, and matured through meditation, the tools of the intellect can be used to communicate this transmitted wisdom. Few in the West realize that training in logic and the use of intellect is closely linked to Tibetan Buddhist spiritual practice. Through practicing the art of debate, for example, students learn to articulate and direct their mental capacities. Grounded in the practice of mindfulness, and energized through concentration, such training strengthens and expands consciousness and leads to the attainment of higher wisdom. As this wisdom is timeless and independent of local circumstances, those who hold it are able to offer a meaningful contribution to the society they participate in, wherever that may be.

In Tibetan education nothing is more important than the continuity of wisdom through the living lineage of enlightened knowledge-holders. The teacher assumes responsibility for the transmission of knowledge to the student, communicating the teachings by word, by gesture, and from mind to mind. In turn, the student assumes responsibility for upholding the enlightened lineage and for embodying and disseminating the Dharma teachings. So long as this transmission from teacher to student continues, the Tibetan Buddhist lineage will stay alive. It is the powerful memory of the lineage holders, which contains the knowledge of texts, practices, teachers, and experiences as well as of the patterns for successful attainment of mastery, that has kept Tibetan Buddhism a living tradition up to the present day.

Remembering the Present

"Listen well, friends," said the Buddha, "The doors of the Dharma number one hundred and eight. . . . Right mindfulness is a luminous door of the Dharma; it leads to no need for memory or fixing the mind on anything."[20] Once we have arrived on the other shore, we no longer need the boat.

An active, clear, and open mind manifests itself in many ways: in an excellent or even photographic memory, in well-developed concentration, even in the capacity to immediately grasp the essence of a situation, predict the future, or read other people's minds. Many relegate these gifts to the realm of fairy tales, or at least assume that they are inaccessible to ordinary humans. Yet they have been described in many historical accounts as normal phenomena. According to Buddhist teachings, mind has the power to penetrate the nature of reality. Almost everything is knowable.

An active and lively awareness produces a rich memory that functions smoothly. Mental engagement is the glue that fixes a fact or event in the mind. We are not likely to forget vivid and dramatic images or things we really care about. Most of us have had experiences of such intense awareness. When we are engaged and fully participating in the present moment, the images we register are powerful and alive. Remembering is effortless; some images last all our lives.

An apathetic or worried mind that remains on the periphery of experience does not register the myriad images of everyday life; when the images are not recorded, the memories that could give richness to life remain blank. We may be busy, but our attention span is narrow and our internal experience is on hold. Our feelings are either sluggish or tense. Days pass in a blur, because the mind is operating under constraint or at half power. Inner dialogues drain our energy. Caught up in mindlessly chewing over the past or the future, we are not connected to the present moment. Complete periods of our lives may pass without being experienced and will thus go unremembered.

Because we are not alert to what is actually happening from moment to moment, gaps in awareness occur in a small way many times each day. On our way from the living room to the kitchen, or from our home to the store, we are likely to be lost in thoughts, making plans or rehashing incidents from earlier in the day. Objects and events along the way fail to attract our attention. Someone may address us without our even noticing. At home we rise from our chair, but immediately forget what we intended to do. We say, "I'm losing my short-term memory," but in reality we were simply unaware.

MINDFULNESS

Exercise: As a mindfulness practice, stroll from one room to another, noticing as many details as possible—the light falling on the windowsill, the pattern of the floor tiles, the missing piece in the frame of a portrait hanging on the wall. When you are mindful in this way, you begin to observe smaller and smaller details. Awareness wakes up and becomes more alert. In the beginning, you may feel like an observer of your own experience, but this is only a transitory feeling. Gradually, as you continue to practice mindfulness, awareness grows engaged, and experience simultaneously deepens and expands. You are less likely to become lost in thoughts, because mindfulness, like a bright lantern on a dark night, penetrates the heaviness of thought and reestablishes a light, open awareness. If you were fully aware in this moment, you would never forget it.

Awareness generates and records our experience in vivid images that are not easily forgotten. The more vivid and dynamic the picture, the more completely an experience registers in our memories. Active scenes and intense colors from important events in our lives are literally imprinted on our minds. When we think about where we live, we can easily give directions to another person, because in our mind's eye we see the neighborhood and the streets in vivid detail. When we think about someone we love, strong impressions, feelings, and images come to mind. For memory the sole criterion is the aliveness of the experience in the moment. A child's birth, the smothering of the flame in a pan, a car stranded in the snow, the murder of an iconic figure, a plane crashing into a skyscraper—these images will never be wiped from the slate of memory. Total mindfulness records everything without effort.

Exercise: Another informal way to practice mindfulness is to cultivate awareness outdoors. You can begin by simply taking a walk. The colors and forms in nature provide an optimal setting for developing mindfulness. As you walk, be attentive to the plants and creatures around you—trees, birds, a tuft of moss. Allow yourself to notice the numerous details—the nuances of color, the soft morning light, the veins of a leaf, a puddle on the path. If you find yourself worrying or trying too hard, take a few deep breaths and let yourself relax. Simply observe without judgment or interpretation, the more details the better.

Walking or driving to school or work, or any other activity you tend to perform automatically can also become an opportunity for practice. Observing previously unnoticed details on a well-worn pathway helps to break our habitual patterns of inattention.

Exercise: Observing your inner landscape is another way to practice mindfulness. This can be difficult at first, since you may encounter uncomfortable feelings and emotions such as irritation, covetousness, jealousy, negativity, self-importance, or apathy alternating with daydreams. Perhaps you notice your stubborn resistance when you feel thwarted, or observe how you panic when someone else acquires something you dream of for yourself. In short, you begin to see the dense jungle of thoughts and emotions you live with every day.

When awareness awakens and we see ourselves in a clear light, the effect can be shocking: "Is this really me?" However, as we familiarize ourselves with our repertoire of automatic reactions, we begin to view them from a different perspective. We recognize a simple pattern: What receives attention becomes reality, what doesn't eventually fades away. Once we understand this dynamic, we can allow mindfulness to prevail. As mindfulness stabilizes the mind, the compulsive pull of our emotional tendencies decreases. We become calm and alert, able to focus on the present and remember our experience in detail. The mind relaxes and softens, becoming more even-minded and peaceful.

Unifying Time and Awareness

Yet another remedy against a weak memory is awakening to time. We usually experience time as an external pressure and our relationship to it is strained. We look at the clock: "Oh my, is it already that late?" We feel time nipping at our heels; it seems there is never enough time. Still, we believe there is plenty of time left before we die, although, in taking time for granted, we are likely to waste it.

When our relationship with time is weakened, our awareness suffers. This can manifest in a tendency to be late: We may often miss the beginning of a meeting or barely make a train. Whatever we undertake requires effort; each new responsibility seems like an additional burden. We often feel exhausted for no good reason. We neglect things that need urgent attention and cannot be bothered to prioritize adequately. "Things will work out," we may say, or "There is always tomorrow." We are full of excuses and alibis.

Alienation from time leaves us waiting for something unknown to happen. We trust that things will resolve themselves somehow, but meanwhile, we wait. Actually, we are holding ourselves back, feeling inhibited and unable to give. Yet without giving we are not really alive.

Time is an ever-present force that we can learn to embrace as a valuable partner. Just as we welcome the sun in the morning, we can welcome time, grateful for another day to live. Simply by paying attention to the clock, an appreciation for time's power and nearness to our lives will grow. We look at our watch, not with a tense eye, but with a glance of recognition. We can also connect our awareness of time to the rhythms of nature by keeping track of the position of the sun or moon. A simple practice is to guess the time and afterwards verify it by looking at a clock. When we bring time to awareness in this way, awareness begins to unite with time.

By holding time in the back of our minds, we learn to extend awareness into time, embracing past and present. We think of time without pressure or strain. Through such practices, a relationship with time develops, and time's vitality connects with our own energy. As awareness and time join together and become unified, intelligence and the power of knowing are activated. Mind becomes more alert, powerful, and creative, no matter what our age or situation. Time's gift comes home to us: Each moment contains a lifetime.

Slowing Down Time

A person who performs at peak level does not experience gaps in awareness. While fully engaged, the mind does not wander or waste time. It knows what matters and when, and what is irrelevant. Awareness is almost meditative, with a sixth sense for problems and a sharp nose for opportunities and possibilities. Seeing encompasses both microcosm and macrocosm, pairing a precise eye for detail with a global view that extends far into time and space. Imagine being the president of a company who, while sitting behind a desk, is able to oversee the entire building and the whole company, including past, present, and future employees, shareholders, and clients—even the competition. This deep and wide awareness knows without having specific information.

In his autobiography, *For the Love of the Game*, Michael Jordan, the greatest basketball player of his time, describes how he secured victory for his team, the Chicago Bulls, in the seventh and final game of the NBA championship. They were down in points with only 4.1 seconds remaining in the game when Jordan caught the ball at midcourt. Time seemed to slow to a halt. With one glance, he saw the location of each player, both teammates and opponents. He knew how many seconds were left until the end of the game. In a flash, he realized which positions each player would take, and understood where the opening would occur. In an ocean of time and through a wide-open space, Jordan moved from mid-court toward the basket and scored the winning points. The clock indicated there were 2.8 seconds left. No one on the opposing team had a player of Jordan's caliber to take advantage of those remaining seconds.

Like athletes in top-level sports, to whom a hundredth of a second may mean the difference between winning a gold or silver medal, we can slow time down and extend awareness out into time and space. When we reduce moments in time to smaller units, we can attune awareness more finely to each infinitesimal point in time.

Our usual notion of time is a linear sequence proceeding from—to. But when we observe the temporal space between "from" and "to" and become aware of the smaller units of time it contains, breaking each moment down into more moments, we discover new worlds of experience. We also find that it is impossible to pinpoint time's movement. When we closely watch the minute hand of an old-fashioned wind-up clock, our experience of time slows down. We might become convinced that the hand does not move, since we never establish when exactly it leaves one position and arrives at the next. In this way, we come to understand that there is no moment when the present becomes the past and the future arrives. As soon as we say, "This is the present moment," the next moment has arrived. There is no transition between moments, and time knows no division of past, present, and future. Only when we are disconnected from the experience of time does time seem to move. That is when we think that time passes. When we condense the experience of time into progressively smaller units, the gaps between awareness and time dissolve. The experience of time is hard to put into words, but a word to describe it might be: zero point. It is time's energy that presents all manifestations and that makes us speak of "time's flow."

The Corridor of Time

Exercise: This practice heals the past by opening the experience of time. In the evening, sit in a quiet spot and review the day in your mind's eye. Let your memory wander through the entire day, from beginning to end. Let your review be as detailed as possible. You woke up, got out of bed, entered the bathroom, got dressed and had breakfast. Be specific: Was breakfast granola and tea? Did you eat standing at the kitchen counter or sitting down at the table? Maybe you looked in your pockets for keys as you stepped out the front door. On the way to work or school, you saw people walking in the street or heard news on the car radio. In this way, go through the whole day, remembering as many details as you can without becoming distracted, until you reach the present moment.

While doing this practice, be mindful of getting caught up in mental fabrication. This may happen, especially when an emotional incident has arrested the flow of experience. When a powerful emotion is not processed at the time it occurs, the moment becomes frozen. Left unresolved, the emotion remains trapped in body and mind. Every time you think about it, you become upset again. Meanwhile, time passes by without your participation: You are not *in* time.

By returning to time and reliving the event completely, scene-by-scene, as if watching a movie in full color and with an abundance of detail, you release the emotion and allow the trapped energy of that moment to flow throughout the body. As you arrive fully into the present moment, the experience of time opens. Tension disappears and the released energy is transformed into fresh vitality.

If you become sleepy while reviewing your day, look to see if you are approaching an unresolved emotional incident. Sleepiness often occurs just at the point when the emotional tension is felt and is on the verge of melting. To stay awake and allow the process of melting to take place, concentrate on finding more details in the memories. Attention to detail expands your perspective and deepens your awareness of feeling. To tell if the emotion has been released, try recalling the incident without becoming distressed. If you can do this, the emotion has returned to pure energy, allowing you once again to participate in time's flow.

After finishing the first round of review, begin right away on a second round. This time you will probably remember more, noticing specific details you were unaware of the first time. As fresh memories arise, small gaps in your awareness close. At the end of the exercise, let go of all the images. Remain very still for a while, without analyzing or interpreting the experience.

You can also reverse the exercise, working backward from the evening to the beginning of the day. If you practice for a few weeks, you can try extending the practice by going still further back into the past. Allow your thoughts to make chronological leaps, from one recollection to the next, from great moments to the most trivial. Remember a party, a sporting event, a gathering with friends, a vacation, the day you moved to a new location. Recall as many memories as possible, of all kinds. One memory is no more important than another, and none is too insignificant to be relived. During your trip through time, you call on an image, glance at it briefly, and then continue on your way. Sometimes take small steps, at other times giant leaps, moving backward in time.

Here is a further extension. In imagination it is possible to explore realms beyond memory's reach: perhaps your mother's womb, or even the unknown world before your conception. Because these realms are part of your personal history, your human inheritance, your mind is capable of bridging the gap between now and then. Try opening the corridor of time to hundreds of years before the day you were born. Picture historical moments, hold the images briefly, and then dive further back in time. Eventually you will find that the images stop coming, and experience has become silent and spacious.

After dwelling in this space for a short while, turn around and go forward through time to the moment of your conception. Picture the nine months in your mother's womb, your birth, infancy, first memories, your childhood bedroom, the school you attended, the relationships with your siblings, and so on, up to today.

Still, do not stop in the present. Turn toward tomorrow, to next week, to events that are already on your agenda—perhaps the upcoming summer holidays, or Christmas, maybe even an event that is planned for a few years from now. Free your imagination by stepping into the future. See yourself grow old; perhaps you are lying on a hospital bed, surrounded by loved ones who have come to say farewell. Imagine how you slide into death, how people mourn for you, and how life goes on, as time continues. Keep tracking time until a hundred years from now, when everyone alive today will be dead. Then go on beyond that, accelerating as you go.[21]

Finally you are so far ahead in time that images no longer come. Let consciousness form a link, a gigantic overarching awareness that unites the experience you had in the distant past with that of the distant future. In the ocean of space and light that opens you may hear the call of an eternal longing, begging to be fulfilled—the longing to live fully in time, without regret.

7

Awakening Mind

In March 1976, a month after my father's retirement, he and my mother moved to Italy. In the preceding years they had carefully planned everything for the time when they would both retire. They sold the family home in Wassenaar, Holland and purchased an apartment in The Hague that would serve as a pied-à-terre. Meanwhile, they built a comfortable bungalow on Elba, a tiny island off the coast of Italy.

Thus began for my father a time of well-deserved retreat. For forty years he had worked hard to build a career and support his family. Now he chose not to take on any board positions or perform volunteer work. His personal interests and hobbies offered enough variety and challenges. He spent most of the time painting, doing yoga, and reading books by the great philosophers; he enjoyed his newfound freedom and felt as if reborn. He had never cared much for socializing, preferring only my mother's company. The solitary character of the rocky island suited him perfectly.

For my mother the situation was very different. She had just turned sixty-three and up to the day of their departure she had led a fully active life. In addition to her position on the board of directors of Pro Senectute, she had an extensive social network, including several clubs, a circle of friends who met purely for pleasure, women in the neighborhood who drank coffee together every Monday morning, and a cluster of friends with whom she had played tennis for years. In short, my mother belonged to a very close-knit social system. Although she had known that moving to Italy would end all of this, the full implications became clear only after she and my father had taken up residence on Elba. From one day to the next, she had nothing to do.

My parents' house on Elba was called *L'Uccello Azzurro*, The Blue Bird. The short story by Maurice Maeterlinck called "The Blue Bird" was one of my father's favorite tales. It tells of two children who, one night, crept out their window to look for a blue bird that had appeared that morning on the windowsill. They searched high and low, but finally had to return empty-handed. My father would end the story by saying, "When they entered their room—imagine their surprise! There, in the open window, was the blue bird. And this is the moral of the story: You may think that happiness is found elsewhere, but it has been right under your nose, at home, all the time." My father seemed to believe that after searching high and low, he and my mother had found their blue bird on this rough tourist island off the Italian coast.

In Holland my mother was like a fish in water, but on the island she seemed stranded on a barren shore. Except for running errands, preparing meals for two, and making coffee and tea, no demands were made on her talents and skills. She did some embroidery and wrote long letters to her children and many of her friends. It had become awfully quiet around her. During morning coffee on the bungalow terrace she received daily visits from a lizard. She fed it jam on a silver spoon. Otherwise, there were few visitors and the telephone rarely rang. Even nature offered little consolation; the feared *sirocco* was always waiting in the wings, a dry desert wind from Africa that threw many of the island's inhabitants into depression. For hours, she would gaze out upon the deep blue sea and the ruins of a fourteenth-century castle where, according to legend, a princess threw herself from the towering walls in despair over a forbidden love.

Before moving to Elba my parents had taken Italian lessons, and my mother spoke well enough to get around. She had hoped to be able to connect with the locals, and maybe even make some friends. During a weekly game of bridge with the woman who owned a vineyard down the road and another neighbor, she had the chance to practice her Italian. Seated at the card table with a bottle of wine and a tray of snacks on hand, my mother did her best to keep conversation going, while my father quietly waited for the next bid. "Bridge is a silent game," he would say.

At the foot of the hill lived a farmer and his wife, from whom my parents had bought their small plot of land. A few times a day my mother waved at them, and now and then, at her insistence, my parents paid the couple a visit. The farmer's wife would sit on the steps leading up to the living room while her husband sat at the dining table. They spoke a dialect almost unintelligible to outsiders. On a bare wall hung a hunting rifle, used to hunt birds, as was the custom on the island. There was hardly a bird left on Elba. During the visit the farmer would descend into the pigsty below the house and come back up with a bottle of homemade wine. When he pulled out the cork, three quarters of the contents spilled out over the table and onto the floor; the rest would be poured into small, grimy glasses. When the farming couple moved to the nearby harbor village, their house remained empty. Only their son would come up now and then to see if a few birds had nested, so he could hunt.

Three of my parents' four sons were living with their families in the United States. The eldest son remained in Holland, but he visited Elba as sporadically as the others. In the beginning, my parents used to visit the United States every year, and at Christmas they would return to the Netherlands for an extended holiday. Then my mother picked up her old friendships where they had left off. Those few weeks would pass by in a blur of excitement. One year, during such a vacation, she wrote me a letter:

The Hague, February 5, 1985

Really, there is nothing special to write, but I just feel like a little chat with you, that's all! How is your little man? Grootvader . . . Oma . . . would he still remember these words? There are so many new things in his life! His little head can't contain all of it—but we can! We had a wonderful time when you all were here—warm

and precious. By the way, we are still having a
wonderful time with many friends and all sorts of
get-togethers.

Five weeks later, this letter arrived from Elba:

Elba, March 12, 1985

Once in a while, we hear the sound of church bells
ringing. They seem to call for prayer—and I really
should try to pray, because I am not happy right now.
I forget a lot—but Daddy is patient. It is best to live
'just in the moment,' but that is not always possible.

My mother did not easily share her feelings about
her new situation. She became more and more quiet
and withdrawn. She had lost her familiar ground and
refuge. During one of my first visits to Elba—after they
had been living there about a year—I encouraged her,
"Tell me, what is in your heart? I think you miss Holland
terribly." Finally she whispered, "Italy . . . your father enjoys it here so much . . ."

My father had begun a new life, and my mother
believed it was her duty to follow him and stay by his
side. To us, their sons, it seemed as if she were waiting for
the bus that would finally take her home—a bus that
might never come. Twelve years later it arrived at last,
and took her back to The Hague, because "mother needs
medical care."

DHARMA AND OLD AGE

In the pre-1959 religious culture of Tibet, where all of life revolved around spirituality and the focal point of every house and tent was an altar, old age was valued as a treasured phase of life, a time to really study and practice the Dharma. When the education of the children was complete, parents devoted themselves to their own spiritual discipline.

If circumstances allowed, many older Tibetans went on pilgrimage or retired to a secluded area in the mountains for a short or long retreat to meditate and perform ceremonies. In cases where a retreat was not possible, an older person was satisfied to stay at home and meditate, chanting mantras and spinning a hand prayer wheel that sent millions of prayers out into the world. Practicing with a prayer wheel could be a person's main activity for many years. There were also other valuable practices for older people. I once met a young lama with a chronic illness whose old father never left his side. He gave his son strength by reciting the texts of the Tibetan Buddhist Canon, called the Kanjur and Tanjur— the direct teachings of the Buddha and the commentaries and texts by masters of the Buddha's lineage. Reciting these texts in their entirety took several months.

This way of life, which held the traditional teachings close to the heart, is still practiced in many Tibetan refugee communities in India, Nepal, and other countries. When they are not on pilgrimage, aged parents usually live with their children and grandchildren, all under one roof. Family members experience birth, death, and everything in between together, as a community. From a very young age, children become familiar with the pain of sickness, the debility of old age, the process of dying—and the value of the Dharma teachings. Elders pass on their wisdom to the younger generation in an unbroken stream, ensuring that the traditions of the Buddha's teachings are honored in the household. Through their influence, respect for the Enlightened Ones, for life and all of nature informs every aspect of daily life.

The purpose of the Dharma teachings is to purify the mind so that the journey through time—our life—becomes meaningful. While the discipline of the Dharma covers many fields of study—including philosophy, cosmology, logic, astronomy, astrology, psychology, medicine, and ceremonial practices—the heart of the Dharma teachings relates to what is true at all times. Studying and practicing the Dharma connects us with what is greater than ourselves. It offers us a chance to mature and be of benefit to others.

Western culture produces many brilliant specialists, but there are few examples of individuals who embody enlightened wisdom. Neither in child-rearing nor in adult education do we aim at the attainment of higher wisdom. Instead, earning a position in society is considered a high priority. People may be vaguely aware of an inner conflict between who they really are and how they think they should be, but without deep introspection—beyond that afforded by exploring emotions or discussing problems with a psychologist—self-knowledge rarely emerges. Our emotions tend to determine our identities: "I feel something, therefore I am." The origin of emotions and how we can deal with them remains a mystery. Most of us are heavily burdened by our self-images, but we have no idea how we came to be this way or how to free ourselves. Wrapped up in our egos, we pass by doors to our inner potential without even noticing them. We do not know who we are or what we are capable of.

In these times of spectacular scientific and technical advances, the book-knowledge we gain during our lives and careers is constantly being superseded. Older people must step aside for younger men and women. Younger workers with more flexibility and with cutting-edge technical skills push many older people out of the work force long before retirement age. The life experience, accumulated expertise, and skills of those in middle age are less valued than the advantages of youth: energy, cheap labor, and openness to change. For numerous elders there may seem to be no other option than meekly fading into the twilight of life's last phase.

No wonder so many people fear old age. No longer being useful or productive provokes feelings of resistance, even despair. Some members of the so-called Old Guard envy the young and bitterly regret missed opportunities. Aches and pains intensify feelings of isolation and vulnerability. As energy wanes, there seems little left to do but live in the past, recalling the days of glory, long ago.

SELF-KNOWLEDGE

Knowledge that enables us to deepen our feelings and increase our wisdom never goes out of date. It actually grows with the passing years. Such knowledge of our deeper selves remains vital and keeps us youthful. Older people are especially well equipped to develop this kind of self-knowledge. As other possibilities fade, love and wisdom begin to matter more. The attraction of day-to-day affairs weakens; prestige, power, and respect start to lose their magic. Seeing the world from a sober distance, mature people may look around and think, "Much ado about nothing!"

With old age a new era begins. How we approach it is up to us. As we grow older, we have the opportunity to distinguish between what is real and what is not, and to focus on what really matters. Rather than dwelling in the past, we can learn to release it without grief or bitterness. Letting go is a healthy part of the aging process. If we find ourselves resting on our laurels or focusing on disappointments, we can gently let go and redirect our awareness to the present moment. "Tomorrow is the first day of the rest of my life," my mother sometimes said. The challenge is to experience the present without holding on to the past or dreaming about the future. We can encourage ourselves to approach each moment eagerly, with curiosity about the unknown that waits just around the corner.

Although the body may become weak and worn, our mental abilities need not deteriorate with age; the mind is not bound by time. Becoming forgetful in old age is not inevitable. It is a myth that memory and mind must fade as we age. It is true that with advancing years brain cells decrease in number, but the loss is negligible compared to the vast number of cells remaining. When brain cells do break down, stimulating the brain creates new contact points that restore the activity of the circuit. The phenomenon of cells increasing in one place to balance cells decreasing elsewhere is called neuroplasticity.[22]

The brain is less subject to deterioration than the other organs of the body, although it is also true that, with advancing age, brain processes slow down because of decreasing blood circulation. Since brain function requires the oxygen supplied by the blood—more so than the other organs—it may take us longer to learn something new when we are older. However, it is not preordained that a healthy brain functioning under normal circumstances declines in performance with age. Curiosity and interest keep us mentally flexible, especially if we take advantage of our later years by doing things we did not take time for when we were younger. The saying, "You can't teach an old dog new tricks," does not apply to human beings.[23]

Mental capacities we have exercised and developed throughout our lives allow us to greet the future with enthusiasm and energy, even at advanced ages. The more expansive our interests, the more challenging our lives will remain. As Bertrand Russell wrote in his autobiography, "The more impersonal one's interests and the more these interests extend beyond the borders of one's own life, the less important the thought becomes that life will end soon. This is the most important element of happiness during old age."[24]

LIGHTNESS OF BEING

Prince Siddhartha, who later became the Buddha, left his parents' palace to embark on the path of self-knowledge when he was still a young man. Yet discovery of this path is not a privilege reserved for the young. The process of exploration is open to us at any age.

This path of knowledge is not a quest for identity or an attempt to find ourselves. Such quests may provide us with new self-images but will not unmask life's masquerade. The path of knowledge is a journey of awakening to our true nature and the highest reality. Our intention to make the journey must be strong and sincere, in order to tame consciousness and open the heart.

In the Tibetan language, the awakened mind is described by the phrase *byang-chub-sems*.[25] The terms in this phrase have been interpreted in a variety of ways, reflected in a range of English translations of these complex concepts. I have been inspired specifically by the translations of works by possibly the greatest Nyingma master, the fourteenth century lama Longchenpa (1308–1364). In these translations the word "byang" points to pure awareness, which remains pristine regardless of the activity in the mind. Awareness is as untouched by negativity or agitation as a mirror by the image reflected in it. Pure awareness accommodates anything presented to it, without distinguishing between good or bad.

Such distinctions have no reality in its realm. Still, joy expands consciousness and makes it light, while jealousy and hatred constrict and obscure it.

In byang-chub-sems the word "chub" refers to the vitalizing power or creative, ever-present energy. "Byang-chub" stands for optimal being and doing: human beings living at the peak of their potential. "Sems" is the mind that radiates the light of awareness. Byang-chub-sems, the awakened mind, is inseparable from Buddha-nature.

In Sanskrit, the word for fully awakened mind is *bodhicitta*. "Bodhi" means enlightenment, and "citta" mind. Bodhicitta is a specific type of Sanskrit compound that blends the two terms into one: Enlightenment-Mind. There are two kinds of bodhicitta: absolute and relative. Absolute bodhicitta refers to the mind that *is* Enlightenment. The mind turned toward enlightenment is relative bodhicitta. Once I heard a teacher say that the path of the Buddha can be summarized as "making everything light." Extrapolating from this teaching, one might describe the term relative bodhicitta as "becoming light," while absolute bodhicitta refers to "being light." Shining unhindered, always, the light of Enlightenment-Mind is our guide, now, in this life, and later, on our journey through death.

TAKING REFUGE

Buddhism suggests that we consider each situation we find ourselves in as if we had chosen it. We can never put the entire blame on external circumstances or on other people. My parents' departure to Elba, even if it could be culturally understood as dictated by one of them, was a shared venture. Both my mother and my father, each for their personal reasons, had wished this dramatic shift in their lives to take place. But once her choice was challenged and the privileged world they had retreated into began to crumble, my mother was left empty-handed. Feeling useless and without the possibility of acknowledging her feelings, she saw no other way out but to withdraw into what seemed to be a depression. Under these circumstances, where could she find refuge? What did she have left to rely on, once her cherished motives and high aspirations fell away?

Taking refuge is the classic phrase in Buddhism used to indicate the resolve to follow the Buddha's example and explore his experience for oneself. Fear of suffering, the need for inner peace, or a wish to be of use to others can all motivate this choice, which involves giving up the conviction that we can rely solely on our own unenlightened mind and mental patterns. Making this decision also entails letting go of the hope of becoming enlightened as well as the fear of not attaining enlightenment. One trusts in the possibility of enlightenment, without hope or fear.

When we are confident that enlightenment is within reach, we can take refuge in the Three Jewels. In reaching this turning point we become a Buddhist. The Buddha, Dharma, and Sangha are called the Three Jewels; they are "found in anyone in whom the wholesome and healthy is rooted, because they are infallible, their powers are inconceivable, they are priceless, never lose their value, and are an ornament for the world."[26] When we take refuge in the Three Jewels, we put our trust in the mind, heart and body of the Buddha, in the enlightenment path of the Dharma, and finally in the Sangha—the community of accomplished and enlightened ones that has followed the Buddha's example.

The Three Jewels are the form, meaning, and essence of enlightenment. When we turn to them, the mind expands and the heart opens. The Buddha provides protection, the Dharma offers structure, and the Sangha gives the power of example, showing that it is possible to embody all Three Jewels. Together, the Three Jewels offer protection from all fear and insecurity, and the guidance needed to follow in the footsteps of the Buddha.

At first these three beacons of light—Buddha, Dharma, and Sangha—appear to be external phenomena that we honor and turn to for guidance, support, nourishment, and comfort. The purpose is to make ourselves healthy in body and mind, and awaken the potential of our inner resources. Eventually we recognize that there is no need for external worship: The Three Jewels stand for qualities that all beings can embody. The Buddha is Enlightenment-Mind experienced as pure awareness. The Dharma is wisdom, love, and compassion in action. The Sangha is the possibility of embodying these qualities, affirming the essential unity of all beings.[27]

Taking refuge may be an unfamiliar concept to us Westerners, but in our daily lives we take refuge all the time. During a piano lesson, we pay attention to the teacher and follow the instructions to the best of our abilities; we have confidence in the teacher's expertise and in the fact that it is possible to learn to play the music. The way we take refuge in our thoughts, trusting that they convey the truth, is much more subtle. We listen to the inner dialogue that informs us of the state of affairs in our lives; we allow its limited repertoire of choices to dictate our behavior: "I want this, I do not want that, I don't care." Our ability to judge which option to choose tends to be our refuge, our so-called safe haven. When we "change our minds," we adjust our references and search for new shelter. Placing confidence in something so unreliable and constantly shifting is like trying to pour the foundation for a house in drifting sands.

Becoming aware is possible under almost any circumstance, no matter how old or weakened we are. A split second can suffice for the realization of the ultimate. At any time we can remind ourselves of the preciousness of life and of the opportunities we have as human beings. The choice to live sincerely is always available to us. At any moment, at any age, we can wake up.

Refuge in The Three Jewels

I take refuge in the highest:
The Buddha, the Dharma, and the Sangha.

Every morning upon awakening, followers of the Buddha may recite this or some other refuge prayer.

The prayer becomes the foundation and background of daily life. It is repeated three times. I think of it this way: The first time we beseech the Three Jewels to appear, the second time we ask to embody them, and the third, final time we request that they be revealed in our conduct.

The Buddha's teachings on karma, the Four Noble Truths, and the Three Jewels have been called "the three securities," or grounds for the three kinds of faith, confidence in those things that are real, have value, and are possible.[28] The Buddha, Dharma and Sangha are guiding lights on the path of transformation. Through taking refuge, our awareness deepens, and we gain the freedom to take charge of our lives, not in a forceful or grasping way, but with confidence.

A common refuge prayer is that taught by Atisha, the great eleventh-century Indian master who traveled to Tibet to share the teachings of the Buddha:

I take refuge in the most excellent Buddha,
Dharma and Sangha
until I reach enlightenment.
Through the merit of my practice of generosity,
discipline, patience, effort, concentration,
and wisdom,
may I become a Buddha for the benefit
of all sentient beings.[29]

Tibetan practitioners often precede this prayer with the invocation: "I take refuge in the Lama" or "I take refuge in the Guru, the guide who dispels darkness."

The Guru's compassion toward us arises because he knows that our awareness and the awakened awareness of the Buddha are of the same nature. It is our conduct rather than our inborn nature that causes disharmony. Thanks to our contact with the Lama we are able to invoke an "inner guru," an open awareness. With time we may even recognize that we "already are a Buddha and always have been, from the very beginning."[30]

8

A Glimpse of Relaxation

The couch, with its three big, soft pillows and rose pattern upholstery, was the centerpiece of our living room. We would often sit there in the afternoons, my mother at one end and I at the other, with Lola, the cat, in my lap. We listened to records—Harry Belafonte, spirituals, Mahalia Jackson, and violin concerts of Beethoven, Tchaikovsky, Bruch, and Mendelssohn. I was a fan of Elvis Presley, and whenever a new record came out my mother would say, "Let's buy it, we'll go fifty-fifty!" When listening to "Wooden Heart," she used to burst out laughing at the German refrain with Elvis' American accent. Sometimes I would lie with my feet in her lap and she would massage them. Meanwhile, we chatted about all sorts of things—I do not remember the details, except that it never seemed to be about her.

As the youngest son, I was the last to leave home. Once in a while, when my father was out on business for dinner, my mother and I would go to a restaurant for steak, French fries, and a salad. We had a few regular places. In the restaurant, surrounded by salesmen and businessmen, I sometimes brought up grievances about my father or brothers. If I had done that to my father, he would have said kindly, "But you should not feel that way." My mother's standard response was, "He doesn't mean it that way." But she listened attentively, so I confided in her.

Looking back on those years, I realize I never really wondered what might have been on her mind. She always seemed cheerful and on top of things, except for one time that I remember well. She was often teased about her cooking. Once, she jumped up angrily from the table and left the house. It was a frightening moment for me. Not knowing what to do, I ran after her into the street. When I caught up with her, I could sense how much she would have liked to really lose her temper.

Emotions were never discussed in our house when I was young, but after my father's retirement, both my parents suddenly began to open up. When we were together, either at Elba or in California, we would talk for hours, especially my mother and I. Yet it was evident that she had become heavy-hearted. When speaking about herself she often choked with feeling, unable to find the words and battling tears. On Elba she seemed to come up against emotions she did not know how to express or bring into balance.

One morning during my annual visit to Elba, at the breakfast table, my father told us of an incident that had happened during the preceding night. He described how my mother had leapt from the bed, screaming with pain, "My legs—my legs!" She had severe cramps. Getting up did not help, and lying down made the cramps even worse. I threw her a glance; her face looked ashen as she mumbled, "I don't remember." I said, "If it happens again, please wake me up." For the rest of the day my mother seemed tired, as if she had endured a major battle.

At two o'clock the following morning my father knocked on my door. "Come quickly!" I ran to their bedroom and saw my mother standing in the middle of the room. She was moaning, "Oh my legs—my legs—" We walked her to the living room. She and I sat down on the couch, one on each end. My father sat in a chair across from both of us. Gently, I took her legs into my lap and started to massage them, just as she used to do for me. She put one hand on her forehead and began to calm down.

"What are you thinking about?" I asked after a while. She answered, "Oh ... before the war ... you know, with Daddy ... it was such fun ... all of us ... together ..."

I encouraged her to go on and she talked about the six years when they were engaged. Tears rolled down her cheeks as I rubbed her ankles. Her energy seemed to soften and suddenly she became still. Resting my hands on her feet, I gestured to my father that she was asleep. Carefully we got her up and walked her back to bed. The next day she remembered nothing of the incident, or of what she had said.

The following two nights were a variation on the same theme. While rubbing her feet, I asked her to talk about the past. Many old memories were full of joyful feelings, but grief and tension arose as well. She expressed how much she missed her children. "You all live so far away; we have grown apart so much." In the silence of the night she could be honest about the past and present, and long-suppressed feelings welled up.

On the island time had little meaning; both present and future were elusive. With no outlet for her energy and creativity, my mother seemed to be sliding down toward a black hole where only the past seemed real. My sense was that fear was stifling her. Yet there was also hope; something was urgently calling for attention, signaling that change was imminent. This was a time for moving forward. But she had no reply to my questions about how she would like the rest of her life to be. She could not summon either the energy or the intention to envision a positive future. She merely asked, "What will become of me?"

THE FOUR NOBLE TRUTHS

Just before the moment of supreme and complete enlightenment, Siddhartha Gautama sat "calmly, not moving so much as an eye, his senses calm, his body unaffected and glorious; free from all passion, hatred, and confusion, unshakable as the king of mountains, neither despondent nor anxious, without weakness, his mind perfectly firm. Having renounced emotionality, he had entered the gate of wisdom."[31]

After reaching enlightenment, the Enlightened One, Shakyamuni Buddha, remained seated for a week under the Bodhi Tree in Bodh Gaya, India. During this time he pondered whether to teach the path of enlightenment to others. He reflected, "The Dharma I have obtained is profound; it is the Dharma of a perfect and profound Buddha. It is peaceful, very peaceful, completely peaceful, full of contentment, difficult to see, difficult to understand. It is not in the realm of reasoning; only the very intelligent ones can grasp it."

Out of respect for the Dharma and the needs of all sentient beings, the Awakened One agreed to teach for the benefit of those who might otherwise be unable to perceive the way to complete enlightenment. In Sarnath, the Buddha set the wheel of the Dharma in motion for the first time. His very first teachings were about human suffering. "Concerning this Teaching not heard before, by setting my mind on the nature of the source of suffering, I produced knowledge, vision, and realization; I produced abundant knowledge, and by setting my mind on the nature of suffering, I discovered the Four Noble Truths. These are: there is suffering, there is a cause of suffering, suffering can be brought to an end, and there is a way that leads to an end of suffering—the Noble Eightfold Path."[32]

First Noble Truth

A human life is characterized by suffering. What is suffering? It is the pain of birth, old age, sickness, and death. It is the pain of not getting what we want. It is the pain we experience when something happens that we resent. Negative emotions such as anger, hatred, sadness, and frustration cause pain, to others and also to ourselves. Positive emotions such as excitement and falling in love cause suffering as well, for they contain the seed of impermanence and will not last.

Second Noble Truth

Suffering has a cause. What is the cause? Suffering is caused by ignorance. We are blind to the state of pure awareness, to non-duality and openness of being; we are blind to the patterns that keep our mind in bondage. Holding on to what is insubstantial and transient, we grasp for solidity where there is none. In our ignorance, we forget the lightness of being, and identify with the darkness of consciousness, or *I*.

The belief in *I* is founded on a notion of separation between *I* and all else, a split between self and other that fosters isolation and confusion. At a deep level, suffering stems from the nature of duality, which conceals the underlying wholeness of all existence. As *I* is merely a mental construct—albeit an enormously powerful one—our belief in it leads us to rely on something that is unstable, transient, and insecure. Identifying with our bodies, feelings, perceptions, ideas and even consciousness—thinking *I* am these and they belong to "me"—we are bound to suffer. Cut off from the deeper truth that could nourish and support us, we are vulnerable to suffering in every aspect of our lives.

Third Noble Truth

Suffering can be brought to an end. How can this be done? By breaking the now interlocked chain of mental processes—beginning with ignorance—that solidify the sense of *I* and perpetuate suffering. Suffering ends as soon as we recognize the insubstantiality of whatever comes to mind—thoughts, images, and emotions—and cease

115

relying on the notion of *I*. The Buddha smiles because he has discovered the path that returns to pure awareness.[33]

Fourth Noble Truth
What is the path that leads to the end of suffering? The Noble Eightfold Path offers a return to the wholeness of being through right view, right motivation, right communication, right action, right livelihood, right effort, right mindfulness, and right concentration.

Restlessness and Suffering

In the West, suffering—in the form of ailments or problems—is accepted as a basic part of human existence, to be endured and borne. Still, much of our time and energy is spent trying to avoid or end it. In spite of all the evidence to the contrary, we continue to believe that once we have obtained what we crave and have eliminated what we fear, all will be well. Why, then, do we still experience endless rounds of pain and frustration?

In Western society, life is suffused with what the Buddhist teachings call the "eight worldly concerns": pursuing gain and avoiding loss, pursuing pleasure and avoiding pain, pursuing praise and avoiding blame, pursuing a good reputation and avoiding a bad one. We are motivated primarily by these concerns, and in our daily lives we rely on them to end our suffering. The Buddha, however, taught that the eight worldly concerns set the stage for suffering. They are unreliable and unstable, and because of their inherent duality they cannot provide lasting inner peace. Instead, the eight worldly concerns perpetuate internal restlessness, which is yet another form of suffering.

According to the teachings of the Buddha, life brings pain and frustration, but is not inextricably bound up with them: "In letting go our belief that suffering is a necessary part of human life, we can take a few steps forward."[34] Buddhism offers a detailed map of the various kinds of human suffering, laying out what sustains them, their root cause, and how they can be countered.

Suffering arises when we ignore what the Buddha called the "codependent origination" of all that arises. Everything that exists is dependent on causes and conditions, on factors that are subject to change. Thus all is transitory and nothing lasts; what is more, nothing is substantial in the sense that it stands by itself. Agitation is the inevitable consequence of ignoring the impermanence and insubstantiality of life.

The Buddha showed in his own being that serenity, light, and wholeness emerge when suffering has ended. But in order to gain victory over suffering, we must deepen our understanding of it. The first step is to recognize suffering in all of its manifestations. The quality of suffering is ever-present in our daily lives— we need only observe our experience to find it. Things that prevent us from maturing as human beings represent suffering, and lacking the right perception is like an ailment of the mind, a mental affliction. A clouded mind causes suffering. Not being able to concentrate, being lost in thoughts, and acting against our better judgment are all forms of suffering. Ignoring our inner voice and adhering to social pressure is also suffering. Regaining our grounding in authentic being signals the end of suffering.

Three Kinds of Suffering

There are three kinds of suffering. All three are caused by wrong perception: We do not understand our own nature or the nature of reality. In the West, we primarily recognize the *suffering of suffering*—pain that has an obvious cause. This kind of suffering includes the physical pain of being born, becoming ill, growing old, and dying. It is the pain of hunger, the discomfort of heat or cold, and the mental anguish of grief and disappointment. We consider this kind of suffering inevitable: "After all, we're only human, aren't we?"

The second kind of suffering is the *suffering of change*. Ignoring the knowledge of our vulnerability, whether consciously or unconsciously, causes unrest. Nothing lasts, neither good times nor bad. This is true for everything that exists and all that plays a role in our lives. All phenomena will one day cease to be. The people, places, and objects dear and familiar to us may vanish abruptly, or gradually fade away like an old photograph. Our bodies too will one day disappear, along with our memories, thoughts, and feelings.

Everything that is born will die.
Everything that has come together will fall apart.

Everything that was acquired will be lost.
Everything that is lifted up will be brought low.
Everything that was created will be destroyed.
What does not die?

The third form of suffering is the *suffering of conditioned existence.* We suffer because we identify with things that have no independent origination. We identify with *I* but the self has no substance, no solidity, no foundation. Like an automobile composed of a frame, engine, tires, and other parts—body, feelings, thoughts, motivation, and consciousness— temporarily brought together. Although *I* identifies with its parts, and considers them to be its property, *I* is not "my" body, nor does this body belong to "me"; *I* is not "my" thoughts, nor do they belong to "me"; *I* is not "my" feelings, nor do they belong to "me". Believing in the self is believing in an illusion that perpetuates the cycles of suffering.

TENSION AND ENERGY

Human beings mature, reach a peak, and deteriorate, until one day life is over. At every stage, we experience tension. Tension leaves the body only after death. While we are alive, tension manifests energy and potential. Without tension, change would be impossible, for the momentum of change is due to tension.

The teachings of modern science are helpful in understanding the causes of suffering in terms of tension and energy. The universe is seething with vitality, manifesting in our lives as time, change, and the freedom to choose. The vitality in the universe is the energy that we inhale and exchange with the environment through the senses, an ongoing embodiment of energy and knowledge taking shape and form. The rhythmic pulse of this process might be experienced as tension.

Tension is a normal, even indispensable phenomenon. Its charge is the motor of everything, and it manifests in all phenomena: the coming and going of the breath, the stream of thoughts, the storing of memories. Everything flows. In nature, tension unfolds in the rhythm of the seasons, the spinning of the earth, and the pull of the moon. Even the condensing and expanding of the universe is a sign of tension.

The tension that often burdens us could be viewed as a promise of strength, the power of our potential. If we tap into it with wisdom and insight, it will empower us. But misdirecting or ignoring it leads to depression and fear. Failing to understand that even the most solid objects consist of moving energies and that matter and energy are equivalent, we disregard our intrinsic connection with the vitality of the universe. When body and mind are not open, exercising fluidly in space, the ongoing "embodiment of energies"[35] is hampered.

Many healing systems point out that psychological problems and most illnesses—including the disease of stress—are related to subtle energy imbalances in body, mind, and senses. These are caused by blockages in our energy system, and undermine fluidity of body and mind.[36]

If the flow of tension is hindered, an energy block-age settles in body and mind. Such blockages are experi-enced as heaviness and stress. Looking for ways to release the tension actually means releasing the blockages and unwinding the stress. Once the blockages are lifted, we will recapture joy, happiness, beauty, splendor, inner peace, and freedom, the natural state of human being, and discover that love, warmth, and creativity are unlimited. A masterwork of art is tension transformed into beauty.

Believing that absence of tension is a major goal in life makes us prone to suffering, as it encourages us to hold back our energy and shut down the senses, which otherwise offer a free exchange with the world around us. Passivity can be mistaken for happiness. Seeing ab-sence of tension as an ideal state of affairs requires clos-ing the heart and living in disharmony with the rhythms of time in space.

RESISTANCE

In a threatening environment, where stress rules, control seems the only defense possible. In a world that places demands on us constantly, we naturally experience block-ages in our energy system. As a result we strive to be in command of each situation. Over the years, grasping for control has become a second nature. We maintain a sense of ownership by holding a tight rein on events, erecting a wall between us and the rest of the world. But our hold is tenuous. A sudden blow, such as a nasty surprise or criti-cism, can knock the breath out of us, causing us to lose control. Our response is likely to be shock, fear, and anxiety. We shrink back—physically, mentally, and emotionally—and quickly try to regain composure. What starts out as a reflexive contraction and withdrawal of energy eventually grows into a pattern of non-stop resistance and defense. We engage the world like an ox pulling a cart: reluctant and far from enthusiastic. Whatever psychological explanations we may offer for our condition, the result remains the same. Our vital energy either moves sluggishly or bolts uncontrollably through the body, manifesting as resistance in body and mind.

Our internal rebellion may be so subtle that we are unconscious of it. Misunderstood and left to its own devices, resistance intensifies. If we really dig in, we grow incapable of warming up to anything. We may genuinely believe ourselves to be willing, while in fact we are constantly hitting the brakes. Sometimes there are clues: Our feelings are surprisingly dull; there is much that eludes us; we tend to be forgetful and listen with only half an ear. Then again, we may erupt unexpectedly in a burst of rage or emotionality that we cannot explain.

In childhood, many people are taught to disregard their feelings and subtle physical energy. No wonder that for those adults awareness remains on the back burner. Hardened from long-term neglect, their senses become coarse, like the skin of an elephant, and they need increasingly strong stimuli to feel anything at all. They have stopped communicating with themselves or listening to others and tend to flare up in irritation or agitation. Mostly they prefer to be left alone. Their own voices ring in their ears, full of aversion and distrust: "Leave me alone!" Their lives are imbued with "No!"

When the door to a negative experience or memory opens, the underlying blockage is approached. At once the underlying pattern of resistance arises, so as to cover deeper feelings like shyness, shame, or isolation. What this means is that precisely in the urge to resist is the gateway to change.

To use the energy of resistance to our advantage, we can focus on feelings and sensations in the body. Encouraging ourselves to stay with the physical experience, we can learn to relax into its depth. At first it may seem we do not feel anything. For instance, when we are frozen with fear or consumed by anger, the deeper feelings will be disguised as a kind of self-control. But if we persist, there is always a feeling that can be exposed, for even density or blankness has a feeling tone.

Communicating with the physical sensations, we can sink into them as if sliding into a warm bath. And by expanding the energy of feelings in the body, regardless of whether they are pleasurable or painful, we stimulate the senses. Our focus shifts; the stories and images we have been hanging on to wear thin. Sensory experiences may sometimes seem overwhelming, but mindfulness of the body lets us find stable ground within our own vitality. Our defences weaken. The protective wall around us becomes transparent. Our consciousness seems softer. By surrendering little by little, we contact our inner being. There is no need for psychological insight in order to melt resistance.

On an energy level, there is no discrimination between negative and positive emotions: Both are manifestations of energy. With practice, the energy of holding patterns is released. Negative and positive emotions are recycled and subtle energy begins to flow throughout body and mind. We wake up mentally, emotionally, and physically. Body and mind can heal.

RELAXING IN THE TENSION

The body in ordinary terms could be considered as a skeletal structure that accommodates the nervous, circulatory, and respiratory systems. But the body is also an energy system. This energy system is intimately related to the subtle energy of the breath. Each cell, each sense, and every aspect of consciousness participates in it. When the energy of the breath circulates evenly to head and heart, our bodies, senses, and minds become integrated and balanced.

When energy does not circulate evenly, the excessive tension that results from subtle energy imbalances can lead to psychological or physical illness, such as burnout. Burnout leaves us feeling empty, left out of our own lives, and unable to imagine any other way of being. Feelings in the body cannot keep up with the head's agitation and excess activity. The energy in the body that the breath and senses draw from the interaction with the environment no longer provides the essential nourishment our body-mind needs for well-being. The whole system is depleted of energy. We have exhausted our own resources.

Excessive tension can find a release in creative work, hobbies, or sports that provide temporary relief. But the relentless drive that we apply in our quest for relaxation may also wear us out. The good feeling passes, and we begin to look for a new fix. Television, alcohol, or sleeping pills seem to provide an instant escape, but this is temporary as well. The best advice is to take time out and allow physical energy to recharge.

My mother found herself on an idyllic island with a pretty view and a partner actively engaged in hobbies, but she had no outlet for her energy or creativity. What could she do? Natural feelings of despair came up, screaming for attention, but they were suppressed, considered inappropriate rather than seen as a cry for help. All she was left with was her pleasure in the environment. But since the interaction between inner and outer was almost nonexistent, what could she do, other than experience her setting as a set of picture postcards? Her whole system collapsed. Internally there was no exchange between body and mind, and externally she was not participating, and her actions were not reciprocated. The stage was set for depression. Often what appear to be symptoms of Alzheimer's disease are actually signs of depression.[37] In such cases the depression can be addressed directly, instead of focusing on slowing down the progression of the illness.

Relaxation is a learning process, to be developed and perfected. The key is learning to relax in a way that supports the integrity of the relationships among body, breath, and mind. When these feed back to each other,

125

each granting the other an equal part, a generous interplay develops that melts tension and pain. Even when relaxation seems almost impossible, as in the case of a serious illness or injury that produces irreparable physical imbalances, it may still be possible to relax the mind and give space to feelings.

Fruitful relaxation requires activating the flow of feeling. When the feelings in the body, even agony and pain, are acknowledged, accommodated, and expanded, mind and breath calm down as well. Once the circulation of energy can develop fully, mind and body become at ease. As anxiety and restlessness in the mind are accepted and faced, breath and body flourish as well. With relaxation of body, breath, or mind, a sense of serenity emerges. We can feel balanced even under difficult circumstances.

Relaxing is not the same as spacing out. It could be considered an activity, an unfolding process that must begin with learning to feel. In becoming conscious of the feelings and sensations in our bodies, we are on the way to relaxation. Mindfulness of our physical experience brings us into contact with our own energy. This is the gate to relaxation.

None of this can happen in a hurry; opening the senses and allowing our energy to calm down and melt down requires time, especially when we are unaccustomed to it.

To consciously and completely *not* do anything is also a way of relaxing, perhaps akin to what Taoism calls *wu wei*. By choosing not to follow inner dialogue, ruminate, or daydream, we step off the treadmill of thinking. We can just concentrate on our bodies instead of on thoughts, and look for feelings even when none are found. Mindfulness of the body allows energy to flow through rarely used channels. The body gently wakes up.

When awareness of physical feelings is enhanced, body and mind begin to communicate. A foot massage or a heart-to-heart talk triggers relaxation and releases energy blockages that developed long ago. When excess tension melts, repressed memories and feelings that were never fully acknowledged float to the surface.

Being able to open up our hearts and express what is on our minds fosters this kind of genuine relaxation, whether it happens in psychotherapy or intimate friendships. The content of the stories that surface at such times does not matter much; ultimately we may even feel the need to revise or revoke them. But they must be expressed first, at the very least to ourselves, to release the energy that comes in their wake. Relaxation occurs when the energy begins to flow again. If we take this process a step further by entering into the flow of feeling, deep transformation may take place.

The key to wellness and wholeness lies in activating our feelings. By truly relaxing, we discover a new way of being.[38] In a universe composed of interdependent relationships, with infinite aspects and layers of existence from the subatomic to the cosmic, human beings play only a tiny role. Nevertheless, our energy is part of the universal energy, a manifestation of one and the same vitality. Nowhere is there separation between inner and outer. When we touch the energy within, we connect with extended fields of energy outside ourselves.

With the body in balance, we experience the external world as a whole, without duality. Isolation and despair, the result of excessive tension, yield to space.

Kum Nye Relaxation

The relaxation that stimulates spiritual growth requires a discipline that engages both body and mind. The Tibetan Buddhist teachings address this need through various forms of yoga (literally, union or integration). The Tibetan lama Tarthang Tulku introduced to the West a traditional form of preparatory healing practices known as Kum Nye relaxation. The aim of Kum Nye relaxation is developing the art of balance, the integration of the energies of body, mind, and senses.[39]

Kum Nye is a natural healing method as well as a tool for deepening meditation. It includes sitting practices, breathing exercises, self-massage, and movement exercises. By stimulating the flow of feeling, the exercises melt feelings and experiences that were frozen. With practice we discover a sensation that is shared by body, breath, and mind—a calm, clear, and profound feeling that relaxes and massages us internally. As we deepen relaxation, feelings open like a lens, letting in more light or energy and creating more comprehensive pictures of experience.[40]

Kum Nye exercises establish inner balance by calming down what is overactive and awakening what is dormant. Ku (sKu) refers to the body—not the physical body, but the subtle energy system and our presence in space. Nye (*mNye*) refers to the internal massage that activates the subtle energy flow. Kum Nye exercises allow relaxing, integrating and transforming the vitality of body and mind.

The practice of Kum Nye guides us through three levels of relaxation. On the surface, mindfulness of bodily sensations reveals a feeling tone, which can seem sad or joyful, warm or cold. This is the first level of relaxation. There may be a sense of flowing, tingling, or pain. There is a duality: I sense my feelings.

By entering these sensations and going deeper, we contact a second layer of energy: a feeling of density and toughness. This layer is characterized by a quality of holding on that blocks the flow of energy. There may be an emerging sense of the exercise doing itself, of an inner massage taking over.

With gentle concentration, we can move through this feeling to the third layer. Here, sensations flow freely: It is as if the body begins to melt. There is no longer a sense of duality. We merge completely with the flow of feeling. Body and mind are freely exercising in space.

At this level of relaxation, our spirit regenerates and revitalizes itself. All experiences, even ingrained emotional tendencies, are being recycled. Emotions we might have felt before starting the Kum Nye practice slip away. In this context an emotion is a blockage of energy, and once the flow of feeling is activated again, the blockage is lifted. Energy in body and mind is refreshing itself. Time and age cannot catch or freeze this energy, as long as it flows. It is actively moving and cultivating itself. It does not belong to us; we are only channels for the energy and the knowledge that it carries. As Tarthang Tulku notes, this process is sometimes called longevity, and its potential lies within the flow of feeling and our senses.[41]

Everything Comes to Life

The relaxation stimulated by regular Kum Nye practice diminishes our reliance upon judgments, interpretations, and the habitual responses that distance us from direct experience. Such responses pull our energy into familiar patterns of accepting and rejecting, hoping and fearing: "I like this." "I don't like that." "I wanted that for myself." "She doesn't like me." "If only I were . . ."

Do we have the courage to briefly interrupt this "minding" and observe what is really happening in our minds? Do we dare to see and feel without interfering? It is all a matter of energy. Resistance and emotions are also a form of energy, generating sensations of heaviness or density, heat or cold. Thoughts too have an undercurrent that originates in the world of feelings, a play of energy. We can consciously contact this undercurrent when we are in the midst of an emotion. But thoughts will pull on us, so we need to encourage ourselves to redirect our focus to feeling the energy in the body. We can touch the energy of emotions and face our resistance, making space for them until their energy begins to flow again.

When energy flows, both mind and senses gain vibrancy. Colors appear brighter, food tastes better, feelings open to intuition, and intelligence becomes empathic. Experience takes on a vital quality, like an exciting adventure. There is no imbalance in our giving and receiving. Inside and outside feed each other. Each one of us is unique, yet part of a whole. This integration is a springboard for exercising our talents to the fullest.

Future Is Past

Is there a relationship between accumulated tension and dementia? Is it conceivable that the chemical processes triggered by relaxation could counter the assault on the brain cells, or perhaps even help to prevent it? That conclusion would be too simple, denying the compound factors that may have contributed to the disease, such as hereditary aspects. Yet it is equally true that total, intense relaxation enables body, breath, and mind to begin a healing process in ways that may seem to be miraculous.

Lack of activity and depression have been shown to be contributory factors to the symptoms of Alzheimer's disease. Inactivity of body and mind can cause energy to stagnate, creating a breeding ground for illness, whereas total involvement promotes the flow of energy. Even the simplest activities make a difference, such as washing the dishes or weeding the garden. Physical engagement enables emotions and memories to circulate. In an active body, tension is less likely to block the flow of energy, while the cycle of vitality may dissolve emotions. Physical activity, performed with total concentration and few thoughts, is a healing method in itself.

Will I become like Uncle Gerard?" my mother sometimes asked. My great-uncle Gerard spent his time in
total solitude, listening to Wagner records for hours on
end, otherwise mentally absent. During the last twenty
years of his life my mother was the only person who visited him regularly.

The prospect of dementia is terrifying to anybody,
young or old. Many people say they would prefer to die
rather than lose control of their mental faculties. Some
even say, "I'd rather kill myself!" without realizing that
once dementia had developed, the consciousness required
for such an act of resolve would probably be absent.

Living in isolation on a little Italian island, my
mother slipped into melancholy. She saw no way to
open up her predicament. When she could not express
herself, part of her energy was blocked. Hopelessness
and depression spiraled downward, perhaps contributing to the progress of Alzheimer's in her brain. In brief
spells of relaxation, old, neglected feelings emerged,
followed by despair: What could she do with her life?
How could she take destiny in her own hands and head in
a new direction?

In her younger years she had been able to work through
the pain of the past, but at this point in her life she could
not allow herself to tap into her vital energy. Therefore,
she was incapable of envisioning new challenges. For her,
the time to reflect on the future was past.

9

Mastering Life

One day at the Nyingma Center in Boulder, Colorado, a stranger arrived. He was about twenty years older than I with a balding head and a wiry frame. "My name is Lino," he announced as I opened the door wide. While knocking the snow off his boots, he said, without further introduction, "I would like to learn more about Tibetan Buddhism." Intrigued by his appearance, I inquired, "Why is that?"

Lino told me his life story. As a boy during World War II, he was held captive in a Yugoslavian concentration camp. Close to starvation, he found a method to get more nourishment from the meager daily ration. Very slowly he would chew the hard bread and dry rice. This way, he would spend at least ten minutes on one grain of rice, realizing intuitively that saliva contains nutrients. As an adult, he became fascinated with alternative nutritional theories. He had studied macrobiotics for years. Only recently he had comprehended that perfect equilibrium requires nurturing the mind as well as the body. Having established the "right diet" for the body, he wondered if perhaps there could be a "right diet" for the mind.

INSPIRED BY MASTERY

In Lino I recognized something of a quality that I had been reading about. When I first encountered it personally, a few years before, I was at a crossroads. Even though I was in my late twenties, already my future seemed predictable. Having worked for five years in the shipping industry in New York and Hong Kong, one day it dawned on me that I was likely to end my career in a Rotterdam office, supervising more and more ships. I envisioned this prospect with complete clarity and had no desire for it to become reality. I was ready for a radical change in my life.

I decided to go my own way, knowing only one thing for certain: I wanted to do something that I wholeheartedly enjoyed. My parents were concerned and tried coaxing me to remain at my job and explore new directions in my free time. But that was out of the question for me; it had to be full time. I was somehow convinced that if I did something I really believed in, somehow I would always make enough money.

Before returning to Holland I went to San Francisco, hoping to remain for a while and explore my interest in music. I took up the flute and devoted most of my time to it. But I also found a new direction. Soon I met people who were on the cutting edge of the search for a more intuitive knowledge; people who believed that the human capacity for knowledge was infinite. It was 1976, and the consciousness-raising movement in California was just gaining momentum. I decided to get involved.

Transformation is often the result of a life crisis. But sometimes the recognition that life must have a deeper meaning can be enough to cause a dramatic shift, so that mind and heart open to new possibilities and respond to life's opportunities in a new way. At such a time, extraordinary people may cross our paths and exert a powerful influence on our lives. This was the case for me.

One morning, I audited a master-class by the French flutist Jean-Pierre Rampal. For months the six participants had each studied one particular piece, such as a Bach sonata or a concerto by Mozart. The first student had played only a few notes when Rampal interrupted her. "You can play notes very well, and that is great. But that does not yet make it music. Listen." He brought his golden flute to his mouth and began playing the same passage. At the first tones my breath stopped: A few yards away, a master was at work. Thereafter, every time I played the flute I imagined Rampal playing.

On that same day I visited the Tibetan Nyingma Institute in Berkeley, which was just a few blocks away from the master flute class; someone had recommended it to me. In the meditation garden, I saw Tarthang Tulku giving instructions for painting prayer wheels. For the second time that day, I felt I was in the presence of a master at work. I enrolled in a weekend seminar that began the next day.

Everything I heard in the seminar was new to me, yet sounded somehow familiar. I do not recall much of the content, but the way I felt all through the weekend is still vivid in my mind. Something in me awoke, and I thought, "This is it. This is what I want to pursue." Without wondering whether I was capable and with no concern for the impact on my life, I dove into the Human Development Program offered at the Nyingma Institute. The subject was self-mastery, becoming a master of one's own life.

In my experience, the way masters work is often invisible to the ordinary eye. Strengthened by inner discipline and having access to unbridled creativity, they work by simply being. From a distance it may seem that they do nothing spectacular. What attracts us is their light-hearted simplicity. They work with their whole being, with infectious dedication. They are at ease. Nothing comes between them and their work—no projections, no self-image, no resistance. Masters are always at work, everywhere. It is hard to explain what defines a master; their exact methods defy words, and masters themselves rarely speak about what they think and do.

The inspiration of mastery is a special theme in the Tibetan Buddhist teachings. The siddha tradition (siddha means "accomplished one") preserves the biographies of eighty-four masters, "the powerful accomplished ones" who are also called the Buddha's Lions.[42] These eighty-four siddhas are living proof of the possibility of becoming enlightened within a single lifetime. Just as the wind dispels clouds, the siddhas transform confusion and ignorance into direct realization of the Buddha's teachings. Through their example they inspire others; their path is uncomplicated and accessible to anyone, even the lowliest in society. To begin, one must have deeply experienced the indescribable suffering of all life on earth or have perfected inner discipline. If these conditions are present, the right situation may occur: the coming together of student, teacher, and method. Then it is possible to realize enlightenment in this life, here and now.

At some point in our lives we may become aware of a persistent restlessness that stirs within us, an inexpressible hollowness, a yearning. Something is missing. The fear that life will slip away with little to show for it may enter into our thoughts. From time to time, we wonder: "Is this all there is? Is this what I have worked so hard for? What is the point?" Such questions, and the feelings that attend them, indicate the need to awaken a new perspective and activate deeper capacities for understanding. Whoever enters a spiritual path has perceived at least a glimpse of a greater truth, something that encourages us and points the way. It is a matter of recognition. Through awareness of transience and the need to find meaning in what we do, we become aware of our potential and of latent opportunities. One day our lives will be over, yet now there is still time to offer to the world our resources of awareness and energy.

The Noble Eightfold Path

The Buddha said human suffering is needless: Fears, frustrations, emotionality, and disappointments have distinct causes that can be eliminated. But we lack the necessary wisdom. With more awareness, our actions can become wiser. When wisdom and action come together, our suffering will end. To help us reach this goal, the Buddha laid out the Noble Eightfold Path that leads toward enlightenment. It is venerated and practiced in all Buddhist traditions.[43]

In some ways the Eightfold Path may seem deceptively simple. Perhaps any great teaching runs the risk of being oversimplified, but the risk is especially great with Buddhist teachings, because they have been introduced to the West relatively recently; within too short a time for profound understanding to develop. The language of the teachings resonates with subtle levels of meaning; if we are not attuned to them, we may miss entire realms of significance.

Studying the themes in the Buddha's teachings out of context may also create confusion. Mixing otherwise unconnected ideas can obscure the underlying structure, making it difficult to assimilate the teachings appropriate to each stage of the path. It is best to listen with unbiased ears, without jumping to conclusions, allowing our minds to absorb the words and messages of the teachings without inner commentary or distortion. The tradition tells us first to listen to the teaching and comprehend what is meant, then to meditate on it, and finally to put it into practice. Only from this foundation can we truly evaluate whether or not the teaching works.

The teachings of the Buddha form a complex whole. The enlightened view and the aspiration to attain it, the far-reaching philosophy and psychological insights, and the meditation practices, rituals, and symbols all work together. When we study and practice them with respect for the whole, a structure emerges that the mind can trust and rely upon. Buddhist teachings do not provide a list of dogmas; they form a guidebook that enables us to recognize and uproot the obscurations of consciousness, step by step. Alleviating suffering is really a matter of refining our inner resources.

In the First Turning of the Wheel, his first set of teachings given at Sarnath in India, the Buddha expounded the Four Noble Truths. The first truth is that all existence has suffering at its core. The second noble truth states that suffering has a cause. The third noble truth is that this suffering can cease. The fourth noble truth points to the path that leads to the cessation of suffering, known to all Buddhists as the Noble Eightfold Path. Following the eight steps, we develop right view, right motivation, right communication, right action, right livelihood, right effort, right mindfulness, and right concentration. The word "right" is not used judgmentally, as opposed to wrong, but in the sense of being complete, genuinely pure, universally beneficial, leading to enlightenment.

The Buddha declared that no one knows how to put an end to suffering.[44] That is why he taught the Eightfold Path. But the path is steep and narrow, and therefore arduous. The view that informs it is profound and subtle, and the Buddha said that even if he were to teach, few would be able to fully understand. Some people tend to interpret its terms lightly, assuming they understand them and already apply them to some extent in their daily lives. They may associate the alleviation of suffering with putting an end to difficulties and obstacles, or easing physical pain. However, difficulties and obstacles are inherent in change; they will always show up, independent of our personal development. Actually, for those with a great mind and heart, ready to take on great goals, difficulties and obstacles may arise exponentially.

There are various kinds of suffering, but the most persistent and limiting forms of suffering are closely linked to the notion of *I*. Lack of wisdom—and therefore, lack of compassion—are reflected in suffering. Wisdom and compassion enable us to transcend our fixation on *I*. But difficulties and obstacles remain, even if we no longer experience the grosser forms of suffering. With growing maturity, we will appreciate our opportunities and be open-minded to the trials and tribulations that come with meaningful living. Following the Noble Eightfold Path implies a maturing of mind, heart, and action, thus reducing suffering each step of the way.

1. Right View
Right view provides the remedy for suffering. We aim to develop right view as the first aspect of the Noble Eightfold Path. We question: Do we have a clear, comprehensive view of ourselves and the nature of reality? Or have we completeley lost sight of the whole, focused as we are on the self?

Wisdom involves renouncing incorrect thoughts, actions, behaviors, and opinions on the one hand, and adopting right view on the other. Suffering is the result of lack of understanding and of incomplete vision. We do something that leads to error and pain, and refrain from doing something that promotes benefit and understanding. Because our perception is muddy, consciousness functions poorly. Entrapped within our own karmic patterns and preoccupied with emotions, we may easily become stranded in the world of samsara.

The pain and frustrations we suffer can be traced to karmic tendencies that accompany us from birth, as well as to the learned responses developed during childhood. As children we are taught how to think and act; there is little space for exploring our own feelings. If our enthusiasm and pain cannot be articulated, we become strangers to ourselves, prone to feelings of guilt and blame. We learn to look first to others—parents, siblings, and teachers—rather than to ourselves. The inevitable formation of *I* in childhood in itself predisposes us to suffering.

Upon reaching adulthood, we may hardly know who we are, apart from our roles and our multiple self-images: as parents, employers, employees, and so on. Caught up in incorrect, incomplete, or impure thoughts, actions, behaviors, and opinions, we are weighed down by an underlying feeling of deep disappointment that signals a loss of personal integrity.

Right view provides a clear image of our true nature and points the way to wisdom. Taking a step back and picturing ourselves in the larger scope of things, we understand that we are not the center of the universe, but part of an integrated whole. Once we have a taste of right view, we are able to stop identifying with *I*. Right view disentangles the personal stories and dramas, letting us keep the greater perspective in mind. When we perceive the nature of mind to be like a mirror, capable of producing both happiness and suffering, we no longer rely on assumptions, but on the openness of mind.

Right view is not something to be possessed—it must be rediscovered again and again. It helps to remember that right view always points to the middle way: not too much and not too little, no extremes of austerity or decadence. Not too hard and not too soft, not too fast, and not too slow. Right view recognizes freedom of mind, not belonging to either determinism or nihilism. It unites wisdom and compassion.

2. Right Motivation

From right view arises right motivation, which inspires the actions that relieve suffering. As long as we lack right view, we act impulsively, unclear about our motivation. We choose the path of least resistance, running on automatic pilot and repeating familiar patterns. Or we may act out our confusion, taking a certain action against our better judgment, going back and forth and in the end, choosing another course entirely. Not sure who we are or what we stand for, we communicate mixed messages, saying "yes" when we mean "no," and vice versa. Because we have no firm ground on which to stand, our motivation is unreliable.

If we were to look more closely, we would see how utterly confused our motives really are. Even when we think we are giving our best, our desire to help may be tainted by hidden agendas and needs. Are we yearning for recognition? Do we want to be seen as a rescuer, the source of another's happiness? An act that feels courageous today may turn out tomorrow to have been shortsighted, even cruel, or perhaps simply useless.

By identifying our thoughts and categorizing them without judgment or guilt, we learn to discriminate between healthy and unhealthy tendencies in our minds. We become familiar with the motives underlying our behavior by examining our opinions and asking questions. If I am totally honest with myself, what are my real motives? Do I want to improve my self-image? Do I secretly hope that others will fail? Why do I need to attract attention? Why would I be holding back, waiting for others to take initiative?

In becoming mindful of our motives, it is important not to judge them as positive or negative. This would tempt us to hold on to the positive ones as good and reject the negative ones as bad, which may not be helpful in the long run. A positive motivation is not necessarily a right motivation, for where self-image is operating, right motivation does not come into play. For us to experience right motivation, we must first experience an inner transformation that moves us closer toward right view. There comes a time when we see clearly that our old motivations are no longer applicable, yet new motivations have not yet evolved. During this time, it may be best to relax in that "space between," to simply wait and be mindful, to continue to observe and question what is universally good. This could be, for example, the genuine wish not to harm anyone or to refrain from unwholesome activities.

Nourished by mindfulness and continued questioning, the foundations of our motivations begin to shift. Right view comes more fully into focus, clarifying the nature of our motivations and enabling right motivation to take root and flourish.

3. Right Communication

Right communication alleviates suffering. From right motivation, right communication is born. What is the use of living if we cannot express who we truly are, if our thoughts and feelings must remain hidden in silence or lies? The magic of words allows us to know ourselves deeply, acknowledging the bonds with our fellow human beings, and bridging whatever separates us. Without this magic, we become strangers to others and ourselves.

Right communication begins with stillness. As the Bible says, "Let your words be few." [45] Grounded in silence, we can sense the intention and quality of our communication. We can see the effects of our lack of caring, observing how even sincere words may create distance or possibly inflict harm. We see that by using words to attach labels and judgments, we may solidify what would otherwise naturally change. Perhaps we judge harshly or assign blame needlessly, talking about others behind their backs. We may say one thing to one person and something else to another, speaking out of both sides of our mouth. We may curse at random, without giving any thought to the effect on those around us. With a few words, even a glance, we may devastate another; in a single burst of anger, we can destroy years of carefully built harmony.

Within silence we recover balance and connect more fully to the inner breath. The right words then come naturally, for speech is married to breath. We discover gentle words that inspire, give new energy and courage. When others speak, we listen from within, hearing not only the words but also the meaning behind the words. Communicating with care, we build bridges, heal old wounds, and open the door to deeper contact with others.

From within silence, we can observe our habitual patterns of communication and gently expand our repertoire of responses. If we are usually introverted, we might try expressing ourselves more often; if we are accustomed to talking, we might occasionally choose to be silent. If we are impelled to make conversation because we feel restless and lonely, we can learn to comfort our heart with the nurturing qualities of silence.

Right communication brings people together and opens realms of possibility beyond words. It is an echo of the truth, so difficult to express in words. Grounded in silence and compassion, a simple gesture may speak louder than a thousand words.

4. Right Action
Right action reduces suffering. Right action is directed by right view and, in turn, manifests right view in the world: One cannot exist without the other. If right view is not developed, we can still extend ourselves toward right action by asking, "How can I contribute?" Right action begins with avoiding harmful behavior. Murder cannot be

right action, even if the life taken is that of an ant that walks across the table. Physical maltreatment—of others or ourselves—is never justified. Similarly, mental abuse, pressure, or pestering, thwarting, or undermining others can only lead to suffering.

But we can go further. We can refrain from weakening another and also offer our support. We can refrain from stealing and also give generously. And instead of being jealous, we can enjoy someone else's success. We can occasionally ask ourselves, "Am I sure that, despite my best intentions, I am not causing harm?"

Ten Wholesome Actions
1. sustaining life
2. engaging in giving
3. maintaining pure ethics
4. speaking the truth
5. speaking harmoniously
6. speaking lovingly
7. talking sensibly
8. cultivating joy for others' prosperity
9. cultivating helpfulness
10. learning correct views

Right action honors the common good and the law of karma. It is not based on blindly following the example of others, but on confidence that our actions will have positive consequences. Wholesome action produces wholesome results, while unwholesome activity leads to more rounds of suffering. The Buddha's path is paved with right action.

There is no simple recipe for right action, for what is needed in each moment is unique to that moment. Sometimes we must refrain from acting; at other times it is best to act without inner debate; on still other occasions we may need to think everything through until no questions remain.

Right action demands sensitivity to time as well, for our response needs to come at the right moment, not too early and not too late. Timing is crucial for right action. When the time for reflection is over, for example, we must act. Our attention is focused not on our own concerns, but on what needs to be done for the common good. If the timing is right, we need not be afraid to act. If a mistake is made, we can repair the damage immediately. That is right action as well.

We learn by doing. Each situation offers us another opportunity to give. We do not need to wait to take action until we are absolutely certain what to do, nor do we need to act rashly. When our actions are right, we will find that we receive more than we give; the more we give, the more we are able to receive. Overall, our actions will be protected by the wish: "May all sentient beings benefit from my actions."

5. Right Livelihood
Right livelihood diminishes suffering. If we work merely for income and status, or to satisfy what others expect of us, we eventually experience feelings of dissatisfaction that gnaw at us from within. Can we imagine a different motivation, one that would bring us joy? I have found

for myself that practicing Dharma and earning money are not mutually exclusive. What if we could enjoy our work and grow from it, while at the same time benefiting others? Enjoying work depends on taking advantage of opportunities that benefit all concerned. In the approach developed by my teacher, Tarthang Tulku, this kind of activity is considered an aspect of what is traditionally known as *skillful means* or *skill in means*.[46] Working with skillful means, we can fulfill all our needs, physical, mental, or spiritual, while making a genuine contribution to the society in which we live.

Perhaps we suspect that right livelihood is the privilege of those in the helping professions or the saintly, like Nelson Mandela or Mother Teresa, but right livelihood is open to everyone. Once we commit ourselves to right livelihood, opportunities begin to arise to make our intention a reality. We may want to achieve more than simply benefit ourselves and our family, and our motivation exceeds the notion of ownership and property. Instead, we focus on participating and being of service in society, for the long haul. We begin to ask: How can the benefit of my work spread to the office, school, town or city, and beyond? We see that in business, with every deal we close, every contract we sign, we can aim to benefit all involved: the client, vendor, company, employees, and shareholders, even the neighborhood in which the company is located. Likewise, the profits of the company can be used to benefit all sentient beings.

Right livelihood is not simply a matter of "giving back," but acting in the name of goodness. It inevitably asks for sacrifice—an offering of our time, money, or self-interest, as these primarily serve the *I.* Mindfulness of right livelihood ensures that everyone benefits from our work. By definition, right livelihood takes into account all sentient beings.

6. Right Effort

Right effort is a cure for suffering. It seems simple—give it all you've got and go for it, one hundred percent. Yet right effort also requires right view and right motivation: knowing what works and what does not, what helps and what is counterproductive. Right effort means pursuing an honorable goal in a way that benefits ourselves as well as others. Working for a good cause by manipulating others is not right effort, nor is working hard to gain praise or avoid blame.

Right view and right effort support one another. Right view gives the right outlook, while right effort provides the energy to head in the appropriate direction. In determining the approach, right effort is pragmatic, taking into account the circumstances, the time available, and the capabilities of the other people involved. Sometimes we need to move ahead assertively or even do battle against inertia or opposition, while at other times we need to be patient and bide our time. Right effort is a balance between fighting and surrendering, without ever giving up.

Love and compassion are the compass for right effort. If we maintain right view we will have abundant energy. Things will move ahead according to their own rhythm, for at its best, right effort is effortless.

Right effort concerns not only our behavior but also our attitudes. As we become familiar with the negative tendencies that undermine our best efforts—which always operate in the arena of *I*—we are able to stop protecting our self-image and actually feel the anxiety and dread that underlie the *I.*

Right effort gives us the courage to crawl out of our cocoon of fear, and confront *I.* We work with our knowledge of cause and effect and embrace the laws of karma. We realize that our suffering is the result of past karma: patterns of frustration and impatience that have continued through time up to the present. Now we must live with the consequences. Yet right effort can turn things around, for its pure power can destroy negative karma. The result defies imagination: Just as right view is unlimited, right effort makes everything possible.

7. Right Mindfulness

Right mindfulness is an antidote for suffering. Right mindfulness brings us into the present. As a buffer between the present and the future, right mindfulness protects us from our tendency to go astray. It shines the light of awareness on our automatic reactions and brings them to a halt. No longer do we mindlessly duplicate patterns of suffering. Right mindfulness creates space for us to creatively pursue what is right.

Mindfulness restores the neutral, spacious quality of reality, enabling us to observe what we otherwise would tend to ignore. When the mind finally opens up, we are free to perceive whatever is happening. We are able to maintain our balance in both good times and bad, for all aspects of experience, suffering too, serve as catalysts for understanding. As our minds become more spacious, time expands, allowing us to determine our course of action with greater ease.

Right mindfulness reveals how needless much of our suffering has been. Knowing that our difficulties result from lack of awareness frees us from clinging to the past and prepares us for a brighter future. With right mindfulness as our physician and awareness of the present as our medicine, we know we are protected from the disease of needless suffering.

8. Right Concentration

Right concentration eases suffering. Right concentration channels awareness and keeps us focused. It is the key to success, a priceless legacy for our children as well as us. The Tibetan word for concentration (*ting-nge-'dzin*),[47] which in English is often translated as "meditation," has a meaning more akin to integration. Elements that were separate come together: body and mind, head and heart, right motivation and right action. The quality of right concentration is relaxed, neither too tight nor too loose, combining an eye for detail with a global overview. Ultimately, this kind of concentration becomes total absorption, which is effortless.

Right concentration differs from concentration motivated by self-concern. When we are intent on earning a great deal of money or protecting our interests, we may have no difficulty staying focused. For example, we do not lose track of the reasons for our grievances and are able to keep them alive for years. Yet this focusing is characterized by an inner unrest that actually hinders concentration and fosters emotional instability. Restlessness breeds worry and worry interferes with concentration, thus creating a vicious cycle that leads to misery and dissatisfaction. This kind of focused vigilance only causes more pain and suffering.

Right concentration empowers the mind and is the springboard to success. It keeps us on the right course. There is no need to flee from difficulties, for right concentration defeats adversity, always finding a way to overcome obstacles. Right concentration mediates between difficulty and contentment, unhappiness and happiness, small mind and greater mind.

EVERYTHING RIGHT

Hours had passed. It had become still around us; outside the snow muffled all sounds. Inside, the stillness was almost palpable. I could not see Lino's eyes since we were seated next to each other, but I felt he was focused and relaxed at the same time. He radiated so much energy that he seemed to be capable of single-handedly changing his DNA. He was living as if today was his last day and he did not intend to waste a single moment.

While Lino and I were talking, my mother was never far from my mind. On an impulse, I told him about her illness and my feelings of powerlessness. He did not hesitate for a second. He jumped up, waving his arms like a samurai, and made it clear that he knew a remedy for her state. "The right diet! No cheese, no salt, no milk, no wine. And absolutely no coffee and eggs," he implored. With a shock I realized that these very foods were the basis of my mother's diet.

Later that same day I wrote my parents a letter. "Please stop eating all those things you take such pleasure in!" We might be able to save my mother by drastically changing her eating habits. It was quite a radical idea. At one fell swoop, all my parents' cozy rituals would be off-limits: the morning cup of coffee, the late afternoon glass of wine, cheese before and with every meal. Still, I had no doubt that my parents would heed my advice without hesitation.

My plea never reached my mother. My father, the captain of their two-person team, told me by telephone, "We are already trying so many things." An extensive summary followed: yoga every morning (even the cobra posture was on their program), as well as reading metaphysical books, especially about the Tao. "Also, the doctor prescribed a pill to take twice a day, but she often forgets to take it."

I could not understand. Why did they not see that this diet was right action? I was desperately trying to be of help. Or was it not right action? Maybe Lino was wrong. Only years later did I realize why my advice fell on deaf ears: The Noble Eightfold Path is a medicine to be chosen, not prescribed. Each must recognize the path for himself.

10

Love Disconnected

They repatriated from Elba. My father's retreat had come to an end. Sociability reentered my mother's life: "So cozy, to see so many lights at night." But they did not come back to The Hague for coziness. Much had changed in twelve years. Three of their four sons lived abroad. The Kaleidoscope was a thing of the past. Volunteering was no longer possible, nor was playing bridge. Of my mother's old activities, only the Monday afternoon teas remained. Every week her friend Joss picked her up in her tiny Fiat so they could go together. "How nice, Joss! Where are we going?" my mother asked every five minutes. Joss answered her patiently every time. During tea and then cocktails, they sat next to each other on the couch, Joss holding my mother's hand in hers. When it became my mother's turn to share, Joss always spoke for her, as if it were about her own loved ones.

I called my parents every Sunday. At first it seemed as if my mother and I were together in the same room, chatting just like in the old days. But gradually the distance became more difficult to bridge. Words seemed to drop into empty space; I often remained uncertain whether they had actually reached her.

One day, as soon as she recognized my voice, she said, "Wait a moment, and I'll call Daddy."

I was perplexed. It was an open secret that my father did not like the telephone, and he would never initiate a call. In contrast, my mother loved to talk on the phone, asking questions and being a good listener. She would speak enthusiastically about everything she was involved with. Our calls would often be long, and they were a good substitute for meeting in person. But now my father joined us and explained that he had purchased a speakerphone so they could both talk with me at the same time. The intimacy of chatting with my mother alone had suddenly vanished.

After that, our telephone calls always involved the three of us, and my mother rarely spoke, except to occasionally reassure me, "I'm still here." In the beginning she responded to some of my questions, but later on my father would answer for her. One day I decided to call at a time when I was sure my father would be out. Monday mornings he played bridge in town.

That Monday my mother answered the phone. "Hi Mom, how is it going?" "Fine," she said, "tell me how you are." I began to talk and once in a while I heard a concurring sound on the other end. Now and then I forgot that it was better not to ask questions and would ask her something. She remained quiet and I sensed that a lot went on inside of her that she was unable to express. It was as if she simply could not find the right words.

Later, when I visited her in The Hague, there were many such moments when she could not articulate her thoughts. She would turn her face to me, squint her eyes, and chuckle. She beamed and made a humming sound from her chest—hmmmmm—or emphatically pressed my arm. Every time she proved that communication is not dependent on words alone.

It was the early eighties and little was known about Alzheimer's disease. We knew age could bring deteriorating memory, possibly dementia—but that sounded so terrible! That could not have anything to do with us, and certainly not with my mother. We ascribed her loss of memory, her decreased ability to react, and her lack of initiative to old age. As time went on, her increasing disorientation and rapidly changing moods made us suspect some kind of illness. But we were unsure of its nature, and had no idea what lay ahead for her or for us.

Alzheimer's Disease

Alzheimer's Disease is not an inevitable product of old age, but results from damage to the brain.[48] The illness is marked by a progressive and irreversible loss of brain functioning, which is thought to be caused by destruction of brain cells and the connections between them. Abnormal protein deposits accumulate in clumps that damage the brain's nerve endings.[49] Brain activity is disturbed, and the ability to think coherently gradually breaks down. Thoughts disappear before they can be articulated. Eventually, the connection between thinking and speaking dissolves.

In my mother's case the senses remained more or less active; hearing, seeing, and feeling were intact, but short-term memory was weakened and at last disappeared. Also, speaking became more difficult, because even the simplest discussion requires a complex set of interconnections within the brain. A conversation felt like jumping from one ice floe to another across a river, with the next patch seemingly out of reach over dark, cold, inhospitable water. But each Alzheimer's patient has different symptoms, often far worse than my mother's.

My mother was no longer able to prepare meals. The various movements required in the kitchen confused her; she would turn on the stove without holding a match to it, or forget that something was cooking. Other household tasks proved difficult as well. One day I proposed that we make the bed together, and she said, "OK," but when we entered her bedroom, she had no idea why we were there. These gaps in awareness were embarrassing for her. We all forget something occasionally, but once we are reminded, we remember. With Alzheimer's, events seem to be engulfed by emptiness and even a reminder does not help. An appointment, visit, or question is not initially registered and therefore cannot be remembered. Having a conversation with my mother became impossible most of the time.

Still, in the first years after we knew she was ill we regularly received signs of life from her: a little note, an airmail letter, or a postcard. Each correspondence would consist of a pressing request for a recent photo, reminiscences of previous visits, and expressions of longing to

157

see us again soon. Each letter also contained some news about the other family members. But as the years wore on, she wrote less. Eventually, we stopped hearing anything from her, only learning about her from other members of the family or from friends.

I never gave up on my mother, but the old closeness had disappeared. I did not witness or experience the changes she underwent, and therefore my love could not evolve with her. Yet it was not only the distance that kept reality from sinking in; this new world in which she now lived was too frightening for me to embrace. I often wondered why I felt so numb. Was that normal? Shouldn't one feel desperate, overwhelmed with grief, or full of pity? Deep inside, I was uneasy. However, I did not explore my feelings of dullness and disconnection further. And no matter how much I thought about my mother, our bond was fading.

Love Is Friendship

"When you really love someone, you must learn to listen well."[50] A good listener understands the meanings behind words. By cultivating a sensitive ear and a gentle eye, we are able to discern what motivates the speaker, and feel directly what warms her heart. We give without expecting anything in return, empathizing with her over a loss, and enjoying her happiness and success. Giving and receiving merge together and become one.

The feeling of love is characteristic of an open mind, which makes no distinction between self and others.

When we are open and receptive, there is no duality— no division between subject and object, no distinction between giver and receiver. Love, and in the Buddhist tradition, friendship as well, involves only subjects. It is not "you and I," but "we." We are both subjects, joined in equality and amity. Free from the tension between subject and object, a circle of affection grows, and feelings of intimacy deepen. In illness and in health, even across thousands of miles, we are together.

The Buddha declared, "One who loves himself will never hurt anyone else." In the Buddhist tradition, the practice of love starts with oneself. In Western society, where a certain degree of self-contempt, poor self-esteem, and arrogance can seem almost normal, it is essential for us to learn to love ourselves before expanding our love to others. When we are able to befriend and love whatever arises in us, we naturally extend those feelings to others.

Feeling Guilty

In the Buddhist teachings, love originates with the desire to be happy, and the wish that others are happy as well. Compassion originates with the wish that others, as well as ourselves, may be free from suffering and the causes of suffering. Such love and compassion are inherent in human consciousness, and thus are always available, even when we are so caught up in negative reactions that we seem cut off from their healing power. At such times, we can simply ask, "What prevents me from experiencing love and compassion?"

If we look closely, we may see that the answer lies in our self-concern and the negative emotions associated with it. Among these negative reactions is the feeling of guilt. Looking back, I realize that I felt guilty all throughout my mother's process of deterioration. Something inside froze, and I became a bystander to her pain instead of a caring son.

While brief pangs of guilt may have a healthy effect by waking us up to ways in which we have ignored our responsibilities, prolonged guilt prevents us from growing. By keeping our attention focused on the past, guilt stops us from living in the moment. Like laziness, it provides an alibi for inaction. For example, while we read our children a story or help them with homework, we may be plagued with guilt about putting a parent in a nursing home. A small inner voice keeps reiterating all that we should have done differently. The powerlessness we feel to change what has happened casts a shadow over our consciousness that dims the light of our present experience and keeps us from fully engaging it. We shortchange ourselves and everyone else in our lives, especially those closest to us. Knowing this fuels additional feelings of guilt that darken our consciousness still further.

On the surface, our feelings of guilt may suggest the desire to make a sincere penance. We feel ashamed of ourselves, but not in a positive way that could effect change, for the shame we feel is rooted in guilt that we have not lived up to our own expectations. Even when it becomes obvious that a situation is more than we can handle, we cling to the belief that we should have been able to take

care of it. At the heart of our guilt is the "childish illusion that we are capable of anything: Deep in our heart,
we believe we are almighty."[51] Our self-condemnation is a
kind of reversed arrogance.

If guilt were related to a genuine awareness of our
lacks and deficiencies, putting forth a greater effort would
help to relieve it. But trying harder does not necessarily
reduce the burden of guilt; in fact, the harder we try, the
more determined we may be to compensate for the guilt
we still feel.[52] Driven by this need, we tend to present an
inflated public image of ourselves, while harboring self-
doubts and fears of discovery within. Nurtured covertly
over time, these fears can erode self-confidence and make
us vulnerable to self-loathing and destructive impulses.

Feeling guilty is stimulated by a sense of powerlessness. We hold an ideal view of the self that we fail to
live up to. We are unable to do what we feel we ought to
be able to do. Low self-esteem, the flip side of overrating,
reveals a lack of insight. Both guilt and low self-esteem
reflect lack of appreciation for what we are and for what
we can become. We fail to recognize that our life, like
all life, offers unique opportunities for fulfillment. This
is precisely what Dharma teachings emphasize: the
preciousness of life.

The Tibetan language has no exact parallel for the
Western concepts of guilt or inferiority, or for lack
of self-esteem.[53] A person brought up in a Buddhist
culture finds it difficult to comprehend that a human
being might suffer from self-loathing or even self-
hatred. Buddhist teachings present remorse and regret as

dynamic concepts, based on recognition of lapses that stimulate the wish to heal. Understood in the light of the Dharma, remorse and regret are purifying feelings, and significant for spiritual growth.[54]

Although feelings of guilt can last a lifetime, there may come a point when we realize that we cannot possibly be as bad as we have judged ourselves to be. We may meet with someone or encounter a teaching that begins to wake us up to the basic goodness of our being. Realizing that the true source of our guilt has been our lack of self-understanding, and seeing that guilt is prolonging our suffering and perhaps even spreading it to others, we begin to feel genuine regret, which ignites the wish to heal. The wish to embrace our situation and to heal the pain it perpetuates reconnects us with love and compassion. We want to set something right. How can we begin?

Healing guilt involves both forgiveness and the resolve to change. At first, it helps to work through our feelings of guilt and express them openly to another who is willing to witness our resolve to change. The next step is to forgive ourselves for our failures and for our harsh treatment of ourselves and others.

By admitting we have failed or have acted inadequately, we open the door to forgiveness. We yearn for remorse and regret; we actively look for ways to make things better regardless of the cause of our suffering. Forgiveness makes it possible to let go of guilt completely and put our full energy into correcting old mistakes. Our options are open: We can reenact the conflict situation differently, in our minds, or perhaps set the past right by making reparations. The questions, "How could I have acted differently?" and "How would I have liked to be?" can inform our current behavior, and counter old negative karma with new positive karma. In this way, we take the first steps toward healing the mistakes of the past.

Opening the Heart

A healthy human being has a warm heart, a balanced state of mind, and a friendly attitude. Emotions prevent many of us from realizing this natural state. Mental afflictions such as envy, fear, and ignorance are illnesses that veil the infinite qualities of pure awareness. Guilt functions in a similar way, obscuring awareness. But awareness is always present, and permanently accessible.

Love is a quality of openness, a matter of being rather than doing. To open our hearts to the love within, we may need to give ourselves a break from active doing. Much of our doing stems from *I*'s need to assert itself. When we are caught up in doing, we live in the world of *I*, which is characterized by polarity: Longing for one object and feeling aversion to another, we are easy prey for thoughts. Gripped by thought, trapped in shadows between self and other, we allow being little space for love.

Free from the influence of emotions, our being naturally reveals love and the connection with all existence. We are alone, but not isolated, for love does not distinguish between yours and mine, friend and foe. "Love your enemy as yourself," said Jesus. We approach unconditional love, an all-encompassing feeling of kinship with all.

163

Sitting still in a quiet place can help us connect to the feelings of love within our hearts. Contact with stillness relieves the restlessness of mind and deepens the experience of being; we feel more at ease with ourselves and more willing to open. Rather than dwelling on feelings of loneliness or isolation, we can direct our attention inward and focus on what is in our hearts. Listening carefully within, not heeding expectations and judgments, we can bring awareness to the body, the heartbeat, and the movement of the breath. Just as eyes are made for seeing and ears for hearing, the heart is the center for feeling. In the heart we can contact feelings of vital energy that release blockages and bring serenity.

Until we have reconciled with the past, it is difficult to open the heart. Negative emotions such as bitterness and self-pity may shield the heart, and block us from feelings of love. They keep us at the periphery of our being, where we can activate only a smidgen of our potential. Yet we can invite the heart center to relax by cultivating positive attitudes and feelings, not as a cover-up for negativity but as a practice that stimulates the deep flow of feeling throughout the body. Since the heart thrives on beauty and the feelings and sensations of our own energy, we can warm the heart with appreciation and nourish it with beauty, until it opens wide and reveals its capacities for love and joy. The more we live in our hearts, the more we can abide in joy and tranquility.

Exercise for cultivating love: Do this exercise when you are feeling balanced, not caught up in the heat of emotion. Sit quietly and close your eyes. Imagine all the people who play or have played a role in your life, one after another. Start with the people closest to you: parents, partner, children, and other family members. Then move on to other relatives, friends, and acquaintances, even people you know only from history books or through the media. Briefly picture each face in your mind's eye, then let it go and turn to the next. Continue without pausing at any thought or memory. Do not skip anyone; do not cling to or avoid anyone.

As your awareness expands to include more people, let the feeling of connectedness grow. A common thread of knowing may emerge, letting you sense the value of being. This is the beginning of unconditional love. This infinite feeling can work like a catalyst, unraveling tight emotionality and restoring the naturalness of being. The openness of love acts like a mirror, reflecting emotion back to you, and reminding you that "all beings are of one nature."[55]

Love is expressed in the sincere wish that others may be healthy and happy:

May all beings be happy
and obtain the causes of happiness.

Every human being desires happiness. Even under the most challenging of circumstances, when everything seems to be working against us, we can answer the question "Do you want to be happy?" in the affirmative. Pursuing happiness is part of our nature.

When we experience love, we are happy and wish the same for others. When we are unable to wish happiness for others, it can only mean that we ourselves are not happy. It is that simple. Feeling fulfilled, we overflow with warmth towards the entire universe. Love and happiness are interchangeable. If we long for love, then we must discover the causes of happiness and pursue them.

THE CAUSES OF HAPPINESS

In The Declaration of Independence of the United States of America, all citizens are said to be endowed with the inalienable right to the pursuit of happiness. If it were our job to discover the causes of happiness, where would we start? Perhaps we could begin by taking a look around us to see what circumstances are associated with happiness. We would see people focusing their desire for happiness on plans for a vacation, a new house, on hopes for a better relationship, or on having a baby. Others might believe that happiness will simply come along one day, that happiness is their birthright and will be bestowed upon them some day in the future.

But that is not enough. If our life depended on finding the causes of happiness, we would investigate further. Soon we might begin to suspect that happiness does not depend on material comforts, or on our degree of success or fame, or on the amount of money we possess. A perfect body does not provide the causes of happiness, for beautiful people suffer just like everyone else. Our research would further show that poor and even sick people can be cheerful and content. Terminal patients may experience great intimacy with themselves and others; they may recognize the purpose of life for the first time, resulting in greater happiness than they have ever known. In the end, we might conclude that happiness is a state of mind that is independent of circumstances. Even bliss is accessible to all. It may come in meditation, just before death, when coming out of a depression, when a second chance in life presents itself, or when the heart opens to unification with the greater. To recognize that the conditions for happiness lie in our own hands is a major step.

Love and happiness depend on taking the right perspective. When we recognize the unique value of others, and a healthy, integrated energy flows throughout body and mind, we are happy. Happy people are sociable, flexible, creative, and more capable of enduring discomfort.[56] They forgive easily, maintain optimistic outlooks, and are kind to all and everything.

If we do not feel happy or loving, it is helpful to remind ourselves that no matter what our customary states of mind, our consciousness can be trained and developed. The brain, for example, is flexible. Brain cells can grow and make new connections. Our feelings, senses, and other kinds of intelligence can also be trained and developed. We can learn to observe more carefully and ask questions. We can sharpen our attention, experience and deepen our feelings, and open our senses. This kind of expansion and growth is natural to our consciousness.

As the mind expands and the senses open, love comes to the foreground.

Buddhist teachings show us how to create a stable base of happiness and contentment. Resolving to be happy and to discover the causes of happiness is the essential first step. It is enough to say, "I want to learn how to be happy and to know what steps to take." As soon as we do this, our lives begin to change.

Step two is to establish a discipline—not a code of behavior, but a way of living that fosters happiness and avoids what hinders it. Such discipline holds us to our goals, and helps us to uproot negative habits. Negative thoughts cannot be transformed simply by a positive affirmation or a good experience. We need to protect ourselves against our own undermining patterns and take responsibility for who we really are. The right discipline creates happiness, even if it may at times involve going against our desire for pleasure and doing something we do not want to do. Pleasure can contribute to our sense of well-being, but unlike true happiness, it is fleeting. A successful discipline must include both body and mind. They are our inner resources, and their functioning determines our happiness. In setting up our discipline, we can rely on our love for the things we value. We can set our own targets and standards and learn which attitudes and actions undermine happiness and which promote it.

The third step is to measure every choice we face by asking ourselves, "Does this contribute to happiness?" Finding happiness requires intelligent effort. Whatever we pay attention to will become real for us; what we ignore will fade away. A suggestion by Longchenpa, the great Nyingma master, can be a guiding principle, "Have few desires and be content with what you have."[57]

There are many doors to the Dharma, and more than one key that opens the door to love and happiness. By dedicating our energy to the discovery of happiness, we will find our own way, knowing that the secrets lie within consciousness.

May all sentient beings be free from hatred.
May all sentient beings be free from sorrow.
May all sentient beings be free from fear.
May all sentient beings be happy
and acquire the causes of happiness.

11

Compassion at Work

My parents and I were taking a day-trip to the Veluwe, a nature park in the center of the Netherlands, with picturesque pine forests and extensive fields of heather. We were looking forward to the fresh air and the chance for my mother to get some exercise in a natural setting. The stillness of nature usually did her good. As we climbed out of the car and walked toward the restaurant, there was a scent of fall in the air. It was a crisp day and leaves blanketed the ground. My father had already plotted a short path through the woods, but first we went inside for a cup of coffee.

There were no free tables next to a window, so we passed through the dining area into a crowded reading room and on into a smoky lounge. We found seats among other guests, who were reading newspapers. A waitress brought coffee. My father and I carefully blew on the steaming liquid, while my mother gulped hers down immediately. She sat looking around and, although her posture was relaxed, her expression was slightly drawn. She seemed puzzled about what she was doing there.

Abruptly my father pushed his chair back and rose, indicating it was time for a stroll. I asked my mother if she wanted to go to the ladies room first. She laughed and said, "What would you know about that?" Nevertheless she followed me to the door that said "Ladies" and went inside. A few seconds later she came out again and looked questioningly at me. "What next?" Her skirt was hiked up; her panties reached halfway to her knees. Unaware of the awkward situation and free of shame, she waited for further instructions. Meanwhile my father had joined us. Softly muttering reassurances, he pushed her back into the bathroom and closed the door behind him.

Excluded

It had become obvious that her memory was doing more than playing tricks on her, for she was increasingly bewildered by what was going on around her. In the beginning her lack of comprehension sometimes had a refreshing quality; she seemed so innocent and everything she said was so spontaneous and unexpected that it was endearing. At first we joked about it, as if this childlike naiveté suited her. Sometimes she said, "Heavens! I'm becoming so forgetful. Is it getting worse?"

Initially, after an embarrassing incident she would take charge, often with a joke. She might roll her eyes the way our family always did when one of us asked a silly question—instead of answering, we would look at each other cross-eyed and burst out laughing. When she did this everything would seem normal again, at least for the moment. But gradually, she found it harder and harder to scramble back onto the road of normalcy. Sometimes

171

the gaps in her awareness were so vast it seemed as if her mind had collapsed, like a huge circus tent. When this happened, she was overwhelmed by waves of panic. After she became calm again she would say, "I am so scared. I feel so useless."

After a while, every event became a test; she lived in increasing uncertainty. As her situation declined over several years, we spoke less with her and more about her. Still, it did not fully dawn on us how frightening it must have been for her to confront a failing memory, the judgments of others, and, on top of everything else, fear of the future. In the end our attention was entirely focused on her physical care. Without hesitating, my father took on this responsibility, twenty-four hours a day. He was almost eighty, and being her caregiver demanded all his strength. He did the household chores, cooked the meals, and did the laundry while closely watching my mother all day long.

It seemed wise not to be overprotective, and to let her take care of herself for as long as was possible. My father laid out her clothes each day, but for a long time she continued to dress herself. We encouraged her to keep up with her hobbies, not really wondering whether this would feel like pressure to her. She had always worked on embroidery, making the most intricate patterns for tablecloths and napkins, tea cozies, or elaborate pieces for birthdays and weddings. But now her embroidery patterns became increasingly simple. She was no longer able to concentrate, and had difficulty maintaining coordination between head and hands.

Still, she had her crystal clear moments, up until the very last day. She would suddenly ask a razorsharp question or articulate something we all felt but would never have said, like, "I'm not good for anything any more." She never asked for help or pity; she hated having become a burden to us. But no one thought of addressing her feelings of insecurity and fear. We simply agreed, "She doesn't know what's going on." "She doesn't remember anything." Little by little, with our help, she was removed from the stream of daily life, in spite of the fact that isolation and mental inactivity would aggravate her condition further. Like many Alzheimer's patients, she eventually reached a point at which, in the eyes of the world, she simply ceased to count.

Loss of I

In the face of her bewildering mental and physical deterioration, my mother experienced a loss of both self-respect and decorum. As the years went by, she completely lost the personality that had allowed her to lead her life with confidence; she seemed to lose herself—her *I*. From her family's perspective, and perhaps from her own, this loss was as tragic as death, or even more so. My mother's name was Cecile, but to her parents, husband, family, and friends she was "Pop," which means, "Doll;" her sons and daughters-in-law called her Mommy. We never stopped calling her by name, although the illness made her unrecognizable as a wife, mother, grandmother, neighbor, friend, and colleague. But we stopped treating her as the

173

Pop and Mommy she had always been, and did not manage to form a new bond with the person she was now.

Still, the disintegration of *I* need not have been a tragedy. Although Alzheimer's devoured the woman we knew and with whom we felt at ease, it did not affect her humanity, her being. It need not have prevented us from having feelings of love and compassion. *I* is actually the least interesting part of a human being: the least essential and the most transient. Outwardly, *I* presents itself as a coherent personality with countless characteristics, capabilities, a sense of humor, and other defining traits. When doing stops and knowing fails, being remains. As long as there is being, we can make contact. The contact from being to being connects us all and is ever-present, always available. This bond among all sentient beings is the basis for compassion. My mother's being, even when mental direction evaporated, was still capable of seeing, hearing, and—especially—*sensing*.

My mother's illness did not bring our family closer. In fact, we grew further apart. During the years of her illness, we rarely saw each other, which made it easy to avoid the painful topic of her condition. We were hardly aware of our feelings of uneasiness—we were too busy with our own lives. In the old days we were reputed to be a model family with close ties. Now it became evident that it had been my mother who had kept communication alive all those years. Like a central source of energy, she had provided the warmth and engagement that kept the channels of communication among all of us open. She was the source of our knowledge about each other's lives. Without her inspiration and caring, family intimacy withered away.

At the time we gave little thought to how the loss of family intimacy must have affected my mother. Her being was left to drift on a dark and lonely sea, without the familiar beacons to comfort her. I myself felt the loss of her loving actions as a pain so deep it could not be acknowledged. As an adult, I might have expected the reversal of roles that often occurs between parent and child as the parent ages. But because of the geographical distance between us, this did not happen in our case. When she became incapable of expressing affection, my love for her and for my family no longer had an outlet. Eventually I became silent, focused increasingly on my own life.

If I had opened my eyes and faced my fears, I might have been able to develop feelings of compassion. Yet it is never too late to awaken the deeper connection that stems from compassion for ourselves and others. The realization that we have been self-centered and oblivious to a loved one's pain can awaken feelings of compassion for ourselves. This helps us to let go of our narrow selfish focus and remember our connection with other beings and with all manifestations in the universe. Compassion for others then arises naturally. Through compassion, we experience our connection to the whole human family.

Self-Knowledge

Accepting ourselves as we are provides a healthy basis for love, wisdom, and compassion. The less we value our façade—our self-image—the wiser and more compassionate we become. We all have our own private worlds that we rarely share with anyone else. In these hideouts we entertain lofty thoughts and indulge our frustrations and resistance. Nobody suspects our deep wishes or depressed moods; no one sees us as we are, or so we believe. In order to grow as human beings, we must dismantle these secret fortresses. In order to develop basic human qualities such as reliability and truthfulness, we must overcome the obstacle of self-deception and stop thinking we are different than we really are. Self-knowledge allows us to acknowledge that our minds are often poisoned by negative thoughts and beliefs that foster unhealthy attitudes and actions. Self-knowledge is the beginning of wisdom.

Self-knowledge supported by compassion for ourselves sets a healing process in motion. Confronting the emotions that rule us, we say to ourselves, "Yes, this is how I was, but from now on I can be different." Like an experienced psychologist, we observe ourselves in awkward situations and ask intelligent questions, without judgment, and with a compassionate heart. Slowly the invisible cracks in our defenses grow wider. In time, compassion for our own small-mindedness warms our hearts, melting inner resistance.

Self-knowledge does not allow us to turn away from a larger sense of responsibility with alibis such as, "That's how I am," or, "I'm only human." On the contrary, the more we see through our own stories, the more our sense of responsibility grows. Our self-knowledge helps us act more effectively in our own lives and contribute more to others as well. We become strong and independent, and gain confidence in our ability to help others. Looking in the mirror we recognize others as well as ourselves, for we are all made of the same stuff. Nothing human is foreign to us.

As we look closely at our efforts to help others, we may observe that at times our care is far from genuine. Helpfulness may provide a cover for negative attitudes like arrogance and contempt. It is easy to mislead others and even deceive ourselves through actions that appear altruistic, but are in truth self-serving: "Look at me, the Good Samaritan!" Expressions of gratitude from others may just spark feelings of self-importance in us.

This is not to say that we should wait to perform helpful actions until we are saints. Instead, we can acknowledge that whatever we do or refrain from doing impacts a situation; every little bit of effort counts. Responsibility is our response to being alive. By taking responsibility for our actions, we become sensitive to the situation we find ourselves in. This will deepen our experience of compassion.

We can begin practicing with small steps at first. If we are caregiver of another who is the recipient of our care—we can use this inequality as a starting point for the practice of compassion. Even if we do not really feel another's suffering deeply, or our own, we can still offer help and analyze our motives later. We can observe the sense of satisfaction we feel when we help others, and ask ourselves how it must feel to be the one who is suffering. When giving money to a homeless person, for example, we can consider for a moment how it would feel to hold out our own hand and receive a few coins. Using our imagination, we deepen our understanding of the value of true help or kindness.

CAUSES OF SUFFERING

Compassion dispels suffering. An understanding gesture, a comforting word, a financial contribution, and a helping hand—all relieve the burden of suffering, at least momentarily. Giving some extra time, showing interest, or simply allowing another person space can make things better. But that is not yet compassion. Compassion is the ability to feel a person or a situation, and then act with wisdom. Compassion assimilates the pain, recognizes the causes of suffering, and aims to alleviate it. Compassion is a path of action.

The Buddha's teaching on the second Noble Truth makes clear that the root cause of suffering is not-knowing. When duality rules the mind, it inevitably generates the causes of suffering. As we see others as separate from ourselves, grasping, desire, and hatred come into existence.

Suffering is exacerbated by our reluctance to acknowledge the implications of impermanence. Blind to the truth that everything is in continuous flux, we do our best to ignore change. This blindness provokes an ongoing restlessness that in turn fuels anxiety. Responding to our own emotionality, we attach ourselves more firmly to shifting and unstable objects. Thus the cycles of suffering continue.

It is sometimes said that Buddhism states that desire is the cause of suffering. It is true that desire is one of the three root poisons, emotions that corrupt all human endeavors. But the Buddhist teachings also recognize that desire, if understood in the sense of yearning or aspiration, can be a positive force in our lives. Desire can motivate us to contribute something useful or beneficial. We may wish for calmness and clarity, for example, or for improvement and beauty, or happiness and the absence of suffering, or especially for enlightenment. If we set our minds on something that is subject to change and contains the kernel of suffering, however, this desire creates negative karma and cannot bring happiness.

Suffering is not caused by desire per se, but by the way the grasping mind functions. When a desire comes to mind, we identify with its object so completely that we fail to observe the dynamic of desire at work. Naively expecting that our grasping will end once our wishes have been fulfilled, we ignore the fact that grasping becomes stronger each time our awareness is wedded to an object of desire.

By steadily observing the mind in operation, we can eventually predict how the process of attachment will occur. We can see how labeling one particular aspect of an experience as desirable leads us to exclude from awareness the rest of what we know and feel. Just as our speech fixes what we think and feel, labeling freezes both feeling and experience, creating knots of suffering.

How can we return experience to its original openness? The traditional advice is to neither accept nor reject, neither hold on nor push away. In the most literal sense of the expression we might say, "Never mind."

Initially we remove the cause of suffering by not paying attention to the contents of the thoughts that whisper in our ears. We discover that it is possible to simply let thoughts come and go as they will. Gradually we learn to find security in space, in the stillness behind the stream of thoughts. The traditional advice of a lama is, "Let go, relax." When pressed by the student's question, "But how can I learn to do this?" the lama maintains, "Just calm the mind; don't be so serious!"

LOVE IN ACTION

May all beings be free from suffering
and the causes of suffering.

A monk was sitting on his meditation pillow, a cloth over his head, crying uncontrollably. When asked about the reason for his sorrow, his teacher spoke for him. "He has only just begun practicing the Dharma. Now that the truth is dawning upon him, the suffering of all beings is overwhelming him."[57]

The Sanskrit word *karuna* is often translated as compassion. The literal meaning of compassion—"feeling with"—can only hint at the full meaning of *karuna*. True compassion is the gateway between ordinary small-mindedness and enlightened awareness. Such compassion begins with the ability to sense another's situation, pain, and lost opportunities, without distinguishing between self and other. The pain can seem unbearable as we realize its needlessness. Still, knowing that suffering does not have a ground helps us to embrace it with love and thus bring ease to the sufferer.

Love and compassion are fused in an indissoluble bond. With love, one wishes all sentient beings to be happy; with compassion, one longs for the end to all suffering. Love enacts the power of positivity, while compassion counteracts negativity. Love is being, compassion is doing. Compassion is love in action.[58]

WISHING TO HELP

Under certain conditions, love and compassion can manifest as emotions that reveal the entanglements of self-interest. Thwarted love can show up as grasping and hatred and can cause harm to all involved. Yearning to express our love, we cling to our beloved, fully prepared to wish unhappiness on her or him if we do not get love in return. Similarly, distortions of compassion manifest as cruelty and despair.

Cruelty is compassion reversed: We crave to see another suffer and would even be willing to add to his or her pain. Despair is compassion thwarted. It originates with being overwhelmed by suffering. What can we possibly do? Paralyzed and powerless, we are caught in a trap with no way out, ready to give up. But if we fall into despair when our loved ones are suffering, our emotion will only burden them further.

181

What they need most is the medicine of compassion. If we cry on their shoulders because their illness overwhelms us, we are incapable of helping them. And compassion begins with a desire to be of help. Letting go of the wish that things were different and the hope that the situation will improve on its own, we surrender to the facts, embracing them as a starting point. Complete acceptance without judgment or expectation brings peace. From within this relaxed, calm state of being, feelings of love awaken, which in turn make a bridge to compassion.

When we silently murmur, "I wish I could help, I really wish I could help," and ask aloud, "How can I help?" the answer is likely to come from an unexpected direction, from within stillness. Sensing another's trouble, we may be given knowledge of the cause of the suffering as well as a remedy, for compassion joins empathy to knowledge of right action. We feel the desire to care for another as if he or she were our own parent or child. This wish connects our hearts to all living beings, and opens the door to the path of compassion walked by the Enlightened Ones of the past, present, and future.

LIKE A MOTHER WITH HER CHILD

To a person raised in a traditional Buddhist culture, our modern habit of tracing our problems to our parents seems mystifying. After all, our parents gave us life, and we owe them nothing less than gratitude. In the Buddhist teachings, a mother's love for her child, a love that begins when the baby is still in the womb, is taken as a model for the development of compassion.

Exercise: In this compassion practice, adapted from traditional teachings,[59] you imagine living in someone else's skin. Begin with your mother, your father, or the person who raised you. Picture her childhood, her life with her parents, and her relationship with her siblings. Next, visit her school, play with her friends, and envision her circumstances. What was it like to live her life? How was it for her to be alone? How was it to look like her? The precise biographical facts do not matter. What counts is the experience of being her. One day she meets your father: What was that like? They marry and have children. How was it for her to give birth to you? See yourself grow up through her eyes.

Repeat this exercise a second time. Experience your mother's life as an adult; imagine her relationship with the rest of her family and with you. As she becomes older, what does it feel like if her mind deteriorates? How is it if the family remains at a distance? What is it like for her to live in a nursing home or hospital? Can you see with her eyes and feel what she might feel?

You can deepen the practice of compassion by imagining how all human beings may once have been your mother, father or child, or will be in the future. In this way, compassion arises for all living beings. Let yourself reflect on the love of a mother for her child. Imagine how, during pregnancy, the mother endures many discomforts for the unborn child's sake. Delivery can be painful, sometimes traumatic or fatal. Immediately after birth, she begins caring for the baby's health. Not worrying about her own fatigue, she constantly keeps an eye on the child, responding to its every need. She gives it love, food, and clean clothes; when the baby is asleep, she checks that the child is still breathing. She changes countless dirty diapers, and, as the baby grows, with endless patience teaches the child to use the toilet and bathe itself. How can one even begin to describe the compassion and love expressed in the many years of tender, loving care that follow? Imagining yourself to be the parents of all sentient beings, you develop a sense of the meaning of unconditional love.

In the Presence of Being

Visiting anyone who is ill or dying, and especially a loved one, gives us an opportunity to deepen our experience of love and compassion. At first we may feel at a loss about what to do in such a situation. Yet when we accept our not-knowing, we stand on the threshold of a greater love. What do we have to offer? There may well be nothing we can do that will restore her to health. In letting go of the need to impose ourselves on the situation, we discover a deep inner calm. Space and stillness bring the essence of the situation to light. We move from thinking to being, from restlessness to silence and openness. We come into contact with her being and begin to experience her.

A natural empathy arises and sets the right tone. We may hold her hand, or we may not. One time we may ask how she is, and another time say nothing. Some days she may want to express everything that is on her mind; at other times she may prefer silence.

The wish to help can be present like an ongoing mantra. The more intense our wish, the more easily the appropriate words and gestures come. It is best not to offer advice. Every person has her own way of being ill and dying. Before we act or speak, it is best to listen, feel, see, and simply pay attention. Can we see her without judgment? Can we hear the meaning behind her words? What *I* can do is unimportant; what matters is what is appropriate in the situation. If we do not find the right approach immediately, we can sense this and make an adjustment. It may be best to simply share the comfort of silence.

FOR THE BENEFIT OF ALL

The capacity for compassion is inherent in every human being, but it lies beyond the domain of *I.* In the same way as egocentrism is a feature of the small mind, compassion is characteristic of the great mind. When we practice compassion, the boundary between self and others begins to dissolve, and the grip of *I* relaxes. We feel clear and at ease. Practice of compassion softens the walls of *I's* fortress, opens the heart, and prepares the mind to awaken.

To develop and strengthen compassion in our daily lives, we can cultivate the wish, "May all sentient beings benefit from my actions, now and in the long term."

We repeat this wish silently as we go about our day, even during the most ordinary activities. While washing the dishes we can request, "May all sentient beings become pure." During meals we can pray, "May all sentient beings still their hunger and thirst." While working we can wish, "May all sentient beings earn their livelihood honorably." In traffic we can think, "May all beings safely reach their destination." In this way, bit by bit, our daily life becomes permeated with empathy and compassion.

With practice we begin to employ compassion as a catalyst to unlock emotions. In times of adversity or when something is amiss in our relationships with others, it is likely that we are too focused on ourselves. Supported by our deepening experience of compassion, we can shift the focus away from ourselves and identify with others instead. For example, we can ask, "How is it for you? Are you able to cope?" A generous gesture naturally challenges our self-concern and opens our awareness to the larger reality within which our emotional reaction is only a part. With empathy we see others and ourselves in a new light.

When someone we love is struck down with an illness, we are given the opportunity to taste the depths of compassion. Individuals afflicted with Alzheimer's disease may have a special need for compassion, for as consciousness ceases to function, they lose not only their life as they have known it, but possibly also the chance to consciously transform the self, or to attain enlightenment in this lifetime.

My mother experienced the gradual loss of who she was, what she had accomplished in her life, and what she was capable of doing. It seemed she had little choice but to wait helplessly and see what else life had in store for her. "What do I have left?" she would ask in a choked voice. She was no longer able to take care of herself, let alone care for others. She could not express her love and warmth. She was not accustomed to making demands, and I, her youngest son, who had been so close to her, was far away and did not often ask myself what her dearest wishes might be. What was she feeling? Where was she? It seemed she was already in a different world, far removed from us. It was as if she was in a little rowboat without oars, being carried by the wind out to the open sea. We were left on shore, helpless. It would not be long before she drifted completely out of sight.

12

Harmony and Balance

During Dutch winters dusk falls around six o'clock. Children playing outside are called in for dinner, while a few people scurry home through the wintry streets. In the windows, lights gleam, but by eleven o'clock they go out one by one, until the empty streets are lined with black blocks of buildings. The city sleeps in silence.

On the sixth floor of one of the dark apartment buildings, a light is suddenly turned on. A woman squints her eyes against the glare, looking confused.

"I wish you would warn me for once," a man says reproachfully, walking around the bed to the other side of it. He bends over her and turns the blankets back. "Come on, let's get up."

"I can't," she moans.

She tries to turn onto her side, but to no avail. He reaches out, takes hold of both her hands and with great effort pulls her to a sitting position, revealing a dark patch on the sheets.

"Now look what you've done," he says.

These are exactly the same words she always used with the cat, while rubbing her nose in the pee so that she would never foul the couch again.

"Everything is wet; please, now you go sit over there." He deftly begins to remove all the sheets, and covers the mattress with a clean plastic pad. She looks on, puzzled.

"Since when do you make the bed? What am I doing here in this chair?" She trembles like a leaf, watching him straightening the sheets. A little while later they are both lying in bed once more, and he turns off the light on the bedtable.

About an hour later, he wakes with a start. The room is pitch black. He hears her call out, "Charles!" Reaching out for the pillow next to him, he finds it empty. Somewhere a choked voice is sobbing, "Help, please help me."

She is lying on her back on the rug, stuck between the wall and the bed. In shock, he rushes to her and starts tugging on her body. But she is too heavy, and does not budge at all.

"Please, don't fall asleep now. Cooperate a little, will you? Please, Pop." As he bends over to take her hands, she starts to laugh.

"Remember how I pushed the car uphill in the snow, with you in it? That was silly too," she says.

So it went, day and night, seven days a week, month after month. How many families, especially those caring for elderly parents or relatives, must face and deal with this kind of suffering? At first, a small "accident" occurred now and then; eventually it happened up to three times a night. My father would wake up and deal with the situation as best he could. Stubbornly he fought a war of attrition against helplessness and exhaustion. The nights seemed endless.

Neither day nor night brought any refuge for my mother and my father. She needed constant supervision to keep her out of harm's way. This, in addition to the need to clean up after her incontinence, kept my father on alert, always braced for another emergency. This situation was arduous and overtaxing. The main burden of care rested on his shoulders; a network of help and caregivers was not in place, except for help with washing her every morning. The strain of constant demands combined with lack of sleep sometimes made him impatient and short-tempered. It was not easy to feel empathy for the person who consistently robbed him of a well-earned night's rest.

Mother's physical care gradually took precedence over everything else. Below the surface, however, a tragedy was taking place: In our concern for her physical needs, we were losing touch with her essential humanity. We were losing contact with her—and with ourselves. Eventually our entire family, even the sons not directly involved in caring for my mother, succumbed to a kind of exhaustion. At the time we did not realize that this burnout could be remedied. The Tibetan Buddhist teachings on the four immeasurable qualities of love, compassion, joy, and equanimity would have helped to bring us all into greater harmony and balance.

The Destructive Course of Alzheimer's

In 1987, the year my parents returned from Elba to Holland, scientists discovered one of the culprits of

Alzheimer's disease in a particle (A-Beta) of a larger molecule (APP). Until that time, general interest in the disease had been marginal, especially since the diagnosis could not be determined until after death, through autopsy of the brain. Even today the direct cause of Alzheimer's disease is still unknown. Scientists agree that the symptoms are at least partially attributable to clusters of protein that settle among brain cells. While healthy people naturally generate a substance that breaks down this protein, in Alzheimer's patients this process is hampered, and an anomalous residue, the smaller protein *amyloid beta* (A-Beta), accumulates in the brain tissue and devours the cells.

When this toxic protein deposit suffocates a healthy brain cell, a chain reaction is set in motion that cumulatively produces what we call Alzheimer's disease.[60] Like a thief in the night, Alzheimer's steals the life force of healthy brain circuits, replacing them with an agglomeration of plaques and tangles (masses of dead neurons). Memory cells as well as other cells are impaired, producing the startling changes in behavior and personality that characterize the illness. The damage is irreversible; medications currently being used or developed can at best slow the process of decline for a few years.

In the United States, more than six percent of people over sixty-five succumb to some form of dementia, of which there are at least sixty types. Among those with dementia, seventy percent are thought to suffer from Alzheimer's disease. Dementia, however, occurs only in the later stages of Alzheimer's; the disease is often active for many years before any symptoms manifest. Onset may occur as early as age twenty or thirty.

Diagnosis

Since the 1990s, brain scans (MRI and PET) have been able to indicate a predisposition to Alzheimer's, or reveal that the degenerative process is already underway. Precise beginnings are difficult to pinpoint, since the disease may pursue its deadly course for years without any external symptoms.

The first symptom is usually a faltering memory. Older recollections may remain vivid, while events of yesterday or even a few moments ago vanish in a gradually thickening fog. A physician is often consulted once family members become concerned about this increasing forgetfulness. In the past, diagnosis was made by exclusion of other ailments; nowadays more direct approaches are employed. The patient must answer questions about mundane topics, such as date of birth or address. A memory test, blood test, and brain scan are made. Soon it becomes clear if concern is warranted. A doctor can confirm, "It is likely that your mother has Alzheimer's disease."

Once the verdict has been rendered, the doctor will sometimes prescribe medicines to slow the progress of the disease. Apart from following some simple guidelines for keeping the mind active as long as possible, there is little else that can be done. Physical exercise, preferably outdoors, is recommended, as it promotes the growth factor that is critical to the production and preservation of brain neurons. Listening to stories read aloud is beneficial, as are playing games and pursuing hobbies. Browsing through old photo albums and reminiscing may activate infrequently used brain cells and stimulate healthy parts of the mind. Reliving even the most ordinary memories and engaging in the simplest activities can serve as gymnastics for the brain. In advanced stages of Alzheimer's, when short-term memory loss has been extensive, it is best to avoid talking about recent events.

These days, scientists recognize three kinds of memory: short term, long term, and procedural. Alzheimer's first obliterates short-term memory, followed by long-term memory. Procedural memory remains intact the longest, as it concerns motor function; we remember by *doing*. We do not learn to ride a bicycle by reading a book or watching a video; the movements are ingrained in memory through repetition. In the beginning stages of Alzheimer's disease, the patient can continue to learn in this manner. Repetitive motions like dance steps or stirring a pot can refresh procedural memory and enrich one's quality of life.

Research is currently being conducted on the relationship between Alzheimer's and nutrition, as well as on the effects of education, lifestyle, and the environment on the disease. There is no doubt but that the brain is influenced by the foods we eat. A healthy diet, low in hydrogenated and saturated fats, sugar, and salt is wholesome for anyone, ill or not. Additionally, people with Alzheimer's are advised to take vitamins C, E, B11, and B12, found in whole-wheat products and specific vegetables like broccoli, spinach, Brussels sprouts, and string beans. Some natural supplements like ginkgo biloba may also be beneficial to a certain extent.

Finally, anti-inflammatory medications such as ibuprofen have proven somewhat effective in limiting the growth of free radicals that overload the immune system.[61] Research is being conducted with medicines intended for other conditions, like high cholesterol or vascular disease. For example, the cholesterol-reducing substance statin seems to decrease plaque formation. Still, its effect can only be limited, as Alzheimer's may have been active for decades before discovery.[62]

Brain Research

With the graying of the population, dementia in general and Alzheimer's disease in particular are becoming increasingly widespread. Keeping the mind sharp has become an urgent topic for millions of people.

Research has shown a connection between memory and imagination. The more active the imagination, the more accurately the impressions are recorded. The storage capacity of the mind is unlimited, but what we remember depends on the quality of the impressions. If the images in our minds are blurred, they will not be recorded. Memory benefits from a vivid and active mind. Mindfulness practice awakens the mind.

For those suffering from dementia and Alzheimer's disease, recent neurological research on the production of new brain cells is of particular interest. Neural stem cells, a specific type of brain cell responsible for generation of new cells, may eventually be harvested to replace damaged brain tissue. For now, however, this research is controversial, because the most suitable stem cells for research come from human embryos.[63]

> *Exercise*: Neurobics is a new word that suggests aerobics for the brain. As you go about your daily activities, begin to exercise your memory by consciously taking in new details. Notice how alive you feel when observing even the smallest detail. You can stimulate the senses by making changes in your home or at work; for example, by introducing new colors or fragrances. You can also try varying an ingrained routine, thus breaking old patterns. These memory and mindfulness exercises result in the production of new neurons, a "neural-buzz" that refreshes the mind.[64]

THE GOLDEN YEARS

Nowadays, the last stage of life is sometimes called the "golden years." To older people who are finally relieved of their responsibilities, the promise of freedom might seem alluring, offering chances for new life chapters filled with exciting and rewarding activities.

Reality, however, often turns out to be less appealing, and it is not unusual for older people to use the phrase ironically. Many people actually experience this time as a period of slow decline in health and ability. Bothersome

ailments appear and do not go away. It becomes difficult
to move about; performing even the smallest tasks can be
tiresome and painful. Appetite decreases, and sound sleep
appears to be a thing of the past. Favorite activities may
no longer be feasible, while new pastimes seem few. Our
once-so-alert brain betrays us, leaving us feeling disori-
ented and vulnerable. The world in which we used to feel
at home becomes increasingly grim and inhospitable.

People in their fifties or sixties often anticipate old
age as a dreadful fate. Many expect to feel excluded from
society as they age, since they no longer have the
energy to keep up with younger generations. Their
talents and abilities become outmoded, and they are not
surprised to find themselves living in increasing isolation,
subject to depression and loneliness. There may seem
to be no recourse but to wait quietly and hope death will
come during sleep.

It is true that, as we age, energy diminishes and the
senses operate more sluggishly. But does this imply that
the functioning of the mind must lose its vitality as well?
Some elderly people still appear young at heart, and are
mentally keen and active. "Use it or lose it" is the popu-
lar saying. If we use our mental capacities well and enjoy
good fortune, we may be spared the loss of mental powers
in our old age.

According to Buddhist teachings, the mind has no age,
form, color, beginning, or end. Although the philosophical issues here are complex, a simple way to think of it is
that there is really no personal mind, neither "my" mind
nor "your" mind, but rather an intrinsic intelligence or

awareness in which we all participate. This vast awareness was here before we were born and will remain after our deaths. Now, in this time between birth and death, we have access to this boundless and timeless awareness and may take part in it. For a person who has reached the advanced stages of a disease like Alzheimer's, this advice is of course useless; there is nothing to be done, since there is no known remedy for reversing the brain damage. At some point the person can no longer add two plus two, and later on does not know what addition is. Eventually, even the number two fades from consciousness. Like a drawing made with a stick on water, knowledge vanishes without leaving a trace.

Once my mother had lost her qualities, talents, social network, and rich inner life, all she had left to hold on to was the familiarity of her surroundings. When this too was taken away from her, she had no frame of reference at all, no anchor except the presence of her husband. Whenever he was absent, she wandered about aimlessly, a poor soul lost in the wasteland of her mind.

For Better or For Worse

When a patient has a terminal disease and nursing back to health is not a realistic aim, caregivers tend to focus on the patient's mental and emotional well-being. It is a well-known fact that on the threshold of death, essential healing of mind and spirit can still take place, and everyone half hopes and half expects to have this good fortune.

Around a deathbed, long-standing issues can be resolved; old wounds can be allowed to mend and shattered relationships can miraculously be put back together. The patient recognizes that time is precious, and former patterns are losing their grip. Loved ones have a precious opportunity to come to terms with their impending loss and set the past straight.

For the Alzheimer's patient, such healing, which arises from awareness and insight, may be impossible. Becoming aware together and sharing on an intimate level is out of the question. With this illness, the emphasis remains on physical care, which for the caregivers can easily become draining and exhausting. Until recently, family members had to manage almost entirely alone, consulting only with a physician. Nowadays there are many resources available, including social support as well as different forms of assistance such as home and day care. Even so, the nonprofessionals—volunteer aides, family members and friends—are often the mainstays of care. If there is a partner, however, the lion's share of the burden is likely to rest on him or her.

"Marriage is for better or for worse," my father used to say. Without ever uttering a complaint, he went about doing what he considered to be his duty. "How useless I am," my mother said when she saw him working. To him it was self-evident that caring for his wife was his job.

Is love able to withstand a hopeless sense of duty? Without the power of love, are compassion and joy still possible? My father performed his tasks devotedly, yet the admiration and gratitude toward the woman to whom he had once said, "You are the light in my eyes," were fading away. "I have said farewell to my wife as I have known her," he said with resignation.

Responsibility

Duty is not the same as responsibility. Duty reflects a sense of obligation; we are committed to do something because we feel we owe it to the situation. Responsibility is our natural *response* to being alive, expressed in an active caring toward everything around us. We respond to whatever needs to be done with our full energy and awareness. A commitment out of true responsibility knows no hesitation—knowing and doing blend harmoniously. Taking responsibility is the essence of being human.

Relying on intuition and a sense of duty may help us deal with whatever we have to do, but it is not enough to support our spirit and sustain our best efforts as a caregiver, especially when we know there is no prospect for the patient to recover.

Full responsibility involves knowledge as well as willingness and enthusiasm—in this case, knowledge of the disease, knowledge of the patient and his or her circumstances, and knowledge of oneself, as partner or caregiver. Familiarity with Alzheimer's disease, for example, makes us aware that our loved one is sinking into a quagmire. Knowledge of our loved one focuses our attention on his or her needs and helps us sense what kinds of support will be most beneficial. Self-knowledge helps us to recognize that we cannot handle this all-consuming task on our own. Caregivers, no matter how self-sacrificing they are, also need care. By acknowledging their own limitations, they allow space for others to help and prevent both helpers and patient from being victimized.

Taking full responsibility for the situation precludes reactions such as impatience, resistance, and resentment from taking control. For if they do, the inevitable result is defeat, followed by the conclusion: "This cannot go on."

Caring for an Alzheimer's patient is an exhausting battle. Things grow worse all the time. Barely have we come to terms with one change for the worse when another blow falls. Bit by bit things fall apart. What used to be pleasant becomes unbearable; activities that once were taken for granted are now out of the question. Yesterday's smooth run becomes today's race full of obstacles. Deterioration continues at its inexorable pace; nobody can do anything about it. Thread by thread the fabric of the family unravels. Under these circumstances, can a caregiver maintain his or her sense of qualities such as equanimity, love, compassion, and joy?

Next to managing the chores adequately twenty-four hours a day, the caregiver's highest priority is to remain aware of him- or herself. Under ideal circumstances, a caregiver is capable of relaxing while working. Once he or she becomes exhausted, however, everything comes to a standstill, like a car with an empty tank. A good night's rest can offer temporary relief. A heart-to-heart talk with a trusted friend or with a professional, may provide respite. Self-pity does not help, but viewing the situation honestly can be refreshing.

The quality of our awareness determines how well we handle adversity. We can strengthen awareness by learning to develop an interest in whatever we are doing, and by paying attention.

Regardless of what we are doing, we can avoid falling into a routine that deadens our mental acumen. Optimal caregiving requires an attentive and interested mind. We can foster these qualities by asking ourselves neutral questions, free from hidden prejudices or emotions: "How can I do my work better?" "Is there something we still need?" "What would benefit her?" Neutral questions like "what," "why not," and "how else," awaken awareness.

Friends, neighbors, and others close to the caregivers and patient can offer help instead of waiting to be asked, keeping at a distance, or complaining and judging. They can make themselves available and offer their services, their time and energy. Feelings of compassion for the caregiver and patient can be strengthened by cultivating the wish to ease the burden. Then it is not difficult to ask, "How can I help?"

Joy

In a strong and open heart, the qualities of love, compassion, joy, and equanimity, known in Buddhism as the Four Immeasurables, are truly immeasurable; their expression has no limits.[65] These qualities, inherent in human nature, arise when our minds and hearts grow more open and spacious. As an enduring part of human potential, they can also be called upon and strengthened.

In the traditional practice of love and compassion we wish:

May all beings be happy and free from suffering.

For the practice of joy, this can be followed with:

And may all beings not be separated from joy.

Joy is inseparable from life's flow, just as rhythm is inseparable from music. All phenomena have their own pace, sometimes moderate (*moderato*) or slow (*largo*), sometimes sprightly and cheerful (*allegro*). When we tap into these natural rhythms, joy manifests in our beings.

If joy is really always available, what keeps us from experiencing joy? Absorbed in its own private concerns, *I* is averse to joining in the melody of life. Whether forcing the tempo or holding back, *I* is not attuned to the rhythm of the whole. True, ego is willing to play its part as long as it receives benefits, but our consciousness and energy tend to be geared toward resistance. Wanting things to be different is characteristic of *I*'s internal monologue: "If only—if only he—if only I had—" "Why me?" or "Why *not* me?" is its favorite tune.

In its interactions with others, *I* acts out a different repertoire—all too often variations on gossip, sarcasm, cynicism, and slander. Although these themes hinder our pursuit of happiness and spoil the joy of others, *I* does not care. There are times when *I* feels more at ease with the dissonant music of suffering than with the harmonies of joy. Unless it can take some credit, *I* resents others' successes; *I* is oblivious to the sound of joy, which finds pleasure in the success of others.

Joy brings a happy, almost elated feeling that inspires gratitude. When we are burdened with sadness and fatigue, even thinking about joy seems artificial and absurd. Yet even under the most challenging circumstances, it is possible to take some small step that reconnects us to the lilt of joy. A loving gesture, a token of appreciation, or a humorous exchange can offer welcome release and provide a sunnier outlook. Scientific research suggests that active appreciation and gratitude stimulate the highest brain functions.[66] Cheerfulness sharpens our intelligence, activating the sword of knowledge that can cut through emotionality, putting the ego out of commission and releasing vital energy. Happy people are not ruled by their emotions.[67]

Inner joy is related to time and the rhythms of time, like those we find in nature. When we are attuned to nature with its changing seasons and shifting light, our aliveness is rekindled. Our breathing becomes balanced and harmonious, for the rhythm of the breath connects consciousness with time. When we move in tune with the fluid rhythm of time, joy emerges naturally, even in times of crisis. The key is being mindful of the present moment. Being on time and tuning into what is timely is a good place to begin.

For lasting joy, it helps to build a conscious relationship with the breath. When we are mindful of the breath, the rhythm of breath becomes part of consciousness. We see the connection between breathing and time—how we take short, shallow breaths when trying to catch up with time, and heave long, deep sighs when time is passing us by. As we bring awareness to the present moment, breathing relaxes and becomes more soft and gentle. Before long a delicate, joyful feeling emerges, fluttering in the back of the throat. Energy flows and the senses open. Feelings of happiness and gratitude fill our being. We are tasting the nectar of joy.

Once we are accustomed to evoking joy, we can use its inner warmth as a catalyst for unlocking emotions such as jealousy and envy. Consciously provoking jealous thoughts, we allow them to mix with joy. Energy that was wasted in negativity and stuck in tension is thus transformed into charismatic activity, aiming for the success of all sentient beings.

Touched by joy, we do not sink into envy at another's success; on the contrary, we rejoice in their good fortune and share in it. We respond with good humor to the subtle ways in which *I* tries to limit our joy, for *I* no longer holds us in thrall. We perceive the sting of jealousy in our frustrated wish to be the source of another's happiness and can gently laugh at ourselves.

Now we are free to pursue our own happiness and appreciate others at the same time, enjoying their successes and pleasures as if they were our own. The result is wisdom: We see that everything is as it should be. Silently we wish, "May they be enlightened now and always, may they never be separated from pleasure and happiness."

EQUANIMITY

Equanimity completes the sequence of the four immeasurable qualities: love, compassion, joy, and equanimity. Equanimity arises when we keep friends and foes at an equal distance in our minds, without gravitating toward one or rejecting the other. In Buddhist practice, equanimity is cultivated by the wish:

May all sentient beings live in equanimity,
without attachment or aversion,
and believe in the equality of all living beings.

When we feel hard pressed, we retreat into the fortress of *I,* barring the door fast. This narrow functioning of our consciousness reveals itself in the distinctions we make between people. We are strongly attracted to some; others we reject and avoid. Yet today's friends may be our worst enemies tomorrow, and those we despise now may later share our interests: In making such distinctions, we are setting ourselves up for disappointment.

Exercise: Imagine yourself surrounded by all the people you have ever known, friends and enemies alike. Allow them to intermingle freely, without any concern for their relationship to you. Instead of turning toward your loved ones and pushing away those you dislike, maintain a neutral attitude toward everyone. Let friend and foe alike be held in mind in the same way, each person the equal of everyone else. This neutral perspective diminishes fear of losing friends, decreases envy, and illuminates the value of others. Partiality lessens, as we develop open-mindedness toward everyone. Both friends and enemies are revealed as individuals, independent of our projections. We become aligned with all the people in our lives.

The tranquil neutrality at the heart of equanimity offers an antidote to self-importance and arrogance, transforming them into wisdom. Once we see the person in front of us clearly, we no longer feel the need for superiority. We realize that all human beings are equal. Furthermore, we recognize that every phenomenon carries wisdom, even attitudes such as arrogance. Within the heart of arrogance lies the seed of equanimity.

The Four Immeasurable Qualities Interplay

When equanimity wanes, indolence takes its place. We say, "Who cares? Let someone else worry about it." Indolence quickly degenerates into apathy. When this happens, we can rely on love to revive consciousness. The immeasurable feeling of love reveals the uniqueness of everything and everybody. One way to evoke love is by listening intently to what others say, discerning not only what is said but also the meaning behind the words. We acknowledge what is important for the other person and what matters to us all.

Feelings of love, as conventionally understood, have a restrictive quality. Once we become attached to someone, we grow possessive. Yet true love is unconditional. Love does not entail the right to manipulate or terrorize. Loved ones cannot disappoint us; if we feel disappointed, it is because we have stopped listening to them, and are hearing instead the voice of our own self-concern.

When the expansiveness of love contracts through self-concern and attachment, compassion can restore the quality of openness. Once we recognize that we have become caught up in self-concern, we can invite the other person—and even all sentient beings—into our consciousness. We can imagine being in the other person's shoes, leading his life, going through his hopes and fears. Instead of asking, "What do I have to gain?" compassion wants to know, "How does it feel to be you?" "What can I do to relieve your suffering, ease your burden?" With compassion we recognize: I am just like you.

The extent of our compassion is expressed in our level of participation in the world. Do we play our part? Making a contribution need not involve complicated actions. Even simple acts such as leaving a space more beautiful than we found it, or respecting the traffic rules, or picking up a piece of litter express a sense of responsibility for the welfare of others. Of course, we make many more substantial contributions to society's welfare, through our family and our work.

No matter how much we contribute, however, there are times when we feel it will never be enough. The misery we encounter in the outside world can become so overwhelming that we are simply unable to face it. We wish we could hide under the covers and weep. It all seems hopeless. At such moments it is time to invoke the immeasurable quality of joy. Even when we are overwhelmed by feelings of hopelessness, there is always the option of doing something constructive. We can all make a difference; even the tiniest positive gesture generates a beneficial change. Taking action gets our energy going again. When our energy begins to flow, the doing awakens a pleasurable rhythm that evokes joy.

When joy degenerates into euphoria—the feeling that everything is just perfect!—a healthy dose of equanimity is required. When equanimity degenerates into indifference and lethargy, we can turn to love to renew awareness. When love contracts to a focus on self, we can awaken compassion, which in turn can be protected by joy. In this way we can continue the cycle. Whatever the situation, we need never feel stuck: Once we recognize the negative fixations of each of the four immeasurable qualities, we can rely upon the momentum of their cycle to restore harmony and balance.

When all four immeasurables are properly applied, negativity cannot take hold in the mind or put a damper on the heart. Like healing balm, the four immeasurables act as medicine for the diseases of hatred, anger, grief, insecurity, fear, and jealousy. Together, they reinforce balance, release the energy invested in emotions, and protect us from further emotionality. At a deeper level, they protect the innate enlightened mind.

When our minds and hearts are relaxed and in balance, all four qualities are naturally in play. But even in the most dire circumstances, the four immeasurables are always available to strengthen and balance us; all we need to do is call upon them. Fortified by their beneficent powers, we find the time and energy to do what is valuable. Under their umbrella, we are protected from darkness and despair, and can tap into the caring, enthusiasm, and willingness we need to do whatever needs to be done, as caregivers, or in any other role in life.

CIRCLE OF HARMONY

Thus a man who by having taken refuge has
become the site for spiritual growth
will cultivate his mind for the welfare
of those who are alive
by letting the flower of compassion
blossom in the soil of love
and tending it with the pure water of equanimity
in the cool shade of joyfulness.[68]

Each of the four immeasurable qualities offers abundant opportunities to strengthen the mind and open the heart. The traditional advice is to start with equanimity. Equanimity is traditionally developed through meditation practice, since calmness and clarity naturally lead to equanimity. The practice of sitting quietly in meditation on a regular basis is still somewhat unusual in our culture, and a meditation practice takes time to develop. Therefore, practice of the four immeasurables in the West may begin with any of the qualities. Since each of the four qualities leads naturally to the next, it does not really matter where we start.

At work, where energy is directed toward a common goal, and time and actions are of the essence, joy is a suitable starting point. Genuine sharing of energy and knowledge can be an everyday source of joy. Through wholehearted cooperation and smooth communication, people literally join forces. Whenever "joining" takes place and what was apart comes together, joy emerges. This becomes an ongoing weaving, a total integration. The ensuing interconnectedness creates a greater whole, in which everything flows smoothly. The vitality of joy has an almost tangible charge. Achieving results, together and on time, creates an extra spark—the joy of working well.[69]

A still deeper union can take place when time is incorporated into our consciousness.[70] When awareness and time become inseparable, we feel we have more time and sense we can do almost anything. Learning to master time, we begin to embody the energy of time and express our freedom in participation and creativity. The union of appreciation and appropriate action releases joy, which will become the fuel for all our accomplishments.

In relationships, love and compassion are qualities especially suitable for practice. A parent, for example, can make an effort to build a special connection with each child, something particular to this individual. Each child holds a unique promise; each has his or her own potential that needs to be cultivated, outside of their role as the eldest, youngest, or most difficult child. When parents connect deeply to the unique qualities of each child, relationships among the children also become more harmonious, because there is little cause for rivalry. Similarly, in our friendships, we can develop love by cultivating interest in our friends' activities and welfare. By being engaged with their lives and willing to put ourselves in their places, we communicate that we are all equal. We all want the same thing: a happy and harmonious life.

When love turns into duty, it is time for compassion. But when witnessing the pain of the loved one becomes too much, the refuge can be joy. We may ask, "How can I generate joy when my partner's situation worsens every day? And her mind is absent most of the time?" The answer lies within. We cannot rely on external circumstances to validate the circle of the four immeasurables or to keep it going.

Our external circumstances can only prompt us to invoke the immeasurable qualities that are part of our human nature. When we invoke these qualities, they act like internal transformers that convert the energies of our heads, hearts, and senses into love, compassion, joy and equanimity. Protected by these immeasurable qualities, we can find harmony and balance in any situation. The choice is ours.

To Ananda, his cousin and most faithful companion, the Buddha said, "Teach these four immeasurable qualities to the young ones. They will feel self-confident, strong, cheerful, and will have no afflictions of body or mind. They will be well equipped for their entire lives."[71]

PRAYER FOR ALL SENTIENT BEINGS
This traditional prayer is used to strengthen the four
immeasurables—love, compassion, joy, and equanimity:

May all human beings be happy
and find the causes of happiness.
May all human beings be free of suffering
and the causes of suffering.
May all human beings not be separated from joy
and may their minds be calm and clear.

13

Finding a Safe Haven

A few days after the doctor's visit, my father brought out a small beige suitcase. After placing it on the bed and opening it, he wordlessly began to pack: some underwear, a nightgown, and a pinafore that my mother used to wear at Elba. On top of these garments, he placed a few knick-knacks and finally a silver frame with a photograph of her as a young woman seated on a couch, surrounded by her four little boys, reading from *Babar*, a story about a baby elephant. He zipped up the suitcase, lifted it off the bed, and walked into the vestibule with her following at his heels. Then he turned and without looking at her, said only, "We have to go." While he helped her into her coat, my mother asked for the umpteenth time, "Where to?" My father locked the door behind them, pressed the elevator button and said, "This can't go on."

Outside, a cold wind was blowing. As always, she slipped her arm through his and he closed his hand over her fingers. In his other hand he carried the suitcase. They took a few shuffling paces before falling into step with one another, a custom acquired during fifty-five years together. The bare trees made silhouettes against the gray sky. In a few weeks, the first spring flowers would pop up from the soil, snowdrops followed by crocuses. In the garden of the house where they had lived together for twenty-nine years, a wild apple tree grew. When in bloom, it resembled a huge wedding bouquet. "I want to go home," she whispered.

Together, they walked to the nursing home, which was only a stone's throw from their apartment. They were walking away from the past, heading into an obscure future. Repeatedly my mother asked, "Where are we going?" "I have told you so many times. They will take good care of you there. I will visit you every day," he replied.

On the third floor a nurse welcomed them. She led the way down a seemingly endless corridor, past an empty auditorium and a row of closed doors. Finally, they entered a small room. Four beds separated by night tables lined one wall. The floor was linoleum and the walls were bare. "This one is your bed," said the nurse. Then she opened the closet, revealing a few metal coat hangers. The young woman arranged the clothes quickly and expertly. She placed the silver picture frame on the night table next to my mother's bed. My parents stood watching, side by side. "It's best this way," my father said at last, and kissed her on the forehead. "I'll be right back."

A Sense of Security

The bottom shelf of the bookcase in their living room contained the photo albums that recorded my parents' married life. Seventeen large albums bore witness to happier times:

the births of children and grandchildren, special occasions, shared trips to Indonesia, Surinam, and, of course, the United States, where three of their four sons lived. At the time all these events had seemed significant and substantial, like steps on a stairway leading higher and higher, toward a happy ending. Since their wedding day my parents had rarely been separated, and it had seemed self-evident that only death could dissolve their bond. Now their partnership, once meaningful and productive, had been ripped apart; a chasm had opened between them. The mentally impaired wife and her husband no longer lived under the same roof.

That day my father walked back from the nursing home alone, to an empty apartment. He called no one to talk about the revolution in his life; he did not look for a shoulder to cry on. He was like a prisoner of war who had survived unspeakable experiences that had frozen his heart. On paper, his life appeared to be in order, with an inflation-proof pension and savings in stocks and bonds. But for what purpose?

Three times each day, he carefully set the table for himself; in the evening, he always cooked the same simple dish. Every morning he dutifully made his way to the nursing home, where his wife waited with her hands in her lap without knowing what she waited for. And what about her? What was her life like? Impersonal nursing home rules and an always changing staff determined the rhythms of each day. Her physical care was in the hands of strangers. Her mind was disintegrating. And her spirit? Who cared for her soul?

When we were small, mother taught Bible lessons to us and other children in the neighborhood. She told parables about the twelve disciples of Jesus, and together we read from a children's Bible. One time, in order to demonstrate how to make an offering, she took the steak for that night's dinner from the refrigerator and helped us to perform a solemn ceremony on the small steps to the kitchen door. Believing in God, however, was not obligatory; each of us determined that for himself on his eighteenth birthday, as was customary in the Baptist circles in which she grew up. No one in our family went to church, except my mother, once or twice a year. While we ate breakfast on Sunday mornings, the church bells would ring, and she would look on wistfully as the neighbors hurried off to morning service. Some formal reflection on the meaning of life would certainly have suited my mother, but it was not a priority.

If awareness of a transcendent reality had been a part of my parents' frame of reference, that knowledge could have supported them during this time of farewell after more than fifty years of marriage. These two old people could have taken comfort in a shared sense of security, and perhaps their last journey together would have been less distressing. They would have understood the meaning of impermanence and could have surrendered to their plight. They might have recognized that everything they had lost during these last years was destined to vanish at some point in their lives.

Once Alzheimer's disease has consumed seemingly everything—the mind, past, present, and future—what is left? What is enduring, and not subject to change? When all else has fallen away, what remains that we can take refuge in?

Spirituality in Daily Life

Tibetan Buddhism does not separate the secular and religious life. Every gesture, thought, and expression is part of a magical show in which everything is important but nothing lasts forever. Only such elements as space and light endure, as well as perennial, timeless truths. Each human life is a precious occasion, every action an offering. Birth and death are neither beginnings nor ends, but simply transitions.

Throughout the Middle Ages, until the Renaissance, Western thinkers and artists employed their minds and talents largely in the service of divinity. The primary aim of art and philosophy was to connect the earthly and heavenly realms, so as to provide a ground in uncertain times. Since the rise of science in the West, scientists have increasingly focused on penetrating and describing phenomena or appearances in the external, physical world, apart from the workings of the human mind. Matters of the spirit have been relegated to religion; only recently has the nature of the human mind been studied in relation to brain function. Today, however, a few philosophers are searching for a "general theory of everything," in which all subjects of study, including religion, have equal value and participate in an integrated whole.[72] Religion is part of this integrative process.

Nevertheless, in our present era, human talents and creativity are employed primarily in attempting to perfect what is actually impermanent. For some, money, prestige, and power are the religions of today. Financial institutions are the temples and the pursuit of meaning is reduced to finding better methods of amassing wealth. From this perspective, social and personal problems are reducible to economic modes of analysis. Since everything revolves around manipulating and controlling the economy, our general welfare is ruled by the desire to possess more and better. As long as we buy—always more, better, bigger—our culture thrives. If the dynamics of desire and money were to come to an abrupt halt, the world as we know it today would collapse.

Self-concern is the norm by which many of us live in today's world. What *I* want and what pleases *me* tends to determine our thoughts and actions. We are capable of generating abundant willpower and discipline—think of the people who work sixteen hours a day to build up their own business—if it serves our sense of self-importance, and of course when it is a matter of survival.

Money, prestige, and power can lose their allure in a split second, when illness and death enter our lives. Everything changes when we are laid off, or when one of our loved ones is diagnosed with a terminal disease or dies on the battlefield. Nothing that ruled our lives before can help us then. The shock can jolt us into becoming a different person. Suddenly we understand what really matters, and solemnly we resolve to live according to this newfound knowledge from now on.

Once the adversity has been overcome or mourning has ended, however, these powerful insights may disappear into the background. Little by little, life returns to normal. It is not that we lose the experience—as a treasure chest of wisdom it remains in the back of our minds—but we seldom open it. Deep down, there may be a nagging regret about letting our resolve slip through our fingers. Now and then the question surfaces whether things might have been different. We wonder: Is it actually possible to live a well-adjusted and successful life while also penetrating more deeply into knowledge of the human condition?

The Time Is Now

Religion invites us to give life meaning and understand the cosmos as a whole, in which human being has its place. The word "religion" originates from the Latin word *religio* (from the verb *ligare*), "that which binds." Religion binds all phenomena that would otherwise appear random and inexplicable together, to form a unity. Some religions teach that human beings can contact an inner sanctum, to be honored above anything else. The teachings of the Buddha point to honoring the truth, being authentic, and respecting the value of all sentient beings and of nature.

One truth we cannot deny is that everything passes. This day will not return. One day we will die. When the time comes, we must say goodbye to what we now hold dear and release what we are now prepared to fight for. But no matter how obvious or imminent change is, the pressing issues of each day and the tempting illusion of *I* tend to hypnotize us into ignoring this truth of life. Many people believe it is morbid to pause and think about their own death.

What if we were to embrace knowledge of impermanence wholeheartedly and live our lives in accord with its fundamental truth? Far from being morose or fatalistic, this approach could serve as a healthy guiding principle. When we internalize the knowledge that everything is temporary, we appreciate the value of this moment and are inspired to make the best of it. This moment offers the opportunity to manifest our highest truth, so we can live without regret. With this outlook, our attitudes toward life gain a quality of urgency that supports authentic thought and action. Every thought can be constructive, every gesture an invitation, every word a bridge. We naturally bear in mind what is good for ourselves and for all sentient beings, now and in the long term.

Living truthfully implies questioning ourselves and daring to act upon the answers we find. It requires courage to acknowledge we have made mistakes. What knowledge can we no longer ignore? What knowledge can we rely on when our worldly security falls away? The answers to these and all other questions lie within our own minds.

GROUND OF BEING

Nyingma Buddhist teachings distinguish nine levels of consciousness.[73] Six of these levels correspond to the senses, including thinking, the sixth sense. These six fields of consciousness determine the content of everyday life. They are characterized by the power of *I*; we say, "I see," "I hear," or, "I think." When we start to fall asleep at night, the six fields of consciousness gradually become less active. We may observe remnants of thoughts or hear sounds as if in the distance, but the mind does not follow their trail. We may be able to observe this quieting of sense consciousness during an afternoon nap, when the transition between waking and sleeping is usually more transparent and therefore more noticeable.

During sleep, before dreaming begins, sense consciousness comes to a standstill. We enter an obscure, still, and unknown territory that is always present, whether the six senses are active or not. It is the ground of our being. Here residues of the past retain their original emotional charge, and act like filters that determine the flavor of every experience. Emotional residues that linger in our consciousness make our energy languid and heavy, provoking an inner resistance so subtle that it is barely discernible. Until the senses and mind relax and open, this torpor contaminates the quality of all experience. In meditation these residues turn up as tension, a blocking energy reflecting the holding of *I*.

Traces of the past, conscious and unconscious remnants of our history, are called latent tendencies or *bag-chags* in Tibetan (*bija* in Sanskrit). When circumstances activate these emotional memories, they set up duplication of old experiences. For example, whenever a person who has once hurt us comes into view, or is merely mentioned by name, we experience an emotional flare-up. We cannot help ourselves—old emotions consume us instantly. We are governed by the unfinished business buried in the deepest layer of the mind.

The more numerous these subconscious traces, the heavier and darker the ground of our being. Still, even if it seems a black hole, the substratum also contains the light of pure awareness, and while subconscious traces impede limpid awareness, they do not affect the light. In meditation, consciousness can yield to the open nature of mind penetrating the opacity of the substratum. We retrieve the light of awareness, and resurface with it, allowing it to illuminate all the senses. In this way, little by little, the open nature of mind is revealed.

Relaxing means putting down our weapons. By letting go of internal resistance to past experiences, we are able to completely feel, understand, and accept each life event. Once a life event is completely assimilated, we release its emotional residues. Consciousness becomes flexible and light. We experience a sense of closure; this particular aspect of *I* can finally be released. We are able to live in the present. We are free from the past; the future is open.

VISUALIZATION

After a near-death experience, people often report having seen an overwhelming light flooding the senses. This could be the essential light of mind that enables us to see. Meditation taps into this light of pure awareness.

It is possible to experience light of awareness directly through visualization. Absorption in the object of visualization penetrates the thought world and consciousness becomes transparent and grows lighter. The thick clouds of thinking that make up consciousness dissipate. Experience that is not channeled through thinking reveals itself as direct experience.

The idea of doing a visualization practice may at first seem foreign. Perhaps we assume that we are supposed to "see" something with the eyes, but visualization practices are intended to awaken the mind's eye. This experience can be one of seeing, but also of sensing. In fact we all visualize constantly throughout the day. It is not difficult to picture our bedrooms or imagine cutting and squeezing a lemon. We can easily conjure up a complex series of motions such as we use in making a bed, or imagine a whole series of interactions in recalling the details of a meeting.

Visualization is more than mental gymnastics or an exercise in creative imagination. The light of awareness that projects the visualized image gradually seeps into all layers of consciousness. However, our tendency to identify with thoughts and perceptions makes it necessary to choose the visualization object with care. In principle, any object will do, but as the practitioner and the object merge, an emotionally laden item, such as a photograph of a loved one, is likely to distract, while a personification of evil, for example, will instill harmful and destructive intentions. A neutral entity such as a flower or a tree, the flame of a candle, or even a stone is preferable. Best of all is when the object is an image of enlightenment, for then visualization invites enlightenment qualities into the mind. By concentrating on the form of the Buddha or Jesus, for examle, our mind mingles with enlightened mind. Religious symbols such as the syllables *Om Ah Hum* are also especially suitable for visualization, because they are empowered symbols of the light of awareness.

Exercise: Choose an object of visualization that you are drawn to. Place it about a foot and a half away from you, at eye level. Allow the object to penetrate your imagination, in order to get a *feeling* from its form. After studying the object for a couple of minutes, close your eyes and bring it to mind; see its contours, colors, and details. Then open your eyes and look at the object, again sensing a feeling from its form. Close your eyes once more, and absorb this feeling, while holding the image in your mind's eye.

In the beginning you may have to force your attention, but soon a balance will emerge between effort that is too strenuous or too lax. As you relax, visualizing will become easier. Eventually the object of visualization will remain in your mind effortlessly. The image penetrates the thought-world, dismantling thinking patterns and uniting consciousness with the power of the object. When you are no longer separate from the object, you are ready to enter pure awareness. Finish the exercise by sending the visualization object away. At the beginning of the exercise you have called on it to appear, and at the end it must be dissolved, so that empty space remains. This is an important moment, since it manifests that space is the basis of all mental events and the foundation of consciousness. Every appearance arises in space and returns to space. Space accommodates all; space is our home. Becoming familiar with space through visualization lessens the attachment to whatever comes to mind and releases us from the tendency to grasp.

As our ability to visualize images improves, we gain confidence in the power of mind, and recognize that there is no limit to what we can realize. With an empowered mind, we can creatively pursue all that is positive, while casting aside needless duplications of suffering, destructive thinking, or limiting mental patterns. Thoughts have less power, for we know we can send them off and settle into the empty space that remains.

By familiarizing the mind with symbols that transcend impermanence, we are preparing ourselves for an encounter with what is not subject to change. Here we find security, even in the midst of turmoil. The light of awareness offers a safe haven. The mind becomes our temple, our sacred sanctum.

14

Neither Here Nor There

Like many people in the United States, I had only about two weeks of vacation each year. Usually I took that time to visit my parents, first in Italy and later in the Netherlands. The year my mother moved to the nursing home was no exception.

After bringing my suitcases to my parents' apartment and talking briefly with my father, I set off for the nursing home. Actually, I ran the whole way, as if hoping to catch a train, slowing down only when the building came in sight. A revolving door pushed me into the hall. A receptionist in a glass cubicle, surrounded by monitors showing empty rooms, pointed the way to the elevator.

What state would I find her in? Did she know I was coming? My father had given me only one piece of advice: "When it is time to leave, just say you have to go get something, then leave quickly. In a little while she won't even remember you were there." Otherwise, I was completely unprepared for my mother's new situation. I expected things between us would be more or less the way they used to be; we were always close. "I can handle it," I thought. "After all, she is my mother. No matter what has happened to her, I will still know her."

Stepping from the elevator, I ran into a strong odor of diapers and vomit, mixed with disinfectant. An oddly joyful nurse directed me, "Third door on the left, that's where your mother is." Meanwhile, a distinguished looking man wearing a gray suit came marching toward me. Only at close range did I notice the hollow look in his eyes. He muttered constantly under his breath as he continued walking past me. My first reaction was to thank heaven my mother was not seeing all of this, before realizing that this was her everyday experience. I walked through the third door on the left and entered a spacious, light-filled ward. Next to the door a woman sat crumpled in her chair, and pitiful-looking people were scattered in clumps around the room. Panicky, I looked around. Where was my mother?

I saw her before she noticed me, and I paused a moment to take in her appearance. She was wearing a garish dress that looked unfamiliar to me. "Clothes don't matter too much here," a nurse would later tell me. Her wavy gray hair was cropped short; her head appeared to have shrunk. With thin hands, she gripped the arms of the chair tightly.

"How lovely to see you," she said when I approached. Her voice was wonderfully familiar. Her eyes, crinkled into little triangles, were beaming as always. She seemed to be the only normal person in the room. Others were mumbling to themselves or sitting stonily like ancient ruins, showing no signs of life. "This is absurd," I thought. "What is she doing here? Isn't it obvious that my mother is not like these poor creatures?"

"Do you know something odd?" she said, after I had pulled up a chair and sat down right in front of her. "When Daddy is here, he will say, 'I need to go get something.' He gets up and leaves, and then he does not return." A wave of desperation swept over me. How could I ever leave? My unwarranted self-confidence completely evaporated.

I took refuge in cheerfulness and reached for her hand. Her soft, strong hands felt bony and gnarled; they had become claws that seemed to be grasping for some shred of security. "How about a walk?" I proposed. She responded happily, "Oh, yes." I offered her my arm, and joyfully she walked next to me into the hall.

A nurse approached us, "Shall I take your mother to the bathroom first?" My mother turned to me with raised eyebrows, as if asking me what to do. When I nodded, she meekly followed the woman and returned a few minutes later. She put her arm through mine again and we continued the trip to the elevator. Every few steps she would come to a complete halt. The hall seemed endless. The man in the suit was heading in our direction; he passed by without greeting us or even noticing that we were there. My mother stopped, turned toward me and said, "I feel so sorry for him—there are so many wretched people living here."

"Are you going outside?" said a voice behind us. "Because if you are, your mother needs a coat. Come with me." We followed the nurse to a room with three small beds. "This must be her bedroom," I thought. Looking at the spot where her head would rest on the pillow, I imagined how she must lie here at night. Did anybody talk to her before she fell asleep? What if she couldn't sleep and lay awake at night? Was there anyone here who knew things like this about her? Was there anyone here who knew her at all?

BARDO

My mother's previous world had vanished, leaving barely a trace. Each morning she woke up in a strange setting that she never got used to, without familiar smells or sounds, without her husband lying beside her. The knowledge she had gained during her lifetime about how to take care of her body and mind was gone. Her consciousness grew weaker every day. The illness made it impossible for her to find security in thoughts, in memories, or in familiar ways of comfort. She had lost her bearings and had nowhere to turn.

In the language of the *Tibetan Book of the Dead*, my mother was in a bardo. Bardo literally means "in between"—an unknown gap between two fixed points. It is a transitional phase, a state of being neither here nor there. In English, the Tibetan word "bardo" is most commonly used to describe states we pass through at the time of death. However, a complementary text by the same author (Padmasambhava) describes six kinds of bardos, each with its own particular characteristics.[74] Specific exercises are traditionally used to penetrate the nature of each bardo.

The first three bardos all occur around the time of death. The first takes place during the dying process, just before death; the second comes immediately after death; and the third happens just prior to rebirth, which might be upon death, or a long time afterwards.

The fourth bardo is life, the period between birth and death. This is the bardo we are currently experiencing. The uncertainty characteristic of a bardo permeates our existence, whether we are aware of it or not, as none of us knows the time of our impending death. The bardo teachings encourage us not to waste this uncertain length of time—our life—in indolence and laziness, but to use it to deepen our understanding of the Dharma and make our lives fruitful.

The fifth bardo is the time of sleeping and dreaming that starts the moment we fall asleep and lasts until we awaken. Our perceptions during sleep and dream time are subject to delusions. What ghosts haunt our dreams? Yet according to Tibetan Buddhist teachings, life is a delusion, just as dreams are. If that were true, how substantial and reliable can the thoughts and opinions be that we rely upon to shape our lives?

The sixth bardo occurs during meditation, when we are progressing through bardos. As meditation deepens, awareness illuminates the process of perception, revealing vast layers of the mind free of conceptual thought. In the thinking mind we experience awareness as if it were split into pieces; we are aware *of* something. Thus duality is created. When meditation deepens, thoughts cease to be our reference. Duality yields to openness. The traditional texts provide maps for the worlds of experience we are entering.

Within the bardo of life, there are many bardos. Whenever something begins or comes to an end—a project, a relationship, or even the day—it is as if we were entering into a bardo. When we are in doubt about what is happening, or what the future may bring, we dwell in a bardo, with uncertainty and confusion as our only points of reference. Perhaps we are not sure if a friend has betrayed us, or we fear for our job, or we are awaiting news of a family member who might be involved in an accident. At such a time, everything is in limbo. The fear of losing everything lurks in the background or takes us over; our whole existence may shake on its foundations. We try to bridge the gap as quickly as possible to prevent getting lost in the frightful chasm. When another experience distracts us, we are relieved and take a deep breath: "That was close!"

Some bardos are so brief that we hardly notice them. If for a single day we remained mindful of our inner life, analyzing our reactions to each internal or external stimulus, we would be surprised at how often bardo experiences in this sense occur. Before a meeting, after a departure, and even at the end of a sentence or gesture, we are momentarily in a bardo. In the moment between picking up the phone and recognizing the voice on the other end, we are in a bardo. When an uncomfortable silence falls in the course of a conversation and we have no idea what to say next—this is a bardo. Arriving in a foreign city, beginning the first day of a new job, entering the room at a party full of strangers: Whenever we have no familiar point of reference, we are in a bardo. The situation makes no sense at all; we seem to be floating in space, not knowing who we are or what is expected of us, knowing only that we do not know.

How do we deal with such uncertainty and the fear that comes in its wake? How do we handle feelings of confusion and panic? We tend to take refuge in the comfort of familiar emotions and thoughts. Strong emotions such as hatred, lust, or pride give a temporary sense of shelter or grounding. We hold on to them for dear life, for they seem more true and real than anything else.

Thoughts allow consciousness to be active, interpreting and making decisions. A succession of thoughts offers temporary refuge from the seemingly empty gaps between them by supplying a thread of logic. As Descartes said, *cogito ergo sum*, I think therefore I am. Yet the security granted by judgments and opinions is illusory, for thoughts are too fickle to be reliable. It is impossible to find stability in phenomena that are characterized by impermanence.

Is it possible to find stability in a bardo? A bardo signals the emptiness between past and future, the present moment. What if we could find a way to relax into this space and feel at home there? What if we were able to practice mindfulness in the all-encompassing present?

The *Tibetan Book of the Dead*,[75] a guide through the bardos, can be understood as a teaching about space. Everything originates in space and eventually returns to space; thoughts come from space and vanish into space. The bardo between thoughts is an opening into space. All appearances occur against the backdrop of space. It is space that accommodates the reality of our lives. Space is our natural habitat.

Our well-being depends on our sense of space: The more intimate our relationship with space, both internal and external, the more expansive our minds. Mind and space are of the same family. Wisdom and balance can grow when awareness is wide and deep.

According to the *Tibetan Book of the Dead,* every human being is confronted with dazzling bardos or openings into space during the process of dying and after death. If we are fortunate enough to be fully conscious at the time of death, we experience a gradual weakening of the senses and the rational mind. Hearing and seeing deteriorate and thoughts vanish as if we were about to fall asleep. If during this process we manage to maintain a clear and stable mind without succumbing to fear, we find that death is not an end, but a transition to an intimate new relationship with space.

FEAR AND AWARENESS

A victim of Alzheimer's disease is unable to sustain sufficient awareness to realize that she is in a bardo. It is uncertain to what degree my mother remained aware, but she clearly lost most of her references. Day after day the holes in her memory grew larger. At times not knowing who she was, or what was happening, she seemed to be a buoy adrift on an ocean of feelings, at the mercy of raging storms. She was especially vulnerable to bouts of intense fear, for which there was no remedy.

Fear is our usual reaction to a bardo experience. Fear is the anchor of the ego, which relies on the separation between subject and object. It waits in the wings wherever there is duality and separation.

When the world of thoughts falls apart, as it does when we are ill, dying, or suffering from dementia, a domain opens up where *I* has no authority. Alone in the dark, without the bearings provided by the subject-object polarity that the thinking mind creates, ego weakens. The willpower and drive with which we normally establish our sanity become immobilized. Feelings of terror and powerlessness that are buried just below the surface of consciousness float up.

Trying to fend off such feelings in the bardo only exacerbates fear. Awareness is the only remedy. By bringing awareness to the feelings of terror, powerlessness, and isolation, and relaxing into them, realizing that all our experiences are projections of our minds, we can learn to feel at home in this emptiness. As we do this, awareness expands into space and is supported by it. We recognize that emptiness is synonymous with space, and that fear is simply a marker for openness. As the sense of separation dissolves into wholeness, fear transforms into a sense of freedom.

On the threshold of the unknown, fear can be a positive sign, an indicator that something new is approaching. Fear simply delivers the message that change and openness are near, that new knowledge is just around the corner. We can acknowledge our fear while simultaneously venturing gently into new territory.

But unless we recognize the hidden power of the fear inside, or have the courage to face it, it will continue to poison our best intentions. To help us face our fears, we can ask, "What is the worst thing that can happen to me?" and follow this thought through to its conclusion. When awareness opens to fear in this way, fear loses its edge.

Like a compass for the healthy mind, fear helps us recognize that we are in a bardo. Such recognition provides security. In a bardo—the space between two people, two situations, two moments, day and night, life and death—space invites us to experience its wholeness. There is no separation. In space the unknown stretches out infinitely. We do not know where we are, what is happening, or how long this insecurity will last.

Now we know that we do not know. Facing this truth, we actually contact our knowing capacity—not knowledge of facts, but the ability to know. This capacity is what we must hold on to when all else fails us. Then the emptiness of space no longer frightens us, and we may even discover that we can feel at home there.

As long as *I* is around, there will be fear. Knowing fear as a friend and ally helps us to face it as it arises. When the time comes for our lives to end, we are better prepared to face our deepest fear, the fear of dying. On the brink of death, nothing and no one can save us. The world we know and treasure fades away, and finally dissolves into space. The final unknown arrives: the bardos of dying and death.

STILLNESS AND SPACE

In between birth and death, our energies are exercising in space. We are a continuous embodiment of energy in space. To learn how space accommodates our changing processes is vital. At ease with openness we may find a safe haven: space as a quality of mind.

Stillness helps us become familiar with space. In the beginning it may take an effort to remain still, because we are so accustomed to activity and noise. Social etiquette requires us to communicate incessantly, and silence is so unsuited to society that when a silence descends in company, the Dutch say, "A vicar is passing by." Even at work there will often be a radio or television playing. Wherever we go, there is likely to be background noise: the sound of traffic or machinery, music in shopping malls, or perhaps the neighbors mowing the lawn.

We can grow accustomed to stillness, in spite of our initial discomfort. We can learn to acknowledge our feelings of restlessness and not give in to them. As we remain still, silence allows us to begin to explore our internal experience.

When we dare to submerge ourselves in silence, we enter a whole new world. Silence gives the mind space to expand, so that mental activity becomes more transparent. When we are good friends with silence, any thoughts and emotions that emerge simply pass by without our involvement. Instead of holding on to the projections of mind, we navigate by the radar of awareness.

MANTRA: PROTECTION OF MIND

In the Tibetan Buddhist tradition no effort is spared to create a harmonious atmosphere. Prayer flags, prayer wheels and incense all imbue space with blessings and goodness. At the construction site of a house or temple, a lama will conduct a ceremony to consecrate the foundations, while participants recite mantras to purify the energies of the environment.

Westerners who traveled to the forbidden land of Tibet at the beginning of the twentieth century often wondered about mantra: Was it perhaps a magical spell? Some questions cannot be answered, and questions about why mantras are effective may fall into this category. We may not know why they work, only that they do. Mantra is like a set of keys capable of unlocking the power of human potential, and of nature. Mantra is enlightened energy coded in syllables and sounds.

Mantra can be compared with music, which also carries inner meaning that cannot be expressed in words. In the West, classical musical techniques and instruments are focused on harmony, melody, and the beauty and purity of sound. In the Tibetan tradition, music is not primarily a form of art, but a means to enlightenment. Through the ages, Tibetans have perfected the knowledge of how sound affects the mind. Melody and musical phrasing play a secondary role. To a Western ear mantra recitations may seem monotonous, but the sound of mantra works in mysterious ways.[76]

237

Like silence, sounds affect the mind. Music can relax, inspire, irritate, or depress; it can soothe the deep sadness and pain that words cannot reach. Melodies can inspire us to dance, compete on the playing field, or fight. In World War II, a bagpipe player would often lead the Scottish regiment. Impelled by the patriotic tones, soldiers marched willingly toward the enemy and death.

Mantra has similar power, but at a deeper level. It restores balance between body and mind, and between humankind and the forces of nature. *Man-* means the essence of mind, and *-tra* refers to the "instrument for" the magical transformation that stimulates the subtle energy of enlightenment.[77] We might say that mantra is the language of pure awareness. When we chant a mantra, our minds and souls find sanctuary in awareness, even amidst violence and chaos.

The primal language of Buddhist mantra consists of archetypal sounds such as *Om, Ah,* and *Hum,* as well as other mantric seed syllables and words in Sanskrit. Their rhythm and sound lead us beyond conceptual images and ordinary speech, appealing to indestructible open awareness. The energy thus released can unwind the knots of emotional tension in body and mind. As a result, the energies of body and mind communicate and become integrated, deepening awareness further.

Mantra is often combined with visualization. While chanting a mantra, we call upon an image of harmony and balance, wisdom and compassion. This combination is particularly fitting for people with crowded agendas and minds, who do not have time to establish a steady sitting meditation practice. Just as meditation promotes calmness and clarity, interaction between mantra and visualization rekindles our energy and opens the heart.

Both mantra and visualization are appropriate anywhere and at any time. They can be used as preparation for meditation or in meditation itself, and also chanted while working, doing household chores, talking on the telephone, during a meeting, or in the middle of a tense conversation. Chanted before or after a meal, mantra invites the food to nourish the goodness in us. When blended with our daily lives, the practice of mantra builds up a positive internal momentum that supports us in good times as well as bad.

There are a great number of Buddhist mantras, suitable for a variety of purposes.[78] In order to benefit from a mantra, we need only chant it, either silently or out loud. When the mantra is chanted, sound merges with awareness and energy, and mind and environment come into harmony.

If chanting the mantra is meant to benefit another, the person to whom it is dedicated does not need to be present, for space knows no boundaries. Even a person who has passed away may benefit from mantra. Mantra cannot alleviate the effects of an illness such as Alzheimer's, but it can console when words and even silence fail to help. Chanting mantra creates space in which patience, love, and wisdom can come to the foreground.

One of the mantras I often chanted for my mother was *Om Mani Padme Hum*. This powerful mantra carries blessings similar to those of a sacrament in the Christian church. It can release us from the suffering we experience as a result of our actions. Residues of emotions such as hatred, jealousy, arrogance, and stupidity are washed away. In this six-syllable prayer, each syllable speaks to specific emotional patterns. *Om* heals ignorance, *Ma* jealousy, *Ni* arrogance, *Pad* insatiable craving, *Me* fear and laziness, and *Hum* heals hatred. The syllable *Hri* is sometimes added at the end, referring to the opening of the heart, the culmination of healing.

The mantra empowers us to forgive both ourselves and others for the pain we or they have caused, either knowingly or unknowingly. When we must let go of the familiar world, *Om Mani Padme Hum Hri* frees us from fear, guides us through the unknown, and supports our journey on the path to the light of unending awareness.

Chanting *Om Mani Padme Hum Hri* with my mother in mind helped alleviate my sadness. During our visits, I would chant for her softly, sometimes inaudibly, while we sat together talking or looking silently out the window. It seemed to quiet my mother; she appeared less tormented. The time spent together grew more intimate. Without words, we met one another, two souls in one immeasurable space.

15

Looking in the Mirror

Once my mother and I had left the nursing home and were out on the sidewalk, I was tempted to head straight home. We could just pretend we had been on a visit to a hospital. Once at home, we would have a cup of tea. When the sun came near the horizon, it would signal the time for the wine glasses to be put on the table, along with some crackers and cheese. After a while, my mother would get up and say, "I'm going to go whip up some dinner." I let go of these thoughts with great effort, while gently ushering her toward a little shopping area.

As we shuffled over the wet leaves on the footpath, my mother would stop every few yards and turn to look at me, her face radiant. She would tighten her grip on my arm as if about to say something, but no words came. Each time, as we continued on our way, we adjusted our paces to one another. Near a tall apartment building that had a panel full of doorbells beside the front entrance, she looked at me naughtily and said, "Shall we ring all the bells at once?" When I began to pull her in the direction of the front door, she exclaimed, "Oh no, we can't really do that!" and burst into giggles. For a brief moment, time stood still as I remembered the old days, when I could always make her laugh. Before I was old enough for official driving lessons, she taught me to drive in her car. With her in the passenger seat, I would honk joyfully at random pedestrians, waving at them as if they were our dearest friends. Our victims tried their best to recognize us, and in the rear view mirror we could see their puzzled attempts to return the greeting as we sped on our way to the next prank. My mother enjoyed this impish behavior, and I seized every opportunity to provoke her giggles. Shaking with laughter, she would still always feel sorry for the objects of our mischief.

Now we sat in rattan chairs on a terrace, drinking tea and letting the late afternoon sun warm our faces. A group of noisy kids passed by. "Which of you will get Alzheimer's when you are old?" I mused. Statistics suggest that in fifty years from now the number of people suffering from dementia will have doubled. Anyone can get Alzheimer's: The former queen of the Netherlands had it, and so did a former president of the United States.

After finishing our tea, we began the trip back to the nursing home, trudging along like two convicts returning to their cells after a scheduled break for fresh air. I worried whether she had to go to the restroom. The sun disappeared behind clouds and the air grew chilly. In the elevator she whispered, "I want to go home." Caressing her gaunt ring-adorned fingers, the rings now far too big, I softly began to hum a mantra.

"Hi Madam, was it nice outside?" the nurse asked. "Are you ready for a bite to eat now?" My mother looked at me questioningly. "Eat? I don't know." While the nurse did her best to ease our separation, my mother and I clumsily embraced each other. "Will you come back? I want to go home too," she said. Slipping away like a shadow, I wondered: Had she already forgotten me?

Signals of Distress

When my mother's forgetfulness grew more serious and it became obvious that she was suffering from an incurable disease, we said, "It runs in the family. Remember Uncle Gerard? He had the same thing. Mother's illness is hereditary. There is nothing anyone can do."

Why did we feel the need to look for explanations? Was it perhaps to exonerate ourselves? Nobody could have prevented this, in the same way that no one could save her now. It was nobody's fault. Even scientists were unable to solve the Alzheimer's mystery. Still, something inside us felt powerless and guilty, and so we gradually turned away from her.

We had no idea how to respond to her signals of distress, and pardoned ourselves by saying, "Mother forgets everything anyway." In the beginning she cried for help by saying, "I feel so useless." Later it became, "I'm so scared," and "I want to go home," and finally, "I want to get out." When we visited the nursing home, we sat with her helplessly until it was time to leave again and we could return to the normality of the day. Her life had become so frightening it made us feel insecure. We took refuge in our powerlessness. What if one of us had spoken up for her and said, "Now wait a minute. How can we really help her?" How could compassion have been made manifest?

Alzheimer's methodically did its job, choking the brain cells, undermining consciousness, and destroying all hope of recovery. Step by step her destiny unfolded. It was a shocking spectacle: The woman we had respected, loved, and admired turned into a frightened, helpless ruin. Still, we had to find a way to live with it, and we did. Our judgments, supported by ignorance and fear, created a logical and watertight story, enabling us to remain at a safe distance.

Judging

Judge not, lest you be judged.
For as you judge, so will you be judged.[79]

Wisdom is inseparable from compassion. It can never offend or cause harm. Judgment, on the contrary, holds little wisdom and no compassion. While compassion bridges the gap between people, judging creates separation, even between the best of friends.

When we criticize, we feel invulnerable, as if we were omniscient. Paying attention only to the dictates of our own minds, we close our eyes and ears to the positions of everyone else. Communication between our heads and hearts falters and closes down. The stronger our attachment to a certain conviction, the more rigid it becomes. Judgment fixes that which is actually subject to constant change and closes what is inherently open. Judgments and strong opinions indicate feelings of insecurity, which have their origins in the small space of the *I*: Why else would we need to assume a superior stance? If we look below the surface, we find that opinions conceal resistance to a greater knowledge. Believing that we know the truth, we disassociate ourselves from a far more complex reality. Judgment provides us with an alibi for not being empathic. It grants permission to stifle our feelings and excuses us from the need for compassion.

This might seem harmless enough if the sole purpose were to relieve our own insecurity. Unfortunately, drawing ill-advised conclusions can cause harm to others.

Without any selfish consideration,
one may, with affection, tell people their defects,
only thinking of their own good.
But although what one says is true
this will ulcerate their hearts.
To say gentle words is my advice from the heart.[80]

When the object of scorn begins to defend him- or herself, we know the criticism has hit home; the damage has been done. We have trampled on another's heart. The verdict carried by a negative judgment may echo indefinitely in heart and mind. The one convicted receives a heavy sentence—sometimes lifelong. Terminal or chronically ill patients must deal with two diagnoses at once: the medical verdict of the doctor and the opinions of others. Even if they are not expressed

245

directly, judgments remain in the air, preventing honest empathy. Each visit can become an ordeal for the patient. Instead of receiving the compassion and love he or she longs for, the patient must carry the heavy burden of the illness alone, tainted with guilt and feelings of inferiority. The energy needed to address the illness becomes sidetracked into emotional distress. It takes great effort to give the illness the attention it requires. Sickness becomes a protracted battle on all levels: physical, mental, and especially spiritual.

*Words that do not touch the other gently
the wise leave aside.*[81]

As the saying goes, "If you can't say something nice, don't say anything at all." For why would we want to judge? Or even to tease, which is a jocular form of judgment? Maybe we judge to emphasize the distance between people; to vent impatience and disdain, or else to reaffirm our feelings of superiority. Thoughts and opinions usually mask a fear of facing rejected parts of ourselves. Do we actually perceive a particular quality in the other person or are we simply projecting? Is what we see really outside us?[82] A good remedy for judging might be the playground reminder, "It takes one to know one!"

Judging also offers opportunities; when we judge, we look in the mirror. Just as a dream betrays the dreamer's secret desires and fears, so a judgment reveals a blueprint of the emotional mind. It provides an intimate glimpse of the unresolved issues polluting our private world.

With practice, we can learn to take advantage of judgment to wake up from within this small world of consciousness, which is hardly more real than the world of dreams.

If we are the objects of criticism, we may feel trapped, with nowhere to turn, like a bee in a jar. Most likely, the feeling of being attacked reinforces existing patterns: This hurt is just another blow, the latest incident in a long line of harsh treatments that have affected our development. We have no idea how to be different, however much we would like to change.

Still, we can rise to the challenge by practicing opening enough to receive the critique. Isn't it true that where there is smoke, there is usually fire? Sometimes the problem is simply a matter of poor communication, we did not take the time to listen, but reacted instantaneouslly. Listening and reflecting, trying to connect with the meaning behind the words, we can perceive the wisdom in them. Most importantly, we ask ourselves, "How can I make it better?" The answer is grounded in self-knowledge. To enhance self-knowledge, the Buddhist tradition offers many methods.

The Wheel of Life

The Tibetan wheel of life (*srid-pa'i 'khor-lo*, literally "wheel of becoming") is one of the best-known representations of the extent of human suffering. It demonstrates how suffering arises, how it is maintained, and how it

247

248

comes to an end.[83] Even without description, the message of the images is powerful. Thorough study imprints them on the mind, providing insight that helps avoid duplication of misery.

In the center of the wheel, three animals go around in circles, holding each other by the tail. These three—the rooster, the snake, and the pig—are symbols of the three poisons that pollute our lives: grasping, aversion, and confusion. One after the other, round and round, each of the three poisons perpetuates the dynamics of suffering.

The metaphor of the wheel portrays how strongly human beings are entwined in patterns that generate suffering. As we continually reenact these patterns, the wheel continues to turn, adding a new round of suffering with each revolution. Yet the situation is not hopeless: The very thing that poisons us can also be the remedy for our troubles. When poison is transformed into wisdom, the wheel comes to a halt, if even for the briefest moment, and suffering ceases.

The Six Realms

In the six spaces defined by the spokes of the wheel, six realms represent basic emotional patterns: hatred and aggression, greed and yearning, dullness and ignorance, passion and desire, paranoia and envy, and self-absorbed pride.[84]

Each realm can be seen in terms that connect well with Western psychology. Human beings tumble from one realm or emotion to another, both literally and figuratively, when trapped in limiting patterns of consciousness that make them and their dear ones suffer.

The *hell realm*, with its extremes of hot and cold, is the most intense realm. The hatred we experience and arouse in others dominates this domain. The corresponding images on the wheel depict hell beings immersed in boiling oil, being torn to pieces by wild animals, and tortured by a variety of other means. These images represent the violence of aggression and hatred that each human being is familiar with. Some beings quake in terror, others shake with rage. Hatred and aggression imprison us in hells of our own making.

The *realm of hungry ghosts (pretas)* represents insatiable greed and craving. The denizens of this realm always want more than they have, and are incapable of enjoying what is already here. They are depicted as ravenous beings with large, swollen bellies and impossibly skinny necks. Tormented by endless needs and desires, they have no hope of ever being satisfied.

The *animal realm* is characterized by dullness and paranoia, and all that follows upon those qualities. Here life is concerned with survival—eat or be eaten. While eating, the animals are afraid that another creature might steal their food. When not hunting or eating, they sleep. Every surprise is regarded with distrust and suspicion. Paranoia is a way of life. Its radar scans all kinds of objects, picks out suspects, and perceives each life experience as a potential threat. In this realm, human beings seek protection from some kind of authority, such as a big brother, the police, a lawyer, consultant, or therapist.[85]

The *human realm* is characterized by arrogance and desire. The *I* avidly seeks pleasure and new experiences, eager to explore but at the same time wanting life to remain predictable. In this realm, desire and skepticism go hand in hand. Human beings are cunning, elusive, and evasive. They like to outwit others. They are too proud to question themselves, and are inclined to blame others for their own carelessness and failure to act. But at the heart of the human realm, passion and the drive to survive are dominant.

Jealousy and anger characterize the beings who inhabit the *realm of the demigods (asuras)*. In their relentless envy of the gods, the demigods strive to sabotage the success of others. They thrive on intrigue and manipulation as well as outright aggression. They are combatants who enjoy witnessing the failure of others. Always wanting something, they are compelled to act in order to get it. They never find any peace.

Finally, the *realm of the gods* is for those who close their eyes to reality. Beings in the god realms are obsessed with comfort and enjoyment and avoid conflict and confrontation. Surrounded by beauty and immersed in all manner of sensory pleasures, they feel immortal, although they are not. Time goes by in a flash; opportunities slip away until suddenly one day they must face the end of all they have known. Then they awaken to the knowledge that they are completely unprepared to face the harder realities of life and death.

At this point there is nothing to hold on to. Overwhelmed by anxiety and panic, the gods plummet down from their

cloud castles, landing in the basest world of consciousness—the hell realm.

KNOWLEDGE OF FREEDOM

*There is nothing either good or bad
but thinking makes it so.* [86]

The wheel of life depicts the human condition. Each of
the six worlds of existence symbolizes a specific mental
entanglement. If left to its own devices consciousness will
be drawn to this drama. However, the teachings of the
wheel also reveal that every realm contains a solution;
each predicament offers an escape route.

In each realm the Buddha holds the medicine that can
heal us. In the hell realm the Buddha purifies hatred with
a flame. In the realm of the hungry ghosts, the Buddha
appears with a bowl of noble foods—wisdom, energy, and
moral discipline—that quiet hunger and craving. In the
world of animals, the Buddha offers a book of wisdom
that dispels lethargy and fear. In the human realm, an
alms bowl is offered to counter arrogance with humil-
ity, encouraging human beings to beg for knowledge of
freedom. The demigods receive a sword to cut through
the delusions of envy and jealousy. In the god realm, the
Buddha plays a lute, not to entertain, but to attract the
pleasure-loving gods to the stirring melody of truth.

CODEPENDENT ORIGINATION

The chain of twelve linked images that comprises the outer rim of the wheel of life represents *codependent origination (pratityasamutpada* in Sanskrit).[87] By reading the images clockwise from the one o'clock position, we gain insight into how ignorance, karma, and emotions set up endless rounds of suffering.

Each link leads to the next, in a self-perpetuating cycle of suffering. The first two links depict the relationship between ignorance and karma. In the first image, a blind man casts about with his stick, searching out the way. In the next image a person compulsively attempts to model clay on a moving pottery wheel, while unable to control either the clay or the tool. Together, ignorance and karma conspire to maintain the cycle of desire, aggression, and confusion.

The narrowing of consciousness that takes place in the first two links continues up through the remaining links of consciousness, name and form, six senses, contact, feeling, craving, grasping, existence, birth, and old age and death, until in the twelfth and final scene a corpse, the symbol of impermanence, is carried off.[88]

At this point we are given the opportunity to understand that our suffering, sleepless nights, and desperate searches for relief ultimately have little value. We have been fooling ourselves. There is no greater power outside of ourselves that maintains this cycle; only our actions and perspectives keep the wheel of suffering turning.

Unfortunately, the impact of this insight does not last. The cycle begins again, because we do not have a clue what else to do. For all we know, we are doing our best and there is nothing more we can do; ignorance has us in its grip and tightens our emotional knots. Thus, out of ignorance we generate a new round of confusion.

As the wheel turns, the next phase appears even before the last one has ended. We are still grappling with the results of previous trouble when new difficulty announces itself. And again, there is an irresistible urge to take action. That is karma: always wanting to do something about something. After taking action, we are satisfied for a while with how *I* has resolved matters, but soon—after an hour, a day, a week—restlessness starts to gnaw at us again. Once more we feel the urge to intervene. Each action provokes a reaction, and thus the wheel keeps turning.

By reading the outer rim of the wheel clockwise, we gain insight into how karma and emotions set up endless rounds of suffering. It becomes clear how confusion tightens emotional knots.

To deepen our understanding of the unraveling of this chain of events, we can also read the images on the wheel counterclockwise. We see that only when we consciously stop reacting is there space for wisdom. If we do not identify with what comes to mind, there is no attachment, no reaction, no grasping. For suffering to end, however, we need to completely disarm the *I*: The wheel of life must come to a standstill. This heralds the cessation of suffering.

The cessation of suffering is not merely a matter of stopping the wheel of life. It depends as well on the insight that happiness and unhappiness are intrinsically not different. A happy face and a sad face are still the same face. From the enlightened vantage point, the consciousness that is behind, underneath, and inside all "minding" is empty. There is no mysterious power that drives everything—the mind is open. Just as a kaleidoscope composes new patterns from only a handful of elements , so the elements that cause suffering can just as well take on the shape of happiness.

The god Yama, a wrathful image of compassion, holds the wheel of life up as a mirror so we can see ourselves and understand what we are doing with our lives. Yama exclaims:

> *We need to start! We need to come out!*
> *We need to involve our self with the Buddha's*
> *teachings.*
> *Just like an elephant in a place thick with reeds,*
> *we must trample the armies of the Lord of Death.*
> *Whoever carries out this Dharma discipline*
> *diligently, with real energy and alertness,*
> *is no longer abandoned to the cycle of rebirth*
> *and will make an end to suffering.*[89]

Being born as a human being we have a unique occasion to become enlightened, but unless we resolve to realize our potential, the wheel of life spins on and karma accumulates. Until we wake up from this dream, the nightmare of suffering continues. The Buddha demonstrated that it is possible to stop the wheel and get off it. He offers us the tools with which to do this.

WAKING UP FROM A DREAM

First be rid of evil.
Then be rid of self.
Finally be rid of thoughts.
Wise is the one who knows this.[90]

Our consciousness usually functions in a limited fashion, keeping our world small. We are obsessed with ourselves: our own discomfort, irritation, disappointment, and success. Our focus is on what we need and want. The needs of others do not touch us deeply. We keep our distance, afraid of being vulnerable to others' suffering. What might it do to us?

If we dare to face the suffering within us, however, the mind expands and deepens, and awareness awakens. Suffering becomes a teacher. Pain and sadness signal that something we usually ignore is asking for attention. Instead of turning away or trying to get rid of these feelings, we can ask, "What is really going on? What am I afraid of? How would I rather be?" By observing dispassionately, we see that growth occurs precisely where suffering resides. Where there is pain, there is hope.

As awareness awakens, love and compassion naturally awaken as well. When our affinity for compassion and love is nourished, awareness opens further. Compassion creates a connection with others through which love can flow: Our heart goes out to them. Seeing their suffering, we allow a bond to be forged between our hearts and theirs. Aversion and fear yield to understanding. We realize that everyone has the same desire: to lead a happy, meaningful life.

In dire circumstances, compassion and love arise spontaneously. Yet we should not rely on this, and certainly not wait for it. We can learn to cultivate compassion, even when we are not in the mood. When our compassion seems phony and forced, we can practice compassion toward ourselves, recognizing that our consc iousness is contracted and narrow.

TONGLEN

In Tibetan Buddhist teachings there is an exercise called *tonglen*, "giving and receiving," which is also described as exchanging oneself for others. This practice can heal the tendency to be critical and judgmental and repair the damage previously inflicted on others.

I close my eyes. In my imagination, I go down the hall. I walk straight to the lounge on the third floor, third door on the left. There she is, her small gray head bent. After giving her a kiss, I take a chair and sit opposite her, our knees touching. I close my eyes and focus on the breath. I breathe in, I breathe out. With each inhalation I draw some of her illness into myself. With each exhalation, I send her more light and patience.

My breath carries her battle-torn mind to mine. I hesitate momentarily—can I handle it? Or will the darkness remain with me? I ignore the fear; the breath does its work without my interference. My mother lets me proceed. For a moment, her familiar smile warms my heart. "You go right ahead," she says.

In my imagination, I open my eyes and look at her, seeing her through eyes of impermanence. She is alone; she does not belong to me. Other patients surround us like wooden crosses in a cemetery, lost in their own minds. I think, "All parents are our parents, all young ones are our children, all living beings are our family."

I breathe in all the suffering in the room, and breathe out light and patience. All the patients in the nursing home and all the attending nurses—I breathe in their suffering as well. My father, brothers, everyone else—sometimes I feel close to bursting. I breathe in the sadness, the fear and despair, like thick black clouds. I breathe out light, patience, and compassion for all living beings. Gradually, everything becomes lighter; colors turn sparkling and fresh. I slowly rise from my chair. Mother is sitting motionless, but opens her eyes when my forehead touches hers. I can feel the best of her flowing into me.

16

There Is No Perfect Time

for Death

My father always walked the same route to see my mother, both ways. He would wear a jacket and tie, covered by either a gray raincoat or a dark blue loden winter coat, depending on the season. On his head he wore a green-checkered hat. At first he never skipped a day. As the months went by, there would occasionally be a reason for him not to go, but he never missed more than one day in a row. "She won't notice anyway," he told himself.

One cold January day, while he was waiting for the elevator, the director of the nursing home passed by and said to him, "Your wife looks for you all the time." Meanwhile the elevator doors had opened and my father moved toward them. The director gripped his shoulder and said, "Maybe it would be better if you didn't come for a while."

Upstairs in the lounge, he found her at the round table next to the window. "Hello, dear," he said. His wife looked fierce and wild, hair standing up straight, fists clenched. Without looking at him, she said, "I want to go home. But you don't want me to." With a bang, her head fell forward onto the table. Shocked, he leapt up and cried for help. Two nurses rushed in and, holding her under the armpits, lifted my mother off the chair and dragged her down the hall, my father following in their wake.

At the end of the hall they opened a door and entered a room with only a bed, nothing else; the yellow window curtains were shut. They pulled her onto the bed with great effort. Her eyes were half closed; she made no sound. While one nurse covered her with a blanket, my father and the other nurse exchanged a glance. "What will happen now?" he asked. Without waiting for her to answer, he turned around and walked down the long corridor back to the elevator, his feet shuffling. "What's going to happen now?" he muttered to himself repeatedly. "What's going to happen now?" At home he took the newspaper from the mailbox and went up to his sixth floor apartment.

The next day he stayed away. The following night a noise woke him up; the light was on and he saw his eldest son standing in the bedroom doorway. "You didn't hear the phone ring. They called us. Mother is not well. We've got to go see her," he said.

She appeared to be in a coma. When he took a chair beside the bed, she blinked her eyes several times. Their eldest son and his wife stood at the foot of the bed. Her breath was halting; sometimes it seemed to take minutes before a new breath came. It felt as if they were gathered in the anteroom of death. Feeling restless, my father began to get up from his seat. Suddenly her voice called out, clear and strong, "Don't leave me alone." After a seemingly endless pause, she exhaled for the last time and left her body behind. Everyone froze. She was gone.

Missed Opportunities

The night my mother passed on, I was thousands of miles away and knew nothing of these changes. I was unaware of all that happened during the last days of her life. Even when my father rushed to the nursing home that night, no one thought to call. Not until the end of the next day, when it was all over, was I notified.

For many years after she died, I would feel a lump in my throat when talking about her illness. My eyes would fill with tears of grief and anger because I had been unable to participate in her last moments. I felt that no one understood my loss. My emotions were stuck and had nowhere to go. When I mentioned that I could not understand why nobody had warned me, people would say, "Let it go," and "Don't hold on to it." But what did they know? For years I had been prepared to rush home to say farewell to my mother on her deathbed. In my imagination I had experienced it many times. Yet no amount of reflection and brooding could turn back the clock.

After she became ill, nothing ran properly in our family. The dynamics of our relationships changed completely. She had been the glue that held the family together. If there were differences among us, she brought us together again. To her, we had all mattered. In her last years, when she could no longer play this central role, she seemed to move from the center of the family to the periphery. Once illness claimed her irrevocably, she occupied a vague, undefined space somehow apart from the family: She was out of the loop. And since I had been absent when she died, was I too excluded from the family? Who else had fallen out of the circle? One of my three brothers had already died of leukemia seven years earlier. The eldest had recently been diagnosed with lung cancer; he died a few years after my mother. My only surviving brother and I were never close. And what about my father? After my mother's death he kept even more to himself. The family was in ruin.

Ten years before she died, on June 3, 1984, my mother wrote me this letter:

> *I have nothing special to tell you, I just long to make contact. This morning your father and I were reminding each other how uncertain life really is—for what do we know about how much time we still have? We always say "carpe diem"—seize the day—but today that somehow is not so easy. Why? I feel we are all so distant from one another! Funny, flown-away family. Suddenly I wish I could "feel" all of you—in real life. And believe me I hope that, if possible, all four of you, with your loved ones, will stand around me the moment I say farewell to this life. How grateful I am for all the love and warmth you have all given me.*

BEING PRESENT WITH THE DYING

I had experienced several times the great intimacy that can occur at a deathbed, and had heard about it from others as well. Some people who have witnessed death up close consider this experience the most beautiful time of their lives.

Proximity to a dying person can also stir up great tension, however, bringing out the worst rather than the best in us. Family members who are facing the loss of their primary source of security may be overcome by fear. Feelings of guilt may alternate with bitter reproach for missed opportunities or jealousy toward siblings or relatives. Rivalries that have been suppressed for a lifetime may come to the surface. The urge to exact some due from another may be uncontrollable. All of this contributes to a chaotic atmosphere that disturbs the consciousness of the dying person. While engaged in what may be the most difficult task of her life, she is torn apart by the bickering and antagonism of those around her.

In spite of the strength of such negative emotions, family members can often set aside their pride and self-interest, at least temporarily. This becomes more likely as they become attuned to the value of savoring their loved one's last moments and gently releasing her. If this happens, energy trapped under the weight of judgment and fear relaxes, and communication becomes gentler. Each family member senses that this is not an appropriate time to push an agenda, and gives others space to contribute in whatever way seems best, seeking simple, unveiled communication that supports closeness and intimacy. Affection for the dying person may foster reconciliation, even when family members must bid a painful farewell to someone who has suffered greatly or dies too young.

During the dying process it is possible that *Alle Menschen werden Brüder*—all people become brothers.[91]

The dying person, whose awareness becomes increasingly naked and supersensitive, craves stillness and harmony. The past fades away, while the present moves into sharp relief. Few things really matter. We may want to try to make her more comfortable: How well did she sleep? What is the best way to position her pillows? Should we coax her to eat at least a tiny bite? But more than anything else, she simply needs our presence. Being is what matters; if any doing is necessary, the situation will reveal the need. It is best to put the urge to act out of the mind, relax as much as possible, and focus on being fully present. Repeating the question, "What matters now?" silently to ourselves can help release any desire we may have to dominate the scene. From the stillness, new and perhaps unusual ways of communicating may arise. The focus is on her.

If the dying person is able to surrender consciously, she may radiate serene bliss, contentment with the past, and acceptance of what will come. Saying goodbye, in its deeper meaning of "God be with you," may seal a spiritual bond between her and her loved ones. If the dying person can no longer speak, or is unconscious or demented, those who stay behind can practice silent communication from mind to mind. Talking to her in our minds as if she understands what we are saying can also be helpful, as can silently chanting mantras. A dying person's mind often seems to extend far beyond the body. Entering her room we feel as if we can touch her even though she may be at a distance of five or ten feet. She may prefer not to be touched, as in her mind we are already very close. Sitting in a chair at the foot of her bed may be quite intimate, as our body touches her mind. Rather than staying at the periphery of this experience, we can visualize her mind as a circle that we can gently enter. By placing our attention in the center of the circle, we create a gateway to intimacy. In these ways we maintain and deepen contact with her being. Our presence is a prayer made of silence and light, our awareness a guide between heaven and earth.

Conversation around the deathbed can be open and honest. There may be a final opportunity for regret and confession, and for expressing sincere feelings of love and appreciation. This is the time to let go, together, of past suffering. Deepest wishes and concerns can be shared and will be heard, as a life is coming to an end. Intimacy deepens between the dying person and those around her, and a common awareness arises, a meeting of minds and hearts. Depending on her beliefs and our own, we may be moved to encourage her to journey toward God, join an already deceased loved one, or go toward the light.

Farewell to a Loved One with Alzheimer's

Reconciliating with an Alzheimer's patient may be impossible, as we may never get any confirmation that our messages are received. We have to trust our best intentions and can only assume that her being is receptive and expressive in its own way.

On the average, Alzheimer's runs an eight-year course. During this time, the entire family fabric may unravel, leaving loose threads that will not be rewoven. If the primary caregiver is a family member, he may be burdened by guilt; despite all his effort he cannot succeed in alleviating the patient's suffering. What is worse, he may sometimes feel resentment and anger. Family members who live far away also have a hard time finding a natural way to deal with the patient or the caregiver. In many cases, after the death of a loved one who suffered from Alzheimer's, the family comes undone.

If a loved one suffers from Alzheimer's, we are continuously saying goodbye. As her condition declines, we are repeatedly forced to part with some aspect of her: the great cook, the impeccable dresser, the one who enjoyed our visits, the woman with a great sense of humor, the mother who telephoned just to stay in touch. Almost daily we say farewell to some familiar aspect of her. We are barely reconciled with the new situation before it deteriorates further. We part ways with the person who could go to the bathroom alone, who still remembered a birthday once in a while, who occasionally spoke and recognized us. It goes on and on, even when we think we have hit rock bottom. In the end we may become numb, no longer thinking, no longer feeling.

For the one afflicted with Alzheimer's disease, consciously letting go at the time of death may not be an option; surrender and realization may be impossible. Parting is not a shared experience, but a time of private resignation and acceptance infused with prayer: "Fare thee well."

Yet even death is not the last farewell. When she finally succumbs to Alzheimer's, the survivors may find it hard to be at peace with her fate. True, we can comfort ourselves with the thought: "At least she no longer suffers." My father reminded himself repeatedly: "It is over. It is best this way. Stop living in the past and focus on the future." Death may be a release from suffering for the one who has passed, but those who remain are often tormented by painful memories and persistent feelings of guilt: "What could I have done differently to alleviate her suffering?"

Final farewells never actually take place. Intermittently the person we loved comes to mind; we think about her at certain times of the day or throughout the year. Many things in the house or neighborhood are a reminder of her. In our minds we talk to her. As life goes on these moments become more sporadic.

What remains of those we have loved and lost to death? Once I expressed my sadness to my teacher that one day he will no longer be here. He answered: "But why, where can I go?" For we say goodbye only to the physical form. There is no difference between "here" and "there." There may be different realms, worlds, and universes, yet all are accommodated by one great space: Ultimately, there is no separation.

Still, mourning has to take place. The conclusion of every phase of life invites a period of mourning; without it, loss remains unprocessed. In our minds, we can relive the ebb and flow of a period in our lives that has passed. What was once primary to us is now history.

The relationship, with all of its ups and downs, has come to an end; it is over. It is time for closure.

At this time it is crucial for those who stay behind to contact the emotions held in the body, rather than engage exclusively in thinking. A process of activating feelings and recycling them throughout the body stimulates healing. With the flow of feeling comes appreciation of impermanence, healing in itself.

Someone once asked a spiritual teacher, "How can we be happy in a world of impermanence where we are unable to protect our loved ones from illness and evil?" The teacher raised his glass and said, "Look at this. This glass does a wonderful job of holding water. It shimmers in the sunlight. When I tap it, it sings. But one day it will be blown off the shelf by a gust of wind, or my elbow will knock it off the table. If you really think about it, this glass is already broken. That is why I enjoy it so immensely now."[92]

The Dying Process

Many Buddhist texts emphasize the imminence of death and the importance of preparing for it. The precise instructions of the *Tibetan Book of the Dead* and its accompanying commentaries—familiar to many Westerners—offer guidance on traversing the land of death. They help us to recognize the signposts along the way, so that we understand how to surrender to the process instead of resisting it out of ignorance and fear.

We are born alone and we die alone. In the Tibet of old, people who were dying were often left alone in their last moments, so they would not be distracted by the sadness and pain of their loved ones. The unmasking of the personality, the releasing of *I*, and the dissolving of the elements of which the body is composed were allowed to happen smoothly, without interruption; the undisguised mind left the body and merged with the light unhindered.

Tibetan Buddhist teachings encourage practitioners to take interest in the dying process while they are still in good health, so they can be of help to others who are dying and simultaneously prepare for the moment when they too will die. A dying person needs to hear the truth in a language he can understand, preferably from someone with whom he has a harmonious or spiritual relationship.

The truth is, he is about to die. The elements of which he is composed are dissolving. A Buddhist practitioner needs to hear: "You are separating from the body. Your senses will fade, you will lose your ability to speak, see, and think. Remember what you have learned about this process: Soon you will enter the bardo of dying. Don't be afraid of what you encounter. Go to the light."

According to the *Tibetan Book of the Dead*, as death approaches, the senses are gradually extinguished. Food loses its flavor and is unappealing, appetite disappears, voices grow fainter, eyesight fails, speech becomes difficult, and thinking grows haphazard. Physical strength diminishes, bodily functions fail and inhibitions vanish.

The process resembles that of an onion being peeled, layer by layer, until nothing remains. During this transitional period, as the dying person gradually relinquishes control, consciousness moves to the foreground and ultimately becomes almost tangible.

The person who is dying feels the vibrations of each movement and every sound. Hallucination may occur. His entire life may flash before his eyes. If he is conscious, he may battle with regret, hatred, or fear. Emotions consume his energy until resistance yields, and he is ready to depart. Pain—like a cloud that briefly covers the sun and then floats on—may alternate with rapture. Openness dawns.

Just before death, there is a fleeting moment of openness, a bardo in which the world of *I* dissipates. The energy on which *I* has fed for a lifetime is released. Once the tension of ego is out of the way, what remains is the light of pure awareness, open and clear. In order to experience this light of pure awareness in the moment just before our own death, we need to train the mind to become familiar with this openness now. During the dying process we may then understand that life was but a dream, and that death is not the end, but a transition.

At the deathbed, a bond forms between caregivers and the dying that lasts beyond death. The deceased's consciousness may remain near for a long time. He continues to live in the minds and hearts of those who shared his last moments, with an intensity rarely found in ordinary relationships. When this intense intimacy begins to fade, survivors often yearn for it.

Purifying the Mind at the Time of Death

How can we prepare for the certainty of death? What will help us when that time approaches? One thing is certain: What preoccupies us now will then lose its meaning. Popularity, mundane knowledge, material wealth, power, and status will provide no guidance or solace during the last moments.

We cannot predict how our lives will end. We may die young or old, in illness or in good health, after completing our life projects or with unfinished business. Death rarely comes at a convenient time. We may be comatose or numb from painkillers. If we are fortunate, we will die consciously and at peace. In Tibet, there are numerous accounts of highly developed people who, as death approached, sat up straight and made the transition in a meditative posture.

It is possible to purify the mind in the face of death, provided consciousness is sufficiently clear and strong. Since no one can predict when death will strike, it is important to prepare now, to be ready when our time comes. In order to die in peace, we need to come to terms with the past.

Once we truly recognize our regrets and past mistakes, we have the opportunity to set them straight. This dedicated process of purification can take place in the mind and heart, through prayer and meditation. Mantra can play an invaluable role. Tibetan Buddhists specifically say that the mantras

Om Ah Hum and *Om Mani Padme Hum* transform residual emotions in the body and harmonize the energies of body and mind, so the process of dying can take place peacefully.

> *Cut all bonds with this life.*
> *When death presents itself,*
> *pray to the three jewels,*
> *The Buddha, Dharma, and Sangha,*
> *because there is your only hope—*
> *Call on the Lama on the dangerous*
> *pathways of the bardo.*
> *Confess all negative deeds of this life*
> *and beg to attain enlightenment*
> *immediately after death.*[93]

FORGIVENESS

"Virtuous action brings happiness, action that is not virtuous brings sorrow." That is a Buddhist axiom. Purification of the mind takes place when we honestly confront the damage we have done in our lives—the hurts we have inflicted on others and on ourselves—and ask for forgiveness. When those concerned are dead or otherwise out of reach, it may seem impossible to ask for their forgiveness. But according to the Buddhist teachings, the mind is the vessel for forgiveness. It is in our own minds that we need to confess our mistakes and ask the Buddhas to forgive all the suffering we have caused, either knowingly or unknowingly.

If we feel we have been wronged, it is likely that we need to work through our resistance to being forgiving: "I did nothing wrong," or "What he did is much worse!" or "Let him make the first move." Perhaps we doggedly look for explanations: "If I could understand why he harmed me, maybe then I could forgive him." The temptation to rationalize is strong: "He's always been stingy," or "Her work is really stressful," or "He never learned how to love others." Looking for reasons in this way—and always finding some—may seem fair-minded and compassionate, but it can also support us in blaming and finding fault with those whom we are unwilling to forgive. On a subtle level we are justifying our decision to maintain distance and separation between them and ourselves.

Even when the desire to set things right is strong, we may simply not know where to begin. Lacking a clear course of action, we may wish for an opportunity to present itself: "If only there was an emergency I wouldn't hesitate to help him," or, "If she were terminally ill, I would take care of her." Or, "If war broke out now, we would instantly be on the same side." We may be convinced that things would change if we could only discuss the issues or start with a clean slate. But all these "ifs" are simply ways of putting off opening our hearts to a deeper truth. As long as we cling to our ordinary understanding, emotions cover over our heart and make it impenetrable. Forgiving is letting go of our version of the truth.

Forgiveness usually takes both time and patience. A first step could be to forget. Although we may initially feel that in giving up our grievances we would betray

273

ourselves, deeper wisdom shows that holding on to our way of seeing things is the cause of our pain.

Forgetting is easier when we focus on the present. By being present, a door opens to appreciation and enjoyment of life. Eventually, appreciation for life warms the heart, melting the icecaps of resentment and hatred.

Self-pity is the breeding ground for resentment, while finding fault in others keeps bitterness alive. Forgiveness is not a display of magnanimity, but the willingness to exonerate small-mindedness.

Forgiveness is wedded to deep regret about what happened. Years after my mother died, I wished from the bottom of my heart that events had turned out differently. The situation could have unfolded differently if I had acted differently, and I now know that I relinquished responsibility. To be able to forgive those who hurt me because they forgot to let me know my mother was dying, I had to be willing to learn. Recognizing that I too had something to set right created space for forgiveness to unfold. Forgiving benefited both me and the others involved, whether they were consciously aware of it or not. At a subtle level, forgiveness permeates body and soul and expands out into space. It is never too late to forgive or be forgiven.

Forgive me for the harm that I have done
knowingly or unknowingly.
I forgive everybody.
I forgive myself.

17

What Is Born Will Die

When I learned that my mother had passed away, I booked the first flight to the Netherlands. KLM had special rates for such urgent family situations. I experienced the trip in a haze, as if under a mild anesthetic, staring through the small window of the plane into the dark night and waiting for dawn. When it finally came, it painted the horizon a deep, electric red. Inside, I felt increasingly cold.

In my father's apartment in The Hague, my wife, son, and I wriggled our way through the narrow entrance hall. My brother greeted me by whispering, "You do the talking at the cremation. But don't make it too religious." Otherwise, there was not much to discuss, and the three of us soon departed for the nursing home. Once there, we stood in a cool marble hall and waited until the doors swung open. We entered a moderately lit room with drawn curtains. The coffin stood between two large electric torches.

I approached the casket cautiously, anxious about how she would appear. At the foot of the open box, I paused. The face before me, surrounded by a halo of gray hair, seemed relaxed and peaceful. Her hands were folded on her chest. I had expected to find an uninhabited body, like an empty cocoon, but she looked startlingly familiar. It would not have surprised me if she had opened her eyes and said, "My, how nice that you're here."

I gently bent to kiss her cold, hard forehead. When I was little, she taught me how butterflies and angels kiss. The lightest, most tender touch of the lips to cheek or forehead is a visiting butterfly, while angels kiss by fluttering their eyelashes against one another. This time, my kiss was more like a stamp or a seal confirming, "It's me."

In Buddhist teachings, being with the dead is an important practice. I tried to remember what I had been taught about this experience and briefly rested my gaze on her skull, a traditional practice for familiarizing oneself with impermanence. While I wondered about the next step, my twelve-year-old son took the lead. He began circumambulating the body clockwise. On the walk over he had picked little flowers, and now he laid these on her as he circled, first on her head, then her heart, then her limbs and torso, until finally her entire body was covered with flowers. All three of us then began walking slowly around the coffin while softly chanting the mantra *Om Mani Padme Hum.*

Afterwards, we sat next to the body in silence. Was she really dead or was this merely a dream? Eventually some gentlemen dressed in black noiselessly entered the room. With velvet gestures, they indicated that the visit had ended. It was time for the coffin to be returned to the freezer. It was a heart-wrenching moment, as if they were taking her away alive.

All the arrangements had been taken care of. My mother had never liked the idea of her body being food for worms and ants, and she had decided long ago that she wanted to be cremated. My father had discussed all the details with the undertaker and had sent the obituary announcement to the newspapers. For the funeral procession, he had ordered three black limousines. They carried us first to the nursing home, where we picked her up for her last trip. It was a wintry morning, and the pavement was covered with a thin film of frost. On the way to the crematory, the procession came to a halt in front of the apartment building where my mother once lived with my father, for a few minutes of silent salute.

In the vestibule of the funeral home, other family members and friends had gathered. As the sanctuary doors opened, we yielded for the exiting party from the previous service, avoiding eye contact with the anonymous mourners. A few minutes later, we entered the auditorium. Surrounded by an ocean of flowers, the casket stood on a podium at the far end of the room. On it rested only my father's wreath of flowers; the children's and grandchildren's tributes were placed beside the coffin on the floor.

When everyone had taken their seats, the room grew silent. In his dark suit, my father seemed like a taciturn master of ceremonies. He was now the sole representative of my parents' former union. Standing upright, his chin lifted proudly, he began to speak. "She has suffered so much—" Then it was my turn. "We do not say farewell." In my hands I held a small azalea tree with four branches, full of flowers. "My mother was the trunk from which four children sprouted, each in turn producing new lives. Through us, and through whoever comes after us, she continues to live."

The day before the ceremony, I had been asked casually about her favorite music; could I suggest a few pieces? The hymns I offered were probably too long, for the music was abbreviated and played hastily, jumping abruptly from a section of "Alle Menschen werden Brüder" into "Jesu, Joy of Men's Desiring."

To the melody of the "Adagio" of Albinoni, the coffin was lowered beneath the floor, abruptly. The lack of preparation for this moment shocked us. It was difficult not to imagine a sinister underworld in the catacombs of the building where workers lounged on caskets, talking, laughing, and smoking cigarettes, surrounded by mounting piles of coffins. Then the ceremony was over. We were ushered past another group of waiting mourners, eyes cast down, into a reception area where coffee and cake were served.

The rushed and skimpy ceremony left us feeling like powerless bystanders. The opportunity to fully participate in the final rite had been denied to us; we were spectators in a ceremony performed by strangers. In many cultures, the family is actively involved in rituals of cremation or burial that allow mourners to express their grief together, transforming heartache into appreciation. Activities such as fabricating paper flowers or birds, chanting mantras, reciting blessings, decorating the coffin, or holding vigil give family members an opportunity to integrate their feelings of grief. Forming a circle around my mother's casket or simply singing the hymns together would have fostered intimacy and sharing among our family and friends.

In the years that followed, I often wondered what had happened to her ashes. Overcome with grief, I had not thought of asking. But soon after the burial, I began missing a headstone to bring flowers to, or a special place to sit and imagine being close to her. All that remained was a radiant portrait on my father's dresser, for years accompanied by a fresh bouquet of flowers.

THE TIBETAN BOOK OF THE DEAD

Where there is life there is hope. No matter how bleak my mother's situation was, while she was still alive there had always been the possibility of a simple, lucid chat or a cup of coffee together; we could even hope for unexpected improvement in her condition or the discovery of a magical remedy. Miracles do happen, after all. Yet suddenly it was definite: She was dead. All hope was wiped out.

"Don't make a fuss about it," a Tibetan lama might say after someone has died. "Stillness and silent prayer are supportive and helpful, but clinging will only confuse a person who is deceased. Anyway, death is not earth-shattering."

What is born will die, what arises will pass away, what is united will separate. These are the truths of life. What do we gain by fighting these truths? And how does our struggle against them help the deceased?

In the West, we are familiar with the concept of life after death; we find comfort in the thought that the unbearable suffering of those who have died has ended and they are at peace. We hope they go to heaven. According to Buddhist teachings on reincarnation suffering does not end with death. The *Tibetan Book of the Dead* describes how after death, the winds of the past propel us into space. The Enlightened Ones find peace everywhere, in all bardos, but the ordinary mind is impelled on and on, into rebirth after rebirth. It will find rest only after karma has been exhausted and suffering has come to an end.

The Tibetan title of the *Tibetan Book of the Dead* is *Bar-do'i thos-grol*, meaning *Liberation in the Bardo through Hearing*. The text is one of the *terma* or hidden treasure texts that were concealed by the great Lama Padmasambhava until the time was right for them to be revealed. Composed in the eighth century by Padmasambhava and written down by his disciple Yeshe Tsogyal, this teaching was discovered in the fourteenth century by Karma Lingpa, a lama from the Nyingma school of Tibetan Buddhism.

The text is a guide during the process of dying and the period immediately after death, one of a series of instructions on six gateways to liberation—through wearing, seeing, remembering, tasting, and touching. The *Tibetan Book of the Dead* belongs to the category of liberation through hearing. During the bardo after death, consciousness functions differently than when it was connected to the body, and can be liberated simply by listening to the recitation of the words of the text. Under the right circumstances, liberation can occur without preparation, without exercises, and even without understanding the meaning of the words. This is possible because the text speaks directly to pure awareness, without interference from *I*.

The book is intended to be read aloud during three consecutive phases: the bardo of approaching death, the bardo immediately after death, and the bardo of the forty-nine days following death. In each of these three phases, the deceased needs to be reminded of the Dharma or truth. In addition, there are specific teachings for each bardo.[94] Recitation of the text allows these teachings to penetrate the mind of the dying or deceased, providing the guidance needed to prevent a return to unending rounds of birth and death.

In the first bardo, the bardo of approaching death, the first opportunity for liberation occurs. This opportunity may last only a fleeting moment. The body has not stopped functioning entirely, but the mind is already becoming detached from it. Although the dying person may sense the presence of family members close by, his consciousness can no longer communicate with them.

Disconnected from the body, the consciousness is in unknown territory, vulnerable to strange and frightening phenomena, yet unable to cry out for help. At this time, the dying person urgently needs reassurance and support. Those who remain behind can help by postponing their grief and continuing to communicate with the dying person. Reading the text of the *Tibetan Book of the Dead* aloud can steady the dying person, help him to relate to the unfamiliar surroundings and prepare him for entering the stages of the bardo.

In the bardo of approaching death, it is tempting for the consciousness to be attracted to a familiar path. This attraction is the result of karma. The patterns we have followed all our lives exert a magnetic force, threatening to pull us back into their field once again. In the chaos and uncertainty that characterize the bardo, familiar patterns seem to provide a soft and seductive reference point, associated with pleasure and safety.

Yet there is only one beneficial course: rejecting the inviting patterns of grasping, aversion, and delusion and choosing the path of light. The light is glaring, even blinding in its intensity. If the dying person knows this is the right path and deliberately chooses the direction of intense light, withstanding the seductive power of karma, he is liberated from his karma and can perceive life as a temporary illusion. The mind, no longer weighed down by the body, becomes light and open. If this chance for liberation is missed, a second bardo will appear.

In the second bardo, immediately after death, the deceased also needs advice and support. The *Tibetan Book of the Dead* describes this bardo as characterized by chaos and cacophony, so there is a great risk of losing the way. It is important not to be frightened by the appearances in this second bardo, whether peaceful or wrathful. They are simply reflections of mind, echoes of past actions, good and bad, that accompany the mind like shadows after death. The deceased must resist being blown off course by the winds of karma, the powerful currents of unresolved actions and emotional patterns of the past. We are advised to let the mind be like a mirror, recognizing that everything is just a projection of mind. If this succeeds, we are liberated.

If liberation does not occur in the first two bardos, there is still a chance to be freed in the third bardo. The mind roams around for as long as forty-nine days or until the moment of rebirth. Here too, karma is almost irresistible. In order to prevent rebirth, or—if this is impossible—at least to choose a fortunate rebirth, we desperately need guidance. Otherwise, the momentum of karma and emotions will set the wheel of life in motion once more.

In the third bardo, the deceased is encouraged to keep the opening to rebirth closed, or if that is impossible, to decide wisely the rebirth to come. In the open space after death, it is easier than during life to disconnect from old patterns and choose a better existence. A positive choice, motivated by the wish to benefit sentient beings, will release the deceased from the effects of past karma. It is possible to achieve a good rebirth by visualizing the Buddha or a lama while passing into a new life. If this is done, the one newly born receives the transmission of their auspicious qualities and will embody them in life.

Like the other bardos, the bardo of this life—the period of time between the two fixed points of birth and death—is a time of great uncertainty, since we do not know how long it will last. The *Tibetan Book of the Dead* offers guidance for this bardo as well. During the bardo of this life, we must abandon the attempt to find certainty in impermanence. The realization that all appearances are temporary and unstable will relax our grasping. What matters is suffusing consciousness and body with light. The capricious contents of thoughts and images are unreal. Seeing this, we are already free.

We can bring our destructive patterns to a halt by choosing to make our lives meaningful and fruitful. However, according to the advice of the *Tibetan Book of the Dead,* we must realize that even if our circumstances change and we adopt an entirely new life, residues of the past will continue to accompany us until karma and emotions lose their power. Karma and emotions last as long as we accept their reality. Until we relinquish attachment to the patterns that drive them, we will continue encountering the same obstacles.

THE ADVANTAGE OF SUFFERING

Suffering is the result of karma, so pain is a reflection of our past behavior. By perpetually duplicating old patterns, we bring about suffering for others and ourselves. This is the iron grip of karma, a vicious cycle from which it seems almost impossible to escape. Unless circumstances inspire or drive us to change, mind and consciousness will stay the same or become more firmly entrenched in negativity and harmful patterns. The momentum of negative karma tends to increase, and, as time passes, the patterns that become established grow harder and harder to change.

Suffering offers a unique opportunity to reconcile with the past and break this momentum. Recognizing how our suffering is connected to the past is the first step in a process of genuine transformation. If we look carefully, we observe how strongly our actions today are influenced by what has happened before. The cumulative energy of all past behavior, our own as well as that of others towards us, no matter how long ago, affects all we understand, think, and do today. For example, the scolding parent may live on in our hidden craving for approval. Even if we do receive appreciation now, contentment eludes us as long as the seed of earlier hurt remains buried deep inside.

How can we reconcile ourselves with the past and release the stored pain that leads to more suffering? At first the restlessness, dissatisfaction, and pain we feel may tempt us to use our willpower to bring a particular instance of suffering to an end. We may try eradicating impatience by suppressing it, but the impatient power has been established over a long time, and will not simply be willed away. Emphasizing the wish to suppress, we are probably reinforcing other negative patterns, such as "I am good for nothing" or "Nobody will love me if I do not succeed." While it is possible to create positive karma in this way, there is also the danger of adding negative karma simultaneously. Once emotions are raging, it is wisest to leave them alone, not engaging in a battle in which we would rely on patterns. Relaxing and refraining from action are more effective.

Even better, we can actively create positive karma. Shifting consciousness in this way requires our full intelligence. We need to recognize what our harmful patterns are and use our inner resources for positive change. Every negative emotion has a positive counterpart, which can function both as an antidote to further suffering and as a means to create what is wholesome. That is a method for generating positive karma. Recognizing that we are hurt by lack of appreciation, for example, we can develop self-respect and acknowledge more fully the value of our lives. The result will be that we are able to relate to others with an open mind, without fear of rejection. Cultivating positive responses in this way neutralizes negative karma and may even dissolve it.

There are many other ways to create positive karma by working with old patterns. We can treat an emotion as a guardian or a spiritual friend, instead of a foe. When criticism causes us to shy away, the resulting contraction in the body can be like an alarm going off. The feeling of accumulating tension puts us on alert, giving a warning that we are heading in the wrong direction. It signals us to take care of ourselves and to look for ground in ourselves, especially in the heart and naval centers. The releasing energy will make us gentler and enable us to be present, sensitive to the situation. Old patterns lose their hold and new ways of participation become possible.

In all my future births,
may I never again have to experience
the maturation of karma and emotionality,
or the suffering that is their result.

May they ripen upon my mind and body
in this birth.
May I never again experience negativities
that will mature later in this lifetime:
May they ripen this year.
May I bring to fruition in this month
what would otherwise ripen this year;
May I ripen today
what would otherwise ripen this month.
May I take on this instant
what would otherwise ripen sometime today.[95]

NOTHING IS IRREVOCABLY FIXED

My mother is gone, but traces of her remain. Even though her physical body no longer exists, each of her actions and thoughts have left an imprint in space and time that lingers like a secret code, testifying to the person she was. The present is filled with the past.

After my mother's death, I read the *Tibetan Book of the Dead* out loud, for forty-nine days, night after night. I secluded myself with the book in a small meditation room where a large electric prayer wheel hummed softly. The only light was that of a candle burning day and night. I painstakingly heeded the instructions in the text, out of respect sitting as straight as I could. Sometimes my mother seemed very close, at other times far away, and on occasion I could not find her at all. Finally, the moment came when I felt she no longer looked back. It seemed she had found her way.

287

In the period shortly after her death, I did not give in to my grief, self-pity, and remorse; those had to wait. I focused my mind on her as though she were making a long trip without either a map or a compass. My mind became centered on the thought that *she must go toward the light.* I encouraged her to resist impulses toward grasping, aversion, and blindness, ingrained tendencies that would push her to choose a hasty rebirth. Whenever I had a moment, I talked with her, read to her, or chanted mantras. I did everything I could think of to wish her a *bon voyage.* This wish gradually became a prayer.

No matter how prepared we are, death always takes us by surprise—suddenly a loved one is gone. A person of prime importance in our lives, someone who filled the entire room with her presence, disappears. Looking away for the briefest moment, we turn back, expecting to find her the same as always—but she is gone for good. We are left alone with the unexpressed words we still wanted to say, or the things we always meant to do. There is a tear in reality, a wrinkle in time.

Lingering memories of a loved one, sweet or painful, exert a powerful influence. We seem to live two different lives: one rooted in the past and another in the present. We are often absent-minded, lost in thought. A subtle sense of dissatisfaction preoccupies us internally. Since the past has not been entirely processed, we cannot live fully in the present. Unsettling memories and residues of hurt, fear, or sadness lodge in our bodies and become twisted into painful knots in our energy system. We try to ignore and suppress the tension they cause, concealing its existence even to ourselves. As hidden emotions continue to wreak havoc in our lives, the knots tighten and harden. Until the moment when we dare to look at the pain and feel the layers of stored energy, much of our lives will be shaped by undigested experiences.

Exploring memories takes time, but if we want to grow and thrive, we must face them. The approach itself does not matter so much. Perhaps we choose a psychological approach that focuses on "processing emotions," or a spiritual approach that focuses on "cleansing" and "forgiving." Both approaches aim to untangle emotional knots, and both support us in relaxing, loosening, and unraveling them. It takes courage to finally face a painful memory, but if we can be present with the pain and go through the feelings we have tried to avoid for so long, the tension releases and disappears.

Healing occurs when old, ignored experiences open to awareness, and the energy held within them begins to flow. A moment of remorse that could not be fully admitted at the time can now be relived and felt through and through. Forgiveness to someone who once did us wrong will release us from our isolated position. Any painful event can be positively redirected: In our imaginations we do what we once failed to do. Memory is not etched in stone: Nothing is irrevocably fixed. As a result of the events surrounding my mother's death, old unacknowledged feelings from childhood had abruptly come to the surface. For me, the hurt of the little boy who felt left out and the agony of rejection were like a wake up call. Inspired by the teachings to embrace the energy of this pain, I creatively began to reshape it.

I close my eyes and let my imagination roam free. My mother lies in semi-darkness on a high, narrow bed. She is on her back, her head resting on a big white pillow. Her eyes are closed. My father is standing beside her.

She seems to lie in state, but once in a while she still takes a breath. My three brothers are also in the room, even the one who died several years before my mother. I am next to her bed. No one moves. We are her witnesses, standing by in her last scene. Yet she is also alone. Her mind appears to hesitate.

She breathes one more time. Though her eyes are closed, it is as if she looks at us. "There you are," she seems to say. Leaning closer, I whisper, "We are all here." "Do you know," she says in a down-to-earth manner, "I want to get out." She is no longer the tiny scared bird of her last years. "Yes, it is over now," she continues. She does not long for the past; she is ready for whatever awaits her. "Dearest Mother," I begin, but she does not hear me. She is already on her way.

18

Farewell to *I*

During increasingly rare visits to my home country, I sometimes toured my favorite childhood places, beginning with a drive along the street where I grew up. In a single glance, I would take in our house with the garden, the brook and the little bridge across it. Then I would visit my old elementary school with the tiled schoolyard, and next, my high school, hidden among the trees. On one such occasion, I wandered through a neighborhood where I used to go skating on frozen tennis courts in winter, ending up in a park belonging to a small castle. In front of the castle was a pond surrounded by tall beech trees. White spots glistened in the moss below the trees. Looking closer, I saw lilies of the valley.

My mother's bridal bouquet was made of lilies of the valley. It was her favorite flower, and she was fond of its sweet perfume. Each stem is like a miniature bouquet, with green leaves enveloping a delicate white nosegay. I bent over and touched the flowers gently, careful not to breathe in their perfume. "This scent is for you," I said aloud. This simple gift of beauty and fragrance made me feel there was something I could do for her, no matter how small.

In my imagination, I took her arm, and we went for a walk. It seemed that nature had rarely been as expressive, and we had eyes for the smallest details: ants marching along their trail, a blackbird stamping its feet to pull a worm from the earth, a small troop of young ducks who ran ahead of us, quacking. They reminded me of the ducklings in our brook, who would climb up the bank as soon as they were strong enough and take over our garden. After a while, they would start begging for bread, and soon they would be eating out of my mother's hand.

In the following days I discovered many more moments we could share in my imagination. Together we listened to Beethoven's violin concerto, one of my mother's favorite pieces. My brothers had always claimed it was excessively romantic, but she and I enjoyed it. She was present when I brought my son to bed at night and chatted about the events of the day. Gradually, these shared moments made her presence an addition to my daily activities, like an extra hand on the piano. My experience deepened, and I felt happier than I had since her death. My relationship with my mother had found a new pathway; I had discovered a way to be grateful, with her, for life. The idea that others can benefit from whatever we do began to take root.

First, in the morning, when you are wide-awake,
develop your intention, thinking: "May all sentient
beings awaken from ignorance!"
When you go out of bed, think: "May all sentient
beings achieve the body of Buddha!"

*As you dress, think: "May all sentient beings
wear the clothing of self-respect and decorum!"
While fastening your belt, think: "May all sentient
beings be tied to the root of goodness!"
When you sit down, think: "May all sentient beings
attain the Vajra Seat!"
When you enter a house, think: May all sentient
beings enter the city of liberation!
When you sleep, think: "May all sentient beings
attain the Dharmakaya of the Buddhas!"*[96]

When concluding a period or project, even at the end
of life, it is wholesome to dedicate the accumulated
merit—positive karma—to a person or cause. Giving to
others the goodness acquired through our action helps
preserve the merit, which otherwise may become
smothered by the grasping of *I*. Since the fate of one
individual is connected to that of all others, independent
of time and place, the released energy can benefit all, even
when the intended beneficiary is deceased or far away. To
offer the benefits of actions most widely, Buddhists may
choose to say: "May the positive energy of this action
benefit all sentient beings."

The Six Paramitas

When the Buddha was asked how to practice the path of
enlightenment in daily life, he answered that the essence
of that practice should be a *paramita*. The word paramita
refers to a practice that helps us to traverse from the world

of suffering to enlightenment-mind; it means, "gone over to the other shore."

The vehicle of the paramitas focuses mind and body—the two inner resources that are the foundation of human development—on attitudes and actions that lead us from the banks of emotionality and negativity to the shores of enlightenment. The active power of the paramitas awakens full intelligence and positive, infinite feelings. If we wholeheartedly practice at least one paramita, karma and emotionality are transformed into goodness.

Buddhist teachings recognize thousands of paramitas[97], six of which are fundamental: generosity, discipline, patience, effort, concentration, and wisdom. The training of those whose life's work is geared towards helping others primarily consists of practicing these six paramitas. The first five culminate in the sixth paramita, which in turn informs the activity of the first five. The Sanskrit word for this wisdom is *prajnaparamita,* enlightened knowledge, known as "the mother of all Buddhas." Such wisdom reveals the perfect inner qualities of a Buddha.

Ordinary consciousness operates according to a fixed set of patterns, receiving and guiding thoughts and impressions in ways that initiate a particular behavior. When we practice a paramita, a different kind of activity is added to the range of possibilities of the thinking mind. Set patterns yield to the new element and loosen their tight grip.

By constantly redirecting consciousness toward a paramita, we create space for wider perspectives and new energy. Inner tendencies that once manifested as emotionality and blocked energy are released, making way for creative, positive actions that bring out the best in us. Ordinary mind and enlightenment-mind begin to intermingle, promoting integration. We say farewell to old patterns and what we know, for we realize our current knowledge is no longer sufficient. Little by little, the old *I* is left behind.

Through the practice of a paramita, we create positive karma and accumulate merit. Practicing the paramitas opens the mind to the energy of enlightenment. Just as making regular deposits in the bank accumulates wealth, so consciously directing the mind toward a paramita accumulates lightness of being. Gradually we grow attuned to enlightenment. Ultimately, we realize there is no difference between ordinary mind and enlightened awareness. The paramitas are activities based on this non-duality, which finds expression in conduct that is generous, disciplined, patient, vigorous, concentrated, and wise.

The antidote to regret, remorse, and resentment is the practice of the paramitas. When our mind, energy, and heart wholeheartedly engage in the six paramitas, we will live without regret.

Through generosity, enjoyment is attained,
and through discipline, happiness,
through patience, beauty, and
through diligence, splendor,

295

through concentration, peace of mind, and through
intelligence you reach freedom.[98]

Although the six paramitas together form a whole, each one contains all of the others. After all, what are generosity, discipline, patience, meditative concentration, and wisdom without effort? And what would effort be without being generous, having a discipline, developing patience, learning to concentrate, and understanding to what goal we are applying effort? Without wisdom, effort may only create confusion. As each paramita encompasses all of the others, practice of the paramitas can begin with any of the six. All culminate in wisdom and compassion.

First Paramita: Generosity
The paramita of generosity helps us leave grasping and stinginess behind and reach the other shore, where we fully participate in life with unbridled energy. All living things participate in both giving and receiving. In nature we see spontaneous cycles of giving and receiving that make no distinctions among giver, recipient, and gift. Space provides a home to all manifestations, good or bad. The sun gives warmth without holding back. The breath is totally life supporting. A flower is willing to receive whatever is being offered—sunlight, water, and other nutrients—and in turn offers beauty, fragrance, and even medicinal powers.

Nature does not resist, hoard, or pass judgments; a plant has no aversion or laziness. It cannot help but do its best to function optimally under any circumstance, fully investing its energy in growing and flourishing. Only human beings can choose to hold back energy or let it flow, to resist or participate. The balance we choose between giving and receiving determines our physical, emotional, mental, and spiritual well-being.

According to the Buddha's teachings, humans were once beings of light. The earth was covered by nectar; there was plenty for all to eat and no such thing as hunger existed. In time, the nectar disappeared, and rice began to grow spontaneously and continuously. But when some began to gather and hoard the harvest for themselves, the rice stopped growing of itself, and beings found it necessary to work the land. Some took more and more for themselves, and hoarding and quarreling increased. Selfishness and greed came into being, and the vices of avarice, jealousy, and envy were born.[99]

Holding on to a gift obstructs the circulation of energy and makes consciousness function narrowly. Saving energy for later or holding back because we fear having too little for ourselves makes it harder to receive. We feel closed off; there is no room for anything new. Just as stagnant drinking water becomes a breeding ground for disease, so blockages in our energy flow lead to suffering. Physical ailments, emotions, obstacles, and spiritual uncertainty take their toll. Participating fully, without reservations restores balance and brings us back into harmony with others and ourselves.

True generosity, like that of the sun, does not judge, keep track, or send bills; it gives without self-interest or hidden agendas, expecting nothing in return. Inspired by such selfless generosity, we may discover that our own apparent open-handedness often has impure aspects. Perhaps we secretly expect something in return, a sign of appreciation or respect. When such recognition does not come, we feel indignant. No wonder others intuitively sense that something is amiss with our seemingly selfless gestures.

Driven by the motto, "And what about me?" our self-interest keeps us holding back. Even in the act of giving, we furtively calculate if there will be enough left over for us. We hope the recipient will notice our generosity, realizing the extent to which we have loosened our purse strings. As tightfisted as we are with money, time, and knowledge, with love we are usually even more stingy; it seems too much to freely give love. Yet without genuine interest, affection, and love we give nothing at all.

Generosity is rooted in concern and care for others and ourselves. A good starting point for the practice of generosity is to ask, "What can I offer?" To help refine our understanding of the true needs of others and thus develop a solid basis for generosity, we can practice mindfulness. Giving attention to what is happening in each moment awakens body, mind, and senses, and increases our sensitivity to others' needs as well as our own. Our feelings of caring grow stronger, and we are able to give more. The more we give, the more we receive. We find that giving deepens our caring and infuses it with joy.

One offering that is always within our power to give is the gift of our presence. Every human being longs for presence. As a child, we want our parents to be present;

partners expect one another to be available and attentive; we hope our friends will be here for us. When we are dying, presence is all that matters. The gift of presence is always available. The paramita of generosity offers joy to the giver as well as the recipient, for giving is like receiving a gift.

Second Paramita: Discipline

> *All unfathomable fear and sorrow*
> *arise from the mind.*
> *Such has been taught*
> *by the Speaker of Truth.*[100]

The paramita of discipline focuses on moral conduct. It transforms bad habits and cultivates instead the positive attitudes and actions that bring us to the shore of perfect well-being. Perfecting discipline requires refining our motivation towards moral conduct and suiting our actions to our words and ideals. Through the discipline this requires, we can mold our own lives, for moral conduct protects body and mind from self-defeating patterns, and ensures that our endeavors bear fruit. We submit to its rule not because we have to, but because we choose to do so. As disciples of our own well-being, we gain inner freedom.

For many people, the word "discipline" carries a negative connotation associated with harsh disciplinary measures, order, and regimentation. We expect to be forced to do something we do not really want to do. Healthy discipline, however, has a light, unforced quality that is based on understanding and caring. Moral conduct is a matter of doing what is beneficial and abstaining from what is harmful. If negative patterns make us veer off course, our hand remains steady at the helm, ready to guide us back to our chosen path.

Discipline helps us to face our worst tendencies with gentleness, and to persevere no matter what our circumstances or feelings. With the help of discipline, we live without extremes, keeping to the middle way.

If we could change our behavior by merely repeating a positive thought or through a simple assertion of will, we would have no need for discipline. But there are far too many factors contributing to our situation for this to be the case. Constructive change is the result of a learning process. It calls for participation, understanding, and perseverance; it takes time.

When we realize that our behavior determines our happiness and feel passionate about the results of our actions, we turn to discipline with relief and gratitude. We want to make the most of our talents and accomplish something of value.

How can we do this without discipline? Discipline helps us to overcome inner obstacles, and lessen the power of our negative emotional patterns. In time, discipline becomes our honored friend and companion, and the key to our success. We find joy in cherishing both our accomplishments and those of others.

Third Paramita: Patience

If there is a remedy,
why be sad?
If no remedy exists,
why be unhappy?[101]

The paramita of patience helps us to leave small-mindedness, short temper, and anger behind and cross to the other shore of perfect harmony and acceptance. Practicing patience is a ripening process: We learn to stay constant in the knowledge that our effort and discipline will eventually bear fruit. Patience allows time, space, and knowledge to unfold to the fullest, supporting the growth of confidence.

Patience is the capacity to see clearly the way things are, endure setbacks courageously, and persevere skillfully in attaining our purpose. This does not mean suppressing our feelings or ignoring our insights, nor does it mean postponing, denying, or stifling anything. Patience helps us to remain calm when we are hurt. We feel the pain, but do not protest, not even inwardly.

In the space provided by patience, emotions dissolve. As the saying goes, a handful of salt that would make a glass of water undrinkable goes unnoticed when thrown into a river.[102] We abide in patience, allowing old patterns to play themselves out, knowing that suffering results from karma. When we are accepting in the face of suffering and go through it, no new karma will be created.

Patience softens the urge to dominate. It entails accepting a situation as it is with equanimity, not simply once, but over and over again. The activity of patience requires intelligence and understanding; it does not mean waiting, but always being prepared and willing to act when the opportunity arises to benefit others. Patience is not simply the result of putting things in perspective; it is active tolerance. Patiently we bear suffering, because we know the law of karma is at work.

Impatience is the response of a small, fearful heart. We are startled when something blocks our way and react with irritation. Impatience can transform even the most calm, good-natured person into an unpredictable angry monster willing to harm both self and others. In a flash, one angry outburst can destroy all the good that has been established over a long time, obliterating friendship, trust, and love.

Impatience shows us where we need to develop patience. The antidote for impatience is self-control, which may imply "taking time out." As soon as we feel impatience arise, we can stop and allow time and space for the heart to calm down. We can step back and consciously observe what is happening inside us, telling ourselves, "Let's see," or better still, "Relax." These attitudes create opportunities for us to investigate the entire situation, and to discern whether it is time for action or whether it is better to wait. If something needs improvement, patience will show us the right time.

By embracing the larger perspective afforded by patience, we transform the smaller view that insists on having things its own way. Fresh perspectives and new ideas emerge, as we become receptive to the opportunities time presents us. We see that there is a right time for everything. Resting in patience, going neither too fast nor too slow, persevering and never giving up, we find the pace and timing that lead to fruition.

Fourth Paramita: Effort

Enlightenment abides in effort:
Just as without movement there is no wind,
enlightenment does not appear without effort.[103]

The paramita of effort helps us to leave laziness and bad habits behind and reach the shore of perfect strength and capability, where struggle is no longer necessary. We simply do what needs to be done. Apart from normal physical tiredness, we no longer feel drained, because our energy is inexhaustible. While working and living we constantly replenish ourselves.

We have all succumbed to a lazy mind that ignores the continual turning of the wheel of life, choosing to forget about the ever-present possibility of death. Laziness is crafty and employs its own logic: "There's plenty of time to do it tomorrow, and no one will notice anyway," or "This will do," or "This is as good as it gets."

How often have we chosen to listen to this little voice rather than put forth effort, even when we want to pursue something of value? Perhaps we have tried to counter our lazy mind by exerting ourselves a little, but minimal effort is insufficient as an antidote to laziness. We do not realize that by indulging in laziness, time passes us by, and suffering increases, especially aversion and resentment. As the Buddha said, we fail to notice that our hair is on fire.

"Now when the bardo of birth is dawning upon me, I will abandon laziness for which life has no time."[104] The paramita of effort means being indefatigable, not giving up no matter how much difficulty we face. There is a sense of urgency, informed by the knowledge that this moment comes only once and will never return. In the larger sense, we know that life is short and time is actually running out. We wield this knowledge, not in a way that creates stressful pressure in body and mind, but as a key that helps us to find effort's natural rhythm.

To exert effort in a balanced way that can be sustained over time, we need to learn the trick of moving a little faster and putting forth slightly more effort than we are inclined to do. If we put forth just five percent more energy and concentration, our patterns of resistance will shatter. Like a novice training in a Japanese monastery, we move quickly in order to leave bad habits behind and release fresh energy.

Effort is related to time. When we are behind or ahead of time, everything requires hard work. Once we are in time, moving with the rhythm of time instead of resisting it, our endeavors become increasingly effortless. As practice of the paramita of effort gains momentum, it becomes self-sustaining.

Fifth Paramita: Concentration

Thus to clear away the obscurations
I will pull back my mind from wrong paths.
I shall always focus on the Truth
and abide in equanimity.[105]

The paramita of concentration helps us leave inner agitation and duality behind and reach the other shore of perfect inner peace. This paramita unifies elements that are usually separate: energy and intelligence, body and mind, inner and outer. In its perfection, the paramita of concentration brings the wheel of life to a standstill, so that further cycles of suffering do not form.

The deeper the level of concentration, the easier it is to maintain. Tibetan Buddhist teachings offer extensive maps for developing concentration, describing many levels of absorption, each clearly marked with references and milestones to establish whether progress is being made.

Systems of meditation in general aim to establish inner calm through concentration. In Buddhist teachings, however, meditation is also practiced to increase clarity. Calm (Sanskrit: *shamata*, Tibetan: *zhi-gnas*) frees the mind from restlessness, but does not eliminate the roots of emotionality. For this, insight (Sanskrit: *vipashyana*, Tibetan: *lhag-mthong*) is indispensable. These two practices, calm paired with insight, lead to the perfection of concentration.

Learning meditation means learning to overcome obstacles. Whatever obstructs stillness and equanimity—

including laziness, forgetting instructions, and excessive enthusiasm—will surface during meditation practice. In order not to be distracted during meditation, we need first to gently tighten our attention or focus. Then we gradually relax. With discipline and effort, a stream of concentration develops, and the mind calms down. In the beginning, we may think that concentration requires great effort and causes stress, but with practice, the paramita of concentration is supported by the energy of relaxation.

Exercise: Try experimenting with two kinds of concentration practices: concentration with an object and concentration without an object.

Concentration with an object allows you to control an agitated mind. Like throwing a lasso around a foal's neck in order to begin taming it, concentrating on an object bridles impatient energy. Traditionally, this practice begins with mindfulness of breath. Focusing lightly on the breath, you observe its comings and goings. When the breath is short, simply notice that it is short; when it is long or choppy, be aware of that, without judgment or manipulation. Let the breath come when it comes; let it go as it goes. Gradually the breath calms down. When the breath is even, the quality of the mind becomes even as well.

You can also choose to concentrate on a specific physical object that promotes calm and composure, such as the flame of a candle or an image of the Buddha. As you focus on the object, identify with it, gradually merging with its qualities. Eventually, the duality between the meditator and the object of meditation dissolves. The serenity of the object merges with your being, bringing deep calm.

Concentration without an object improves presence of mind and brings you into the present moment. With your body relaxed and as still as a mountain, let your attention expand as if into a vast open plain. The eyes can be half open, or else open wide, which will produce a different experience. Looking out into space, allow a panoramic openness to unfold. Nothing escapes you; nothing disturbs your quiet, expansive glance. Awareness and space become one and foster an alert presence. You enter the realm of direct experience.

Sustaining either of these exercises for five minutes without being distracted is a milestone. From this point onward, concentration deepens. It is said that there are nine levels of concentration, culminating in *samadhi*, the integration of immeasurable space with unfathomable awareness.

There are countless types and levels of samadhi, but all move toward a state in which understanding becomes wisdom, and wisdom manifests in appropriate action, called skillful means.[106]

Sixth Paramita: Wisdom

All these branches of the Teaching
the great sage taught for the sake of wisdom.
Therefore, all who wish for peace and an end to misery
should generate this wisdom.[107]

The paramita of wisdom enables us to leave needless suffering behind and reach the other shore, where absolute truth is unveiled. The paramita of wisdom is sometimes called the paramita of intelligence, referring to an active knowing that presents itself spontaneously, containing everything and excluding nothing. When we open our minds and hearts completely, such dynamic wisdom is naturally present. Although it is always available, it cannot be owned. It must be rediscovered over and over again.

The limitations that impede us are self-imposed. Emotions such as frustration, fear, and doubt signal the unstable intelligence that lies behind them, and alert us to the fact that we are not applying the knowledge available to us. In general, emotions and karmic action can be understood as malfunctioning wisdom and intelligence. The Buddha teaches that it is possible to lift the veils imposed by such limited intelligence and awaken the higher knowing within.

The paramitas are best considered as active verbs—giving, self-disciplining, accepting, exerting, concentrating, and comprehensive knowing—that collectively lead to transformation. As we practice the paramitas, our activity becomes focused on the welfare of all sentient

beings, and ego no longer serves as the center of attention. The duality between self and other dissolves, allowing wisdom to emerge.

When we practice any of the first five paramitas,
wisdom begins to awaken and move toward the sixth
perfection, all-knowing wisdom. Only through awakened
intelligence is it possible to contact the highest truth.
Fully awakened wisdom is "unimaginable, indescribable
and ungraspable. It is unborn and has no end; it is like
space. Only the awakened mind can contain it."[108]

Relative and Absolute Truth

Relative and absolute,
these are accepted to be the Two Truths.
The Absolute is not within the reach of intellect,
for intellect is bound to the relative.[109]

Buddhism teaches that there are two kinds of truth,
the relative and the absolute. A fully awakened awareness comprehends both truths simultaneously. Relative,
conventional truth is characterized by acceptance of
assumptions we have not questioned or fully explored.
Such truth is subject to conditions and therefore, impermanent by nature.

The law of karma, the concept of impermanence,
and the belief in the possibility of awakening all belong
to the realm of relative truth. The Four Noble Truths
and the Noble Eightfold Path, as well as the concept of

codepedent origination, also belong to this realm. From the perspective of the absolute, there is no wheel of life, no suffering and no enlightenment. There is no Buddha, no Dharma, no Sangha. There is no subject or object, and the concept of taking refuge drops away.[110] Ultimately, these are all notions that serve as rungs on a ladder, helping us climb higher and higher until we arrive at absolute truth.

Then is there nothing, we may ask, that is true under all circumstances? A Mahayana Buddhist teacher might answer this question with a single Sanskrit word: *shunyata* (Tibetan: *stong-pa-nyid*).

Since the introduction of Buddhism to the West, this word has given translators difficulty. Shunyata is not an intellectual construct and words fail to describe it. In English, it is usually translated as "emptiness" or "nothingness," but these terms are misleading. For example, the texts make clear that shunyata is not empty; it is neither a vacuum nor the absence of something or everything. Nothing can be said about shunyata because every word we choose excludes its opposite: "empty" excludes "full;" "nothing" excludes "something." Shunyata has also been referred to as "the open dimension of being," but this excludes a "closed dimension of being." As one author suggests, "in shunyata there is room for every possibility and everything fits perfectly."[111]

In the Heart Sutra, a concise teaching by the Buddha regularly recited in Buddhist monasteries, shunyata is described as inseparable from appearance, in a series of statements that begins: "Form is shunyata and shunyata is form." The absolute and the conventional are inseparable; Absolute reality exists nowhere other than within conventional reality: every appearance expresses shunyata. This insight is also conveyed in the Sanskrit mantra found in the Heart Sutra: *Gate Gate Paragate Parasamgate Bodhi Svaha,* which invokes the complete absence of duality: "gone, gone, completely gone, completely gone beyond, enlightenment, so be it."

In daily life, shunyata can be viewed as verifying our intrinsic freedom. Freedom is not something to attain, but to rediscover and recapture. We are already free. But what about our karma? Our karma will last as long as we believe in it.

TATHAGATA-GARBHA

Buddhist texts say that everything we see and experience is like a dream, a mirage, an echo, a cloud formation in the sky, a rainbow, a reflection of the moon in water.[112] So let us not hold onto our experience and observations; they are nothing but ephemeral magic. Let us not identify with our thoughts; they are only a wave of energy. Everything is open. We are free to change. Every situation is malleable and can be improved. It is a matter of perception—and action.

Our minds begin functioning differently as soon as the vehicle of the paramitas gains momentum. We have been blind, but now our eyes are open, and we slowly grow accustomed to the light. We contact the intrinsic nature that makes us Buddhas: *Tathagata-garbha.*

This Sanskrit word points to the potential for enlightenment that exists in all sentient beings. "Tathagata" means "thus come, thus gone," and refers to the indescribable nature of a Buddha. "Garbha" literally means "womb," the potentializing matrix for Buddha-nature to manifest. The two words combined "Tathagata-garbha" suggest a dynamic, creative impulse toward expression: Our nature is Buddha nature.

Ultimately, there is nothing to do but delve deeply within, to mine what is most precious in us. We accomplish this by uniting our intelligence with compassion, embodying the knowledge that flows from a warm and strong heart. We may not be free of suffering, but we are less burdened by our suffering, because we are devoted to the truth, to the welfare of others, and to what is most important in human life. Thus we are able to be of more service to others.

The last of the twenty-five rings of the temple bell reverberates and dissipates in the darkness of space—the ceremony is over. I let go of the clapper, and turn around to descend the steps. May my mother rest in peace. May my continuing path of inner transformation be of help to others who wish to travel the same road. May the benefit of the work that was invested in this book help the sick and ailing, and guide those who care for them.

May our work and presence, care and dedication, knowledge and compassion, flourish and benefit all sentient beings. This is the path of heroes.

In the beginning nothing comes.
In the middle nothing stays.
In the end nothing goes.
—Milarepa

Notes

1 Tarthang Tulku, *Mind over Matter: Reflections on Buddhism in the West* (Berkeley, CA: Dharma Publishing, 2002), 3.

2 Tarthang Tulku, *Openness Mind* (Berkeley, CA: Dharma Publishing, 1978), 8.

3 Longchenpa, *Kindly Bent to Ease Us, Part One: Mind*, trans. Herbert V. Guenther (Berkeley, CA: Dharma Publishing, 1975), 6.

4 Also refer to Longchenpa, *Kindly Bent to Ease Us, Part One: Mind*, Herbert V. Guenther (Berkeley, CA: Dharma Publishing, 1975); Zhechen Gyaltsab, *Path of Heroes*, trans. Deborah Black (Berkeley, CA: Dharma Publishing, 1995); Paltrul Rinpoche, *Kun-zang La-may Zhal-lung*, trans. Sonam T. Kazi (Upper Montclair, NJ: Diamond Lotus Publishing, 1989).

5 See also Dalai Lama & Daniel Goleman, *Destructive Emotions* (New York: Bantam Books, 2003), 3–27.

6 *Dhammapada*, trans. Dharma Publishing Staff (Berkeley, CA: Dharma Publishing, 1985), 3.

7 Ye-shes rGyal-mtshan, *Mind in Buddhist Psychology*, trans. Herbert V. Guenther and Leslie S. Kawamura (Berkeley, CA: Dharma Publishing, 1975).

8 Majid Fotuhi, *The Memory Cure* (New York: McGraw Hill, 2003), 15.

9 Ye-shes rGyal-mtshan, *Mind in Buddhist Psychology*, trans.
   Herbert V. Guenther and Leslie S. Kawamura (Berkeley, CA:
   Dharma Publishing, 1975), 38–39.

10 Ye-shes rGyal-mtshan, *Mind in Buddhist Psychology*, trans.
   Herbert V. Guenther and Leslie S. Kawamura (Berkeley, CA:
   Dharma Publishing, 1975), 38.

11 See also Paltrul Rinpoche, *Kun-zang La-may Zhal-lung*
   (Upper Montclair, NJ: Diamond Lotus Publishing, 1989), 16.

12 *Ways of Enlightenment* (Berkeley, CA: Dharma Publishing,
   1993), xx.

13 Richard C. Saltus, "Evaluating Your Brain's CEO,"
   International Herald Tribune (August 28, 2003), 7.

14 Majid Fotuhi, *The Memory Cure* (New York: McGraw Hill,
   2003), 4.

15 *Ways of Enlightenment* (Berkeley, CA: Dharma Publishing,
   1993), 176–90.

16 *Footsteps on the Diamond Path, Crystal Mirror Series I-III,
   revised and expanded* (Berkeley, CA: Dharma Publishing,
   1992), 202-5.

17 *Rose Center for Earth and Space*, American Museum of Natural
   History.

18 Ecclesiastes 3:19.

19 Majid Fotuhi, *The Memory Cure* (New York: McGraw Hill,
   2003), 27.

20 *Lalitavistara Sutra, The Voice of the Buddha*, vol. I, trans.
   Gwendolyn Bays (Berkeley, CA: Dharma Publishing, 1983), 61.

21 Tarthang Tulku, *Time, Space and Knowledge: A New Vision of
   Reality* (Berkeley, CA: Dharma Publishing, 1977), 177.

22 Rita Levi Montalcini, *Ouderdom bestaat niet* (Amsterdam:
   Contact, 1999), 12, 52.

23 Majid Fotuhi, *The Memory Cure* (New York: McGraw Hill, 2003), 177.

24 Rita Levi Montalcini, *Ouderdom bestaat nièt* (Amsterdam: Contact, 1999), 109.

25 Longchenpa, *Kindly Bent to Ease Us, Part One: Mind,* trans. Herbert V. Guenther (Berkeley, CA: Dharma Publishing, 1975), 258.

26 *Ibid.,* 274.

27 Tarthang Tulku, *Openness Mind* (Berkeley, CA: Dharma Publishing, 1978), 141–45.

28 Ye-shes rGyal-mtshan, *Mind in Buddhist Psychology,* trans. Herbert V. Guenther and Leslie S. Kawamura (Berkeley, CA: Dharma Publishing, 1975), 38–39.

29 Sangs-rgyas chos-dang tshogs-kyi mchog-rnams-la

    (Sangyay cho dang tsok kyi chok nam la)

    Byang-chub bar-du bdag-ni skyabs-su-mchi

    (Chang chup bar du dak ni kyab su chi)

    Dag-gi sbyin-sogs bgyis-pa'i bsod-nams kyis

    (dak ki chin sok gyi pay so nam kyi)

    'gro-la phan-phyir sangs-rgyas 'grub-par-shog

    (dro la pen shir sangyay drup par shok)

30 *Sacred Art of Tibet* (Berkeley, CA: Dharma Publishing, 1972), 6.

31 *Lalitavistara Sutra, The Voice of the Buddha,* vol. II, trans. Gwendolyn Bays (Berkeley, CA: Dharma Publishing, 1983), 487.

32 *Ibid.,* 628–32.

33 Thich Nhat Hanh, *The Heart of the Buddha* (New York: Broadway Books, 1999), 173.

34 Tarthang Tulku, *Knowledge of Freedom* (Berkeley, CA: Dharma Publishing, 1984), 159.

35 Tarthang Tulku, *Kum Nye Relaxation, Part 2* (Berkeley, CA: Dharma Publishing, 1978), 282.

36 *Ibid.,* 202

37 Majid Fotuhi, *The Memory Cure* (New York: McGraw Hill, 2003), 62-64

38 Tarthang Tulku, *Kum Nye Relaxation, Part 1* (Berkeley, CA: Dharma Publishing, 1978), 1–15.

39 Tarthang Tulku, *Kum Nye Relaxation, Parts 1 and 2* (Berkeley, CA: Dharma Publishing, 1978) and *Tibetan Relaxation* (Berkeley, CA: Dharma Publishing, 2003).

40 Tarthang Tulku, *Kum Nye Relaxation, Part 1* (Berkeley, CA: Dharma Publishing, 1978), 8.

41 Ibid., 14.

42 Abhayadatta, *Buddha's Lions*, trans. James B. Robinson (Berkeley, CA: Dharma Publishing, 1979).

43 *Crystal Mirror, vol. VI* (Berkeley, CA: Dharma Publishing, 1984); *see also* Thich Nhat Hanh, *The Heart of the Buddha* (New York: Broadway Books, 1999).

44 *Lalitavistara Sutra, The Voice of the Buddha*, vol. II, trans. Gwendolyn Bays (Berkeley, CA: Dharma Publishing, 1983), 518.

45 Ecclesiastes 5:1

46 Tarthang Tulku, *Skillful Means* (Berkeley, CA: Dharma Publishing, 1991), and *Mastering Successful Work* (Berkeley, CA: Dharma Publishing, 1994); *Ways of Work* (Berkeley, CA: Dharma Publishing, 1987); Arnaud Maitland, *MasterWork: Mastering Time* (Berkeley, CA: Dharma Publishing, 2000).

47 Longchenpa, *Kindly Bent to Ease Us, Part One: Mind*, trans. Herbert V. Guenther (Berkeley, CA: Dharma Publishing, 1975), 268, n.13.

48 Majid Fotuhi, *The Memory Cure* (New York: McGraw Hill, 2003), ix.

49 *NRC-Handelsblad* (December 30, 2002), 43.

50 Thich Nhat Hanh, *The Heart of the Buddha* (New York: Broadway Books, 1999), 87.

51 H.Buijssen, *De heldere eenvoud van dementie* (De Stiel 2002), 149.

52 *Ibid.,* 143

53 Dalai Lama XIV and H. Cutler, *The Art of Happiness* (London: Coronet, 1998), 134.

54 Zhechen Gyaltsab, *Path of Heroes,* trans. Deborah Black (Berkeley, CA: Dharma Publishing, 1995), 424.

55 Pythagoras, *Golden Verses.*

56 Dalai Lama XIV and H. Cutler, *The Art of Happiness* (London: Coronet, 1998), 6.

57 Thich Nhat Hanh, *The Heart of the Buddha* (New York: Broadway Books, 1999).

58 Longchenpa, *Kindly Bent to Ease Us, Part One: Mind,* trans. Herbert V. Guenther (Berkeley, CA: Dharma Publishing, 1975), 113-122; *see also* Tarthang Tulku, *Gesture of Balance* (Berkeley, CA: Dharma Publishing, 1977), 37–44.

59 Longchenpa, *Kindly Bent to Ease Us, Part One: Mind,* trans. Herbert V. Guenther (Berkeley, CA: Dharma Publishing, 1975), 117.

60 *Newsweek* (June 24, 2002); special report on the brain in *NRC Thema Dementie* November 2, 2002); Majid Fotuhi, *The Memory Cure* (New York: McGraw Hill, 2003), 49.

61 Majid Fotuhi, *The Memory Cure* (New York: McGraw Hill, 2003), 130-33.

62 *San Francisco Chronicle,* Section E (June 2, 2002; *Newsweek* (July 14, 2003).

63 *Newsweek* (December 30, 2002), 51.

64 *Ibid.*, 56–57.

65 See also B.Alan Wallace, *The Four Immeasurables-Cultivating a Boundless Heart*, Ithaca (New York: Snow Lion 1999) and Longchenpa, *Kindly Bent to Ease Us, Part One: Mind*, trans. Herbert V. Guenther (Berkeley, CA: Dharma Publishing, 1975), 13-122.

66 neocortale prefontale.

67 *Time Magazine* (February 17, 2003), 54.

68 Longchenpa, *Kindly Bent to Ease Us, Part One: Mind*, trans. Herbert V. Guenther (Berkeley, CA: Dharma Publishing, 1975), 113.

69 Tarthang Tulku, *Mastering Successful Work* (Berkeley, CA: Dharma Publishing, 1994), 65-93

70 Arnaud Maitland, *MasterWork: Mastering Time* (Berkeley, CA: Dharma Publishing, 2000), 109.

71 Thich Nhat Hanh, *The Heart of the Buddha* (New York: Broadway Books, 1999), 170.

72 Ken Wilber, *A Brief History of Everything* (Boston: Shambhala, 2000) and *A Theory of Everything* (Boston: Shambhala, 2001).

73 Longchenpa, *Kindly Bent to Ease Us, Part One: Mind*, trans. Herbert V. Guenther (Berkeley, CA: Dharma Publishing, 1975), 56-59.

74 *Natural Liberation, Padmasambhava's Teachings on the Six Bardos* (Boston:Wisdom Publications 1998), commentary by Gyatrul Rinpoche, transl. B. Alan Wallace.

75 Padmasambhava, *Tibetan Book of the Dead: The Great Liberation through hearing in the Bardo*, trans. By Francesca Fremantle & commentary by Chogyam Trungpa (Boston: Shambhala, 1975).

76 Tarthang Tulku, *Hidden Mind of Freedom* (Berkeley, CA: Dharma Publishing 1981), 39

77 *Ibid.,* 39-42.

78 *Ibid.,* 40-41.

79 Matthew 7:2.

80 Longchenpa, *Thirty Pieces of Advice from the Heart*,(Tiwari's Pilgrims bookhouse),7.

81 Zhechen Gyaltsab, *Path of Heroes*, trans. Deborah Black (Berkeley, CA: Dharma Publishing 1995), 486.

82 B. Alan Wallace, *Buddhism with an Attitude* (Ithaca, New York: Snow Lion 2001, 242-3.

83 *Footsteps on the Diamond Path, Crystal Mirror series I-III revised and expanded* (Berkeley, CA: Dharma Publishing 1992), 226.

84 *Ways of Enlightenment* (Berkeley, CA: Dharma Publishing, 1993), 208.

85 Padmasambhava, *Tibetan Book of the Dead: The Great Liberation through hearing in the Bardo,* trans. By Francesca Fremantle & commentary by Chogyam Trungpa (Boston: Shambhala 1975), 1-29.

86 William Shakespeare, *Hamlet,* Act 2, scene 2.

87 Sanskrit, *Pratityasamutpada*, in Tibetan, *rTen-'brel.*

88 *Ways of Enlightenment* (Berkeley, CA: Dharma Publishing, 1993), 176-190

89 *Footsteps on the Diamond Path, Crystal Mirror series I-III revised and expanded* (Berkeley, Ca:Dharma Publishing 1992), 226.

90 Aryadeva, quoted in Dalai Lama XIV, *A Flash of Lightning in the Dark of the Night* (Boston: Shambhala, 1994), 20.

91 After one of my mother's favorite music pieces: Beethoven's Ninth Symphony, chorale.

92 Ajahn Chah.

93 Dudjom Rinpoche, *Counsels from my Heart* (Boston: Shambhala, 2001), 68.

94 *Ibid.*, 64-73; *Tibetan Book of the Dead: The Great Liberation through Hearing in the Bardo, Padmasambhava,* translation *Francesca Fremantle & commentary Chogyam Trungpa* (Boston: Shambhala, 1975).

95 Zhechen Gyaltsab, *Path of Heroes,* trans. Deborah Black (Berkeley, CA: Dharma Publishing 1995), 348.

96 Rigdzin Jigme Lingpa, "Entering into the Path of Enlightenment: Taking Daily Activities as the Path, According to the Unified Approach of Sutra and Tantra," in *Enlightened Living,* trans. Tulku Thondup (Boston, Shambhala, 1997), 130.

97 *Bhadrakalpika Sutra: The Fortunate Aeon* (Berkeley, CA: Dharma Publishing, 1986) 15.

98 Longchenpa, *Kindly Bent to Ease Us, Part One: Mind,* trans. Herbert V. Guenther (Berkeley, CA: Dharma Publishing, 1975), 67-68.

99 *Crystal Mirror VII* (Berkeley, Ca: Dharma Publishing, 1984), 13-14.

100 Shantideva, *Bodhicaryavatara* 5:6, trans. by Deborah Black of the Yeshe De Project Translation Team.

101 Shantideva, *Bodhicaryavatara* 6:10, trans. by Deborah Black of the Yeshe De Project Translation Team.

102 Thich Nhat Hanh, *The Heart of the Buddha* (New York: Broadway books 1999), 198.

103 Shantideva, *Bodhicaryavatara* 7:1, trans. by Deborah Black of the Yeshe De Project Translation Team.

104 Padmasambhava, *Tibetan Book of the Dead: The Great Liberation through Hearing in the Bardo,* trans. by Francesca

Fremantle & commentary by Chogyam Trungpa (Boston: Shambhala 1975), 98.

105 Shantideva, *Bodhicaryavatara* 8:187, trans. by Deborah Black of the Yeshe De Project Translation Team.

106 Lama Mipham, *Calm and Clear* (Berkeley, CA: Dharma Publishing, 1973), 82-84.

107 Shantideva, *Bodhicaryavatara* 9:1, trans. by Deborah Black of the Yeshe De Project Translation Team.

108 Dalai Lama, *A Flash of Lightening in the Dark of the Night* (Boston, Shambala 1994), 118.

109 Shantideva, *Bodhicaryavatara* 9:2, trans. by Deborah Black of the Yeshe De Project Translation Team.

110 See also Tarthang Tulku, *Openness Mind* (Berkeley, CA: Dharma Publishing 1990), 144.

111 Tarthang Tulku, *Hidden Mind of Freedom* (Berkeley, CA: Dharma Publishing, 1981), 92-93.

112 Longchenpa, *Kindly Bent to Ease Us, Part Two: Meditation,* trans. Herbert V. Guenther (Berkeley, CA: Dharma Publishing, 1976).

Index

An international lecturer, retreat leader, Nyingma teacher, meditation instructor and Skillful Means consultant, Arnaud Maitland brings the ancient teachings of the Tibetan Buddhist Nyingma lineage into the mainstream of contemporary culture and life—both in the personal and professional spheres. A longtime student of the venerable Tibetan Lama Tarthang Tulku, he leads us to discover that we already possess the knowledge to create a meaningful, successful and happy life.

Maitland's writings and teachings are reaching a wide and diverse audience. In addition to being the subject of the Dutch television (BOS) documentary *Living without a Shadow*, he has been interviewed on CNN and NBC as well as by the founder of New Dimensions, Michael Toms.

Holding both a Law Degree and a Master's in Tibetan Buddhist Philosophy & Psychology, Maitland shares his knowledge in individual and group instructions, classes, and retreats as well as books, on-line coaching and CDs. His first book, *MasterWork–Mastering Time* (Dharma Publishing 2000) describes his years as director of a printing company that was managed according to Tibetan Buddhist principles.

For information about programs on *Living without Regret* please inquire at Dharma Publishing (phone 707-847 3717). Or contact us at dpinfo@dharmapublishing.com.

All proceeds from this book benefit the Tibetan text preservation, translation, and research sponsored by the Yeshe De Project, Berkeley CA.

"Maitland sees suffering in the context of Tibetan Buddhism: his perspective on the important questions of aging and pain among the elderly is unusual and important."
— *Library Journal*

"Enhanced by a foreword by Tarthang Tulku, nuggets of Buddhist wisdom, and guided meditations, this poignant and enlightening book is valuable for anyone touched by life-threatening diseases and death. For it is never too late: We can still heal the past, and live "without regret." This book also helps one to face one's own death with deeper insight and without apprehension and fear."
— *BookWire Review*

"Not just a moving report on the illness and departure of his mother, but also an excellent introduction into Buddhism, on a level that is comparable to the books of the Dalai Lama and Sogyal Rinpoche."
— *General Press Services, The Netherlands*

"As an authority in his field — having worked for over twenty-five years in the US with the Tibetan Lama Tarthang Tulku — through an exceptionally lucid style Maitland succeeds in touching and uplifting the reader with clear metaphors. He has an outstanding ability to sketch complicated matters in a condensed and accessible way. In these times of graying population this is a book of great actuality, and of rare quality."
— *Central Library Service, The Netherlands*

"This book will grip, disturb, and also encourage you. It is written for everyone — those who are suffering or dying presently and those are called to tend to them and who can still look forward to their own old age. His presentation of Buddhist teachings is vivid and superb. It is written with great passion, but also enormous clarity. Highly recommended."
— *Traditional Yoga Journal*

"All those who read this book will reflect on their own relationships with loved ones."
— *Publisher's Weekly*

"A moving book about impermanence. Highly recommended."
— *Mandala*